DIY Style

Dress, Body, Culture

Series Editor: Joanne B. Eicher, *Regents' Professor, University of Minnesota*

Advisory Board:
Ruth Barnes, *Ashmolean Museum, University of Oxford*
James Hall, *University of Illinois at Chicago*
Ted Polhemus, *Curator, "Street Style" Exhibition, Victoria and Albert Museum*
Griselda Pollock, *University of Leeds*
Valerie Steele, *The Museum at the Fashion Institute of Technology*
Lou Taylor, *University of Brighton*
John Wright, *University of Minnesota*

Books in this provocative series seek to articulate the connections between culture and dress, which is defined here in its broadest possible sense as any modification or supplement to the body. Interdisciplinary in approach, the series highlights the dialogue between identity and dress, cosmetics, coiffure and body alternations as manifested in practices as varied as plastic surgery, tattooing, and ritual scarification. The series aims, in particular, to analyze the meaning of dress in relation to popular culture and gender issues and will include works grounded in anthropology, sociology, history, art history, literature, and folklore.

ISSN: 1360–466X

Previously Published in the Series

Helen Bradley Foster, *"New Raiments of Self": African American Clothing in the Antebellum South*
Claudine Griggs, *S/he: Changing Sex and Changing Clothes*
Michaele Thurgood Haynes, *Dressing Up Debutantes; Pageantry and Glitz in Texas*
Anne Brydon and Sandra Niessen, *Consuming Fashion: Adorning the Transnational Body*
Dani Cavallaro and Alexandra Warwick, *Fashioning the Frame: Boundaries, Dress and the Body*
Judith Perani and Norma H. Wolff, *Cloth, Dress and Art Patronage in Africa*
Linda B. Arthur, *Religion, Dress and the Body*
Paul Jobling, *Fashion Spreads: Word and Image in Fashion Photography*
Fadwa El Guindi, *Veil: Modesty, Privacy and Resistance*
Thomas S. Abler, *Hinterland Warriors and Military Dress: European Empires and Exotic Uniforms*
Linda Welters, *Folk Dress in Europe and Anatolia: Beliefs about Protection and Fertility*
Kim K.P. Johnson and Sharron J. Lennon, *Appearance and Power*
Barbara Burman, *The Culture of Sewing*
Annette Lynch, *Dress, Gender and Cultural Change*
Antonia Young, *Women Who Become Men*
David Muggleton, *Inside Subculture: The Postmodern Meaning of Style*
Nicola White, *Reconstructing Italian Fashion: America and the Development of the Italian Fashion Industry*
Brian J. McVeigh, *Wearing Ideology: The Uniformity of Self-Presentation in Japan*
Shaun Cole, *Don We Now Our Gay Apparel: Gay Men's Dress in the Twentieth Century*
Kate Ince, *Orlan: Millennial Female*
Nicola White and Ian Griffiths, *The Fashion Business: Theory, Practice, Image*
Ali Guy, Eileen Green and Maura Banim, *Through the Wardrobe: Women's Relationships with their Clothes*
Linda B. Arthur, *Undressing Religion: Commitment and Conversion from a Cross-Cultural Perspective*
William J.F. Keenan, *Dressed to Impress: Looking the Part*
Joanne Entwistle and Elizabeth Wilson, *Body Dressing*
Leigh Summers, *Bound to Please: A History of the Victorian Corset*
Paul Hodkinson, *Goth: Identity, Style and Subculture*
Leslie W. Rabine, *The Global Circulation of African Fashion*
Michael Carter, *Fashion Classics from Carlyle to Barthes*
Sandra Niessen, Ann Marie Leshkowich and Carla Jones, *Re-Orienting Fashion: The Globalization of Asian Dress*
Kim K. P. Johnson, Susan J. Torntore and Joanne B. Eicher, *Fashion Foundations: Early Writings on Fashion and Dress*
Helen Bradley Foster and Donald Clay Johnson, *Wedding Dress Across Cultures*
Eugenia Paulicelli, *Fashion under Fascism: Beyond the Black Shirt*
Charlotte Suthrell, *Unzipping Gender: Sex, Cross-Dressing and Culture*
Irene Guenther, *Nazi Chic? Fashioning Women in the Third Reich*
Yuniya Kawamura, *The Japanese Revolution in Paris Fashion*
Patricia Calefato, *The Clothed Body*
Ruth Barcan, *Nudity: A Cultural Anatomy*
Samantha Holland, *Alternative Femininities: Body, Age and Identity*
Alexandra Palmer and Hazel Clark, *Old Clothes, New Looks: Second Hand Fashion*
Yuniya Kawamura, *Fashion-ology: An Introduction to Fashion Studies*
Regina A. Root, *The Latin American Fashion Reader*
Linda Welters and Patricia A. Cunningham, *Twentieth-Century American Fashion*
Jennifer Craik, *Uniforms Exposed: From Conformity to Transgression*
Alison L. Goodrum, *The National Fabric: Fashion, Britishness, Globalization*
Annette Lynch and Mitchell D. Strauss, *Changing Fashion: A Critical Introduction to Trend Analysis and Meaning*
Catherine M. Roach, *Stripping, Sex and Popular Culture*
Marybeth C. Stalp, *Quilting: The Fabric of Everyday Life*
Jonathan S. Marion, *Ballroom: Culture and Costume in Competitive Dance*
Dunja Brill, *Goth Culture: Gender, Sexuality and Style*
Joanne Entwistle, *The Aesthetic Economy of Fashion: Markets and Value in Clothing and Modelling*
Juanjuan Wu, *Chinese Fashion: From Mao to Now*

DIY Style
Fashion, Music and Global Digital Cultures

Brent Luvaas

London • New York

English edition
First published in 2012 by
Berg
Editorial offices:
50 Bedford Square, London WC1B 3DP, UK
175 Fifth Avenue, New York, NY 10010, USA

Berg is an imprint of Bloomsbury Publishing Plc.

Library of Congress Cataloging-in-Publication Data

A catalogue record for this book is available from the Library of Congress.

British Library Cataloguing-in-Publication Data

A catalogue record for this book is available from the British Library.

ISBN 978 0 85785 039 3 (Cloth)
       978 0 85785 040 9 (Paper)
e-ISBN 978 0 85785 294 6 (ePDF)
       978 0 85785 047 8 (epub)

Typeset by Apex CoVantage, LLC, Madison, WI, USA.
Printed in the UK by the MPG Books Group
Cover design inspired by a design by UNKL347.

www.bergpublishers.com

For Jessica and Esme—
with love and squalor

Contents

List of Illustrations

Acknowledgments

There's no such thing as DIY; at least, if doing it yourself means doing it all by yourself. As with any individual endeavor, this book was very much a collaborative effort—though the final responsibility for getting facts, sentiments, and details right was entirely my own. Those who deserve credit for their time, energy, and inspiration are so numerous I am inevitably going to overlook some of them. I apologize in advance to anyone whom I inadvertently leave out.

In particular, I am indebted to the many participants in Indonesia's DIY/indie scene who welcomed me in, hung out with me deep into many long lush tropical nights, and made me feel like I was part of something quite special, a real cultural movement with far-reaching consequences that are still only beginning to become clear to me. I want to single-out several people for particular acknowledgement. These include Dendy Darman of Unkl347 for his generosity and time, and for providing the design inspiration for the cover of this book; Adhari Adegreden Donora of Reddoor Distro, Pipuangpu, and the House of Natural Fiber, for being such a great friend, guide, and informant; Sudjud Dartanto and Adhe Maruf for numerous thought-provoking conversations; and, finally, Gustaff Hariman Iskandar of Common Room Networks Foundation for taking me in, giving me a place to live and work, and serving as a critical mentor for carrying out this project. I also want to give special thanks to friends/interlocutors/accomplices Dede Anonim, Michael Rusli, Erik Wiryanata, Ryan Koesuma, Elang Eby, Diana Slackers, Uchok Suave, Meggie "Megadeath" May, Ardi Chambers, Tbonk Starcross, Ahmad Marin, Helvi Sjarifudin, Febby Lorentz, Helmy Fast Forward, Idhar Resmadi, Dicky Sukmana, Argha Mahendra, Parvatae Pungkal, Agnessy Simorangkir, Nadya Asteria, Anggito Rahman, Novan Maltuvanie, Ainu Rofiq, Hamid Ariwinata, Yudhi Groovy, Venus Salient Insanity, Rully Shabara, Ekky RNRM, Reina Wulansari, Dame Siahaan, Chain Smoking Bastard, and the rest of the gang at Common Room. In addition, I want to thank Satria N.B., W. Satrio Adjie, Ridho Fatwerks Alhadi, Doni Arena, Dadan Ketu, Andaru Nanonine, David Tarigan, Arian Arifin, Wendi Putranto, Felix Dass, Anto Arief, Rekti Yoewono, Dina Dellyana, Venzha Kristiawan, Dimas Ario, Muslim Seven Souls, Arina Ephipania Simangunsong, and Riko Prayitno for taking time to talk and/or hang out with me. A special shout out to the kids from Reddoor Distro, as well as those who work or are associated with the following distros and clothing labels: Pipuangpu, Triggers Syndicate, Moly, 308, Starcross, Groovy, Wazzup, Broadway, Pimp, Pleasure Rock Shop, Nimco, Whatever, Mailbox, Slackers, Moof

Roof, Affairs, and Seven Souls De Arcade in Yogyakarta, Chambers in Makassar, Endorse, Nanonine, and Satellite Castle in Jakarta, and Unkl347, Monik/Celtic, Wadezig!, Airplane Systm, Invictus, Evil, No Label Stuff, Arena, Rockmen, 16 D-Scale, Riotic, and Anonim in Bandung. Thanks to the staff and crew of the publications *Ripple, ELV, Suave, Outmagz,* and *Zek!* Thanks also to the following bands: Mocca, The Upstairs, The S.I.G.I.T., Pure Saturday, Burgerkill, diSko, Nervous, Anggisluka, Jenny, Shaggy Dog, Captain Jack, Death Vomit, End of Julia, Rock N Roll Mafia, Polyester Embassy, Homogenic, Dojihatori, Jeruji, Salient Insanity, Airport Radio, Mortal Combat, bottlesmoker, Seek Six Sick, Sleepless Angel, Vincent Vega, 70s Orgasm Club, and Zoo.

I would also like to express my heartfelt thanks to those mentors and colleagues who gave me input on various stages of this book, as well as inspiration and insight that helped shape the final product. I am especially grateful to have had the opportunity to work with the inimitable Sherry B. Ortner, my adviser and friend, as well as an awesome doctoral committee that included Maureen Mahon, Douglas Hollan, Geoffrey Robinson, and Timothy D. Taylor. I am also grateful for the feedback

Figure 1   Unkl347 distro in Bandung, West Java, Indonesia.

and support of my colleagues: Wendy Fonarow, Devon Powers, Jeremy Wallach, Mary Ebeling, R. Diyah Larasati, Wesley Shumar, Constantine Nakassis, Gustaff Iskandar, and Sudjud Dartanto. Thanks also to Mike Fortun and Kim Fortun, Michele Ford, Liam Buckley, and the anonymous reviewers at Berg, *Cultural Anthropology, Inside Indonesia,* and *Visual Anthropology Review.* Thanks to Anna Wright and Joanne Eicher from Berg—who have been terrific—as well as my colleague Joe Hancock, who took the trouble to introduce me to them. Finally, I want to thank my wife, partner, and best friend Jessica Curtaz, who has supplied her shrewd commentary and keen insight to numerous pieces and incarnations of this book, and, of course, put up with endless babble about it for years now.

Funding for this research was provided by Fulbright-Hays and the University of California Pacific Rim Research Program. Some additional travel funds were provided by the Department of Anthropology at the University of California, Los Angeles, and the Department of Culture and Communication at Drexel University. Universitas Islam Indonesia was my host institution in Yogyakarta. Universitas Atma Jaya in Yogyakarta also provided some additional resources. Thanks to Edi, Yono, and Cici and the rest of the crew at CILACS, Nelly Paliama and the gang from AMINEF, and the folks at Lembaga Ilmu Pengetahuan Indonesia for sponsoring the research.

An earlier version of Chapter Five originally appeared in *Visual Anthropology Review.* An earlier version of Chapter Six appeared in *Cultural Anthropology.* A few scattered sentences and paragraphs, in true DIY fashion, have been shamelessly cut and pasted from pieces I originally published in *Inside Indonesia.*

Preface

Shouts from the Sidelines

As cheap digital technologies have brought the tools of media production into the hands of more and more people worldwide, a generation of youth from New York to Manila have taken up the old punk rock credo of "do it yourself" (DIY) and become amateur producers in their own right. Millions of young people, tired of sitting on the sidelines as cultural production happens elsewhere, have begun cranking out their own low- to no-budget media—from self-published zines to fan websites, bedroom-recorded rock albums and homemade fashion—and inserting them into public view, often with little hope of mainstream recognition and no expectation of financial reward (Duncombe 1997; Spencer 2005; Moore 2007; Oakes 2009; Gauntlett 2011).

This book is an on-the-ground investigation of global DIY culture through a detailed ethnographic case study of one highly prolific, if relatively unknown, DIY movement: the Indonesian "indie scene,"[1] a network of youth throughout the Southeast Asian island nation, who use new media technologies, pirated software, and an arsenal of copy machines and silkscreens to create their own clothing lines, magazines, and record labels outside corporate channels of production and distribution. Based on interviews with Indonesian fashion designers, label owners, musicians, bloggers, and zine writers, and over a year of participant-observation in the indie hangouts of urban Indonesia, this book analyzes how young Indonesians have used DIY fashion, music, and media to carve out their places in a rapidly changing society, challenge existing conceptions of national and regional identity, and assert themselves onto the world stage "on their own terms"; that is, as active members of a global community, rather than as marginalized youth on the periphery of the industrialized world.

DIY is a vast and varied field of production. I could have focused on any number of forms of DIY in this book from hand-crafting to biohacking, zine writing to graffiti bombing, the Arts and Crafts Movement to the global anti-capitalist movement, and while I make mention of many of these related streams of DIY culture, and tie them in through common sensibilities and motivations, the bulk of this book is devoted to just two media: fashion and music. I am not asserting that these are more important than other forms of DIY culture. They simply happen to be those forms of DIY that have most caught, and kept, *my* attention. These are, after all, two of DIY's most visible—and audible—forms. The title of this book, then, *DIY Style,* refers to the application of the do-it-yourself model of production to aesthetics. It also, however, refers to the general sensibility behind this model: doing something, as so many articles both online and off implore us to do these days, in a DIY fashion. *Wired* talks about "Transcending the Human, DIY Style" (Borland 2010). *Popular Mechanics* reports on "Combating Satellite Terrorism, DIY Style" (Shachtman 2009). In both instances, DIY is more than a method of operation; it is an attitude, a philosophy, and a stance. In other words, it is an ethos. This book investigates that ethos, its meanings and expressions, and its broad-sweeping cultural implications.

Why Indonesia?

I draw examples in this book from DIY movements in a variety of cultural and historical contexts, but Indonesia is my primary case study, for several significant reasons. For one, Indonesia has one of the biggest DIY movements anywhere, despite being almost completely unknown among similar movements elsewhere. Its indie scene operates on a scale and with a degree of national public visibility unlike any comparable scene I have witnessed in any other country. Though it has precedents dating back hundreds of years, to village handicraft and urban art, it has risen, over the course of the last decade, to a status that is itself unprecedented, becoming one of the most active and influential forms of cultural production in the archipelago, and churning out enormous quantities of clothing, cassettes, CDs, and magazines, among other products. It seems quite appropriate, then, that the region of Indonesia in which I conducted the majority of this research goes by the official title of "DIY," an acronym for *Daerah Istimewa Yogyakarta,* or the Special District of Yogyakarta. It may as well stand for "do it yourself."

For another, as a recently deregulated economy, an emergent postindustrial producer, and a new consumer society, Indonesia is a rich example of the social and cultural consequences of late capitalist principles put into practice, and, hence, helps illustrate the complex, and often contradictory, connections between evolving DIY ethics and hyper-capitalistic economics, a theme that will recur throughout this book.

Moreover, as the world's fourth-largest nation, with the largest majority Muslim population, and second-greatest number of users of social networking websites such as Twitter and Facebook, Indonesia is a fascinating locale to investigate the impact of new media technology, and new organizations of cultural and economic production, on youth culture, more generally.

Finally, the focus on Indonesia confronts and rejects the implicit Western bias behind previous literature on indie, punk, and other related DIY music and fashion movements. It demonstrates the international nature of the phenomenon and helps de-center the academic conversation around such styles of production away from the usual suspects of the United States and the UK.

This book does not, however, gloss all forms of DIY production as part of a single monolithic movement. Nor does it attribute the global growth of DIY culture to a single causative source. It testifies, instead, to the specificity and idiosyncrasy of individual DIY movements, even while identifying certain common convergences of factors that ignite and inspire them. Indonesia's indie scene is presented as one rich illustration of a social process happening in many other parts of the world, but this book situates it within its own specific, historical, political, and cultural dynamics, fully recognizing that DIY takes other forms and holds different nuances wherever it is practiced and enacted. Indonesia helps demonstrate, then, both the flows and discontinuities in DIY culture as it develops and circulates throughout the globe. It is both example and counter-example.

On the Perspectives and Motivations of the Author

Woven throughout this work is a concern with how youth, in Indonesia and the rest of the industrial and postindustrial world, are remaking themselves and their societies in light of profound social, economic, and technological transformation. In my discipline of anthropology, as in cultural studies, sociology, and related disciplines, there has been a marked tendency to either valorize youth practice as resistant to the hegemony of global capital, or, alternatively, to depict it as impotent and ineffectual, subjected to the disciplines and dictates of an established transnational order. In this book, I hope to navigate a path between these two extremes, presenting a cautiously optimistic account of DIY practice as an alternative form of capitalism—similar to what Mason (2008) would label "punk capitalism"—but a form of capitalism nonetheless, with all of its moral ambiguities and cultural contradictions still intact. DIYers are pushing the boundaries of capitalistic culture, I argue, slowly but surely transforming it into something else. At the same time, they themselves are being transformed by it.

My own biases in regards to DIY culture are fairly obvious in this work, and I make every effort to present them honestly and forthrightly to the reader. I have spent a good part of my life involved in indie, punk, or "alternative" scenes similar to those described here. I like similar music, dress in a roughly similar manner, and hold similar values to those people who appear in these pages. I consider many of them my friends as well as my colleagues and informants. I have a great deal of respect and admiration for the work they do, the struggles they are engaged in, and the ideals they hold dear. But I do not naively overestimate their influence on global capitalism, nor do I fail to recognize the internal contradictions in the discourses they produce.

Independence is more an ideal than a lived reality. DIY movements, wherever they pop up, maintain a variety of linkages with the "mainstream" commercial culture toward which they pose themselves in opposition. Moreover, there are clear hierarchies that exist within scenes, despite their common rhetoric of egalitarianism and democratization. In Indonesia, for instance, the more established bands and brands have much more sway over the direction of the scene than do the young upstarts, and even though women are assuming more and more prominent positions within the scene, it is still clearly dominated by the activities and concerns of men.

Most significantly, perhaps, and for me the most troubling, many of the DIY modes of production described in this book fundamentally depend on the labors of menial workers such as apparel manufacturers, package deliverers, and domestic laborers, whose contributions to production go largely unnoticed, unacknowledged, and unappreciated by indie producers. It can certainly be argued that the very term "do-it-yourself" often masks the actual human labor behind such forms of production, and thus works to perpetuate a stark social hierarchy between the privileged middle-classes, who can more easily afford to participate actively in "nonalienated" forms of labor (Duncombe 1997), and the working poor, who, lacking such resources, are forced to sell their labor power for a small financial compensation (Marx and Engels [1849] 1998). The raw materials of DIY production, after all, including fabric, silicon, paper, and ink, continue to be produced in factories, many of whose working conditions exist in stark contrast to the ideals held by indie scenesters. The do-it-yourself claim of indie producers, then, is still very much a work in progress.

Moreover, not all participants in global DIY culture contribute equally to its growth, its aesthetic, or its values. The social and cultural impact of the Indonesian indie scene, despite reaching rather impressive heights within Indonesia, remains decidedly small in the global arena. The fact remains that while Western (and arguably Japanese, Chinese, Indian, and Korean) youth cultural trends exert a great deal of influence over Indonesian youth, Indonesian youth have very little impact on the global production of those trends.

My hope, as is the hope of the numerous young designers, musicians, and producers who fill these pages, is that innovative uses of new technologies like the Internet and open-source software, as well as more and more expansive cooperation across borders, will begin to level the playing field, making transnational cultural production truly global, egalitarian, and democratic in scope. But realization of this ideal, despite all sorts of politicized rhetoric to the contrary, is still a long way off. This book, thus, is about the efforts of young people throughout the industrial and industrializing world to overthrow the legacy of colonialism and the entrenchment of corporate capitalism and participate, as fully as possible, in the production of transnational popular culture. It chronicles their struggles and documents their still limited victories.

On Methodology

The bulk of my research for this book on global DIY style was conducted in two cities: Bandung in West Java, widely acknowledged to be the birthplace of Indonesia's indie scene, and Yogyakarta in Central Java, a university city that has developed a substantial DIY movement of its own in recent years. I also visited Jakarta, Makassar, Malang, and Bali during the course of my fieldwork to better understand the interrelationship between the various outposts of the scene. No doubt, these are very different cities. Yogyakarta, often described as the cultural capital of Central Java, and Bandung, a Dutch colonial city nestled into the highlands of Sunda, or West Java, have very distinct histories, industries, and cultural affiliations. These differences are important, and have, of course, shaped the trajectories of DIY culture in both places. I pay attention to those differences in this account. But too often, as Boellstorff (2005) has argued, anthropologists have fixated on difference, ignoring the basic samenesses and homologies that unite differently situated actors within common experience. Unlike most previous ethnographies conducted in Indonesia, then, I do not take one specific "ethnolocality" (Boellstorff 2005), such as Java, Sunda, or Bali, as the subject of my research. Instead, I explore the cultural formations developing through interactions between places and cultures, those built commonalities that span distance, thriving in and through networks of youth. It is a major contention of this book, in fact, that earlier configurations of ethnicity and locality, tied as they are with projects of colonialism and nation-building (see chapters 1 and 6), are being actively contested through DIY styles of production. Scenes are simply not so easily pinned down.

The primary research methodology of this book can be summed up with one term: ethnography. Ethnography, of course, can mean different things to different researchers. "Minimally, however," as Ortner has argued, "it has always meant the attempt to understand another life world using the self—as much of it as possible—as the instrument of knowing" (Ortner 2006: 42). That is what I have attempted to do here. My own perspectives and experiences, firsthand encounters with DIY culture, and complicated feelings and opinions about it, have informed every aspect of this book. In a sense, then, like all ethnographies, this book reveals nearly as much about me, the researcher, as it does about the people and institutions I researched. I do not see this as a weakness. The DIY ethos is not simply the subject of this book; it has also helped shape the subject who wrote it, that is, me. I attempt to use that fact as an asset in this work, a source of critical insight and reflection. Too often, I would argue, social scientists mask their own biases and preoccupations behind a carefully crafted veneer of objectivity (Tyler 1986; Latour 2005). Whatever other weaknesses it may have, this book does not pretend to be strictly objective. It is written in a more colloquial and conversational tone than is the average ethnographic account, with the intention that my own voice, my own situated perspective, will be rendered utterly transparent to the reader. Ethnography, after all, "does not claim to produce an objective or truthful account of reality" (Pink 2007: 22). Such an account is not possible. It aims, instead, "to offer visions of ethnographers' experiences of reality that are as loyal as possible to the context, negotiations and intersubjectivities through which the knowledge was produced" (Pink 2007).

At its best, ethnography is a self-critical medium of research. It is always partial and preliminary (Clifford and Marcus 1986), recognizing its own limitations and remaining humble in its ambitions. For this very reason, ethnography also tends to be a highly "promiscuous" (Geertz 2000: 107) practice, borrowing from as many sources as it can to supplement its always—by definition—limited perspective. I, too, employed a variety of methods, from participant-observation to open-ended interviews, textual analysis, and historical research in the writing of this book, but I did so within the larger rubric of ethnography, maintaining, as my first commitment, the ethnographic foregrounding of direct experience. The situatedness and embeddedness of ethnography, the complex positionalities it enacts and entangles, and the messy, self-conscious approach it takes to what it studies, are the very things that make ethnography a valuable tool for understanding culture as a lived practice. Along with Ortner (2006), Geertz (2000), and a long line of like-minded anthropologists, then, I see immersive ethnographic fieldwork as the only defense social scientists have against rendering the complex conditions under which culture is lived and produced as "thin" or abstracted facsimiles of themselves. Ethnographers strive for something more, "thick descriptions" (Geertz 1973) of a place and a moment in time, full of detailed observations, feelings, textures, and tensions, the kinds of insights that can only be acquired through direct subjective experience. In practical terms, carrying out an ethnographic project means spending lots of time with our informants. It means detailed notetaking, constant question-asking, continual self-interrogation, and, of course, accumulating piles of photographic and primary source documentation. Geertz once shorthanded this method of inquiry as "deep hanging out" (Geertz 2000), and it seems an apt description of what I spent my time doing in Indonesia, months of late night concerts and conversations, followed by late morning sessions of sitting and scribbling in neighborhood coffee shops.

The primary fieldsites of this project, those locations where most of my "deep hanging out" took place, were *distros*. Short for "distribution outlet," *distro* is a term originally used to describe collectives or distributors of zines (low production value, self-published magazines) in the United States and Europe (Duncombe 1997; Spencer 2005; Wrekk 2005; Uttu 2006). In Indonesia, distro tends to describe mainly distributors of independent clothing and music. Distros come in all shapes and sizes, from small ramshackle shops covered in stickers and fliers to large upscale boutiques with clean posh interiors. Some are run like ordinary businesses, with normal business hours and a permanent staff of hired employees, others more like collectives, with groups of friends taking turns designing, marketing, selling, and hanging out long into the night. They do, however, share a common approach to production and distribution, and it is this approach that is at the heart of this work, an attitude of individual expression and cooperative capitalism that I refer to throughout this book simply as "the *DIY ethos*."

Introduction: The DIY Ethos

First and foremost, we have here a discourse that is authoritarian: one *has to* express oneself, one *has to* speak, communicate, cooperate, and so forth.

—Maurizio Lazzarato, *Immaterial Labour*

Creating by Any Means Necessary

"We've been cut and paste from the beginning," Dendy Darman told me, as we chatted in the repurposed warehouse that serves as the office for his clothing company, Unkl347, in southern Bandung, West Java, Indonesia, "and now is the era of cut and paste." Digital technology and a range of new media resources have made remixing and reworking other peoples' cultural labors easier than ever before. From mashed-up pop songs to satirical auto-tuned news broadcasts, cut and paste, it seems, the digital generation's answer to *bricolage* (Lévi-Strauss 1966), has become the default mode of production for youth nearly everywhere (Turkle 1995; Manovich 2001; Lessig 2009; Luvaas 2010). For Dendy, cut and paste is a kind of mantra, a reiterative call to action that implicates anyone too lazy to take part. It declares not only his company's design aesthetic, but also Dendy's personal philosophy. Cut and paste, after all, is something anyone can do. It takes little skill, little knowledge, and not even much technological savvy. The only thing necessary is passion and intent. Design for Dendy means "doing what's in [his] heart without worrying about what will sell," or even whether it's any good. It means mining his current preoccupations and refashioning them into fashion, making stuff he likes out of stuff he likes.

Unkl347 samples from the icons and imagery circulating through the global "mediascape" (Appadurai 1996), tweaks them, distorts them, stamps their own brand name on them, and makes them their own. Call it a method of critical appropriation, a variety of commercial satire, even a defiant assertion of the social nature of production over the individual rights of "the author." Or call it a clever marketing ploy, a way to draw attention to themselves through controversy or lure in costumers to their expanding label through already familiar brand names. In any case, Unkl347 has built its business out of cut and paste. It specializes in the art of the fashion remix, of conscious pastiche, producing vividly colored T-shirts, hoodies, jackets, and jeans, full of explicit references to bands and brands that have come before them. A recent design in their T-shirt line, for instance, features the trisected circular logo of British post-punk band Public Image Ltd., with the letters of Unkl's own brand name (U-N-K-L) crammed within the three black and white sections. Another manages to sample both the Olympics logo and a modified NBA logo within the same design. Yet another features the Lacoste alligator icon, turned upside down and eating Unkl347's former brand name, "EAT". Their denim line, similarly, features the famous Rolling Stones mouth and tongue icon on its jeans' fly buttons, with labels composed out of two Andy Warhol bananas intersecting into a V. This is pop art recycled, a copy of a copy of a copy. It's not original, it's not complicated, and it's not meant to be.

Unkl347 has come to exemplify an increasingly widespread attitude in Indonesia and just about everywhere else in the world touched by global capitalism and digital technology: *creating by any means necessary*. Design, for them, is a mandate too pressing to be easily ignored. It has weight and needs material resolution. His company, which Dendy prefers to think of more as a "creative collective" than as a business, is a rag-tag crew of skaters, surfers, artists, and musicians, including Adhi, guitarist for the "legendary" local indie pop band Pure Saturday, and Ucok, the MC and provocateur behind the Marxist hip hop outfit Homicide. None of them have any formal training in fashion design. None of them have any experience in the business world. What they do have is an impulse to connect and create, a relentless drive that has pushed Unkl347 to the top of an increasingly long roster of Indonesian independent clothing labels. Unkl347 has become probably the best-known brand emerging from the Indonesian "indie scene," one of hundreds of like-minded production houses founded on the ethos of "do it yourself" (DIY).

This book is about that scene—the political, economic, and cultural context out of which it emerges—and the DIY ethos it shares with numerous, similar scenes the world over.

Beyond Consumerism

For decades now, Indonesianist scholars, religious leaders, and journalists alike have described the emergent consumer culture of Indonesia's growing middle class as if it were a coming plague. Echoing familiar arguments from the American and European academic left about the individualism (Campbell 1987; Giddens 1991; Beck 1992), narcissism (Lasch 1979), and destructiveness of contemporary consumerism, these critics outline, in sometimes sanctimonious detail, the moral and cultural damage this "neo-imperialism" is inflicting on the values and institutions of Indonesian society. Dick has argued that a "class consciousness" has developed among an emergent sector of Indonesia's urban population, organized around a "modern, Westernised lifestyle," which, he claims, "has, to a considerable extent, been based on role models fashioned and propagated by the national mass media" (Dick 1990: 65). Other observers have chronicled the rise of *"kaum yuppie"* (*The Jakarta Post* 1999) or "metrosexuals" (Wibowo 2006), those members of the professional/managerial sector eager to leave behind the constraints of tradition for the imagined Utopia of Western-style hedonism.

These writers frequently lament the debased, materialistic values of contemporary Indonesian youth, worrying that generations are being lost to unbridled consumerist greed. This concern is understandable. The capital city of Jakarta's landscape is pockmarked with new malls, some the size of small villages, with fake blue skies shining overhead, as in a Las Vegas casino hotel. Massive plastic banners (*spanduk*) advertising hot new nightclubs, heavy metal concerts, and slick new digital cameras are draped over the roadways. And every major street now has at least one coffee shop or convenience store, with teenagers hanging out in front until the early hours of the morning, texting friends from constantly activated cell phones and swigging imported beer. In Indonesia, like so much of the industrialized world, consumerism is rampant. It is visible nearly everywhere.

But all of this rancorous ranting about consumerism tends to overstate its case. Simply put, the youth push toward consumerism has never been the passive succumbing to Western spectacle that these scholars fear. Young people in Indonesia, like everywhere else in the world, are highly selective in what they consume, how they consume it, and the meanings they construct surrounding the objects of their consumption (Hall 1980; Ang 1996; Jenkins 1997; Fiske 1987; Hahn 2002). They employ popular culture in larger projects of personal transformation and social-status-making (Diehl 2002; Liechty 2003; Baulch 2007), fit it into existing cultural frameworks for understanding the world (Miller 1992; Condry 2001; Kulick and Willson 2002). Consumption is, and has always been, an active process of selective appropriation and creative interpretation. Media products no doubt exert a powerful influence over the perceptions and worldviews of those who imbibe them, but they do not, as the most strident opponents of consumerism might argue, remake their audiences in their own image. Audiences, rather, continually remake, localize, and implant such products with meanings other than those the producers intended (Fiske 1987; Jenkins 1997).

And consumerism is not the whole story here, anyway. Apart from the louder, flashier narrative of flagrant materialism that animates contemporary social critique, there has been another story gradually unfolding, a shift throughout much of the industrial and industrializing world away from old class-based obsessions with "conspicuous consumption" (Veblen 1994) and toward more engaged participation in processes of production, from an emphasis on consumerism, as it were, toward what is sometimes called "prosumerism," or "prosumption" (Toffler 1980), the blurring of the very categories of production and consumption, and the ascendance of the amateur producer to new heights in the public realm. Status, in Indonesia and throughout the interconnected nodes of global capitalism, is increasingly about *conspicuous creative production* and active participation, shedding old boundaries of place and space and old divisions between producer and consumer. It is about connection

(Maffesoli 1996; Gauntlett 2011) rather than merely "distinction" (Bourdieu 1984), extending one's own personal boundaries beyond national and regional borders, crossing over from passive to active, and staking claim on one's place in the less and less rarified field of international cultural production (see chapter 4). These days, the coolest people aren't the ones with the most gadgets; they are the ones making their own stuff.

In Indonesia alone, there are now hundreds of self-published zines and magazines cluttering the shelves of bookstores; dozens of independent record labels competing with the transnational giants; hundreds of small, collectively-owned retail outlets (distros) selling limited-edition clothing, CDs, and other goods that are designed, manufactured, and distributed by local youth; and who knows how many home-recorded rock bands, clogging the airwaves, lining the record shelves, and blasting their music through the dense tropical air. Dig beneath the surface of contemporary Indonesian youth culture, garbed as it is in Converse and denim, and what used to look like pure consumerist spectacle becomes something very different: a push to express, engage, be part of an active youth movement, not simply defined by wearing the right clothes or hanging out in the right spots, but by participating in cultural production in one's own right.

Indonesia is not unique in this sense. If anything, it is a rather typical example of the reach and influence of digital culture, global capitalism, and the new "creative economy" (Florida 2002; McRobbie 2004; Hesmondhalgh 2007). It illustrates a process happening all over the capitalist universe, as new technologies make once-elite activities the providence of a far wider network of participants, and new conditions of production more and more prominently emphasize creative and immaterial forms of labor (Lazzarato 1996; Hardt and Negri 2001). The very circulation of media content across borders and competing media economies now "depends heavily on consumers' active participation" (Jenkins 2006: 3). We (as in, the global "we" of contemporary consumer capitalism) have crossed the line from a "Read Only Culture" to a "Read/Write Culture" (Lessig 2009: 28), a "sit back and be told" culture to a "making and doing" culture (Gauntlett 2011: 8), pushing thoroughly into the mainstream the once marginal practices of cutting and pasting, mashing up, and remixing (McLeod 2007; Lessig 2009; Mason 2008). Pirated computer software, the ready availability of the Internet, and the collaborative resourcefulness of youth have made "doing it yourself" easier than ever before (Spencer 2005: 12). And a new imperative to do just that has crept up into international moral consciousness.

The DIY Ethos—By Way of a Definition

What I refer to as "the DIY ethos" in this book is the "structure of feeling" (Williams 1977) underlying DIY production, the attitude that fuels it, the sentiments that surround it, and the logic that guides it. It is a set of shared "meanings and values" "actively lived and felt"(Williams 1977: 132) that shapes the way DIYers understand the world around them and choose to act within it.

Spencer uses the term "DIY ethos" to describe the attitude behind the production of low-budget, self-distributed zines in the United States and Europe, that is, "the urge to create a new cultural form and transmit it to others on your own terms" (2005: 12). Moore, an American zine writer, describes the rationale behind her own production as "living a life of intentionality" (2007: 3), of putting conscious thought and attention into how one engages with commercial culture. Rock critic Greil Marcus describes the ethos behind punk rock as the impulse "to live not as an object, but as a subject of history" (Marcus 1989: 6). I use the term "DIY ethos" in this book to capture each of these related sensibilities, but I am not limiting its use to any of them. The DIY ethos, as I conceive of it and as it appears in popular discourse, is too fluid a concept to be defined, or confined, in such a way.

In fact, in the span of a single week in November 2010, just as I was sitting down to write the introduction to this book, I came across, quite by accident, three very different usages of the term "DIY." A box of holiday cookie mix at the American specialty grocery chain Trader Joes advertised itself as "DIY," and two separate articles in *The New York Times* online edition used "DIY" in their titles. One of these articles, on the Tea Party movement inspiring millions of "previously apolitical" conservatives across the United States, labeled rightwing grassroots politics as "DIY." The other, on small-scale foreign aid providers, discussed DIY as a new model of philanthropy. DIY, here, is more than some fringe mode of cultural production. It is a buzzword, a floating, hype-inducing signifier with a variety of vague, and not always, related meanings. DIY, apparently, is the quality that unites disgruntled activists, do-gooder citizens, and amateur bakers, alike. It is at once a tool of empowerment, a weapon against malaise, and a cooking method that bridges making it from scratch and getting it out of the box.

All this points to the fact that DIY has come to have a much broader meaning in American society and, as we shall see, Indonesian society than it once held within fiercely independent circles of punk bands and zine writers. Among other things, DIY is now a home improvement channel on American cable television, a popular title for a series of large-print illustrated "self-help" books, a marketing term for Toyota's highly customizable Scion automobile, a regular feature in design and decoration magazines, and a catchphrase on hundreds of business brochures. DIY is as much the ethos of management conferences as it is of garage rockers and anarchist activists. It has become, one could argue, a recurrent theme of our era, an era that is defined by risk (Beck 1992), flexibility (Martin 1994; Ong 1999; Lloyd 2006) and global capitalist dis-integration (Lash and Urry 1994), in other words, an era where doing it yourself is often the only course of action possible.

For those of us who adopt it as a way of life, DIY means taking our lives into our own hands, assuming responsibility for our own success, and dictating the terms of our own commodification. It means fixing our car without paying a mechanic, adding on a new bathroom without consulting a contractor, or building an online craft empire out of beaded knickknacks and handknit scarves. DIY is all of these things and more. It is an adjective, a verb, and perhaps most of all, an imperative. Go out and do it yourself! insist legions of fanzine writers, fashion bloggers, YouTube filmmakers, and hedge fund managers. Don't wait for opportunity to come your way! Don't waste your time with intermediaries! And don't trust your engine to a mechanic!

As a descriptive term, DIY has been applied to such a diverse set of tasks as to sometimes seem to mean little of anything. After all, anything can be DIY, just so long as it is you who is doing it. Haven't we, then, been doing it ourselves since we've been doing anything at all? Are stone tools not DIY? Was the printing press?

As an attitude, though, a philosophy, a moral discourse, and a call to action, that is, as an ethos, DIY has a much more specific history, inseparable from the conditions of labor and production of advanced industrial, and now postindustrial, capitalism. DIY, of course, only takes on meaning as an ethos when it has a significant counterpoint, something it is not. Over the course of the nineteenth and twentieth centuries, as the following sections will demonstrate, that something it is not emerged in the form of alienated labor, of working for someone else, producing stuff for which we have no claim to authorship and even less to fair compensation. And it emerged in the form of passive consumption, of letting other people make stuff for us in exchange for cold hard cash. DIY is, in a sense, a cultural reaction against living in a consumer society where we hire others to build our houses, design our clothes, and fix our appliances, and where the final products of our own labors are shipped off, sold off, and profited from by a whole series of intermediaries who likely get more credit for it (and money from it) than we do. DIY, in this context, is the attempt to counter anomie (Durkheim 1984) and alienation (Marx [1849] 1998). It is "nonalienated labor" (Duncombe 1997), labor claimed and reconfigured as self-conscious practice.

It would be a mistake, though, to hold up the DIY ethos as an idealistic alternative to the logic of contemporary capitalism. DIY, I argue in this book, is also one of the very ideological pillars upon which contemporary capitalism rests, that creative, experimental, go-getter, and be-yourself spirit that drives innovation and fuels ever more active modes of consumption. The DIY ethos, then, has a good deal in common with the "creative ethos" (Florida 2002) circulating through popular nonfiction and academic circles alike. A wide variety of authors have argued, in fact, that we are entering a new era of global capitalism in which the labor and service sectors are rapidly giving way to an intellectual labor pool, a transnational think tank of artists, marketers, and designers, each trying to outdo the other in the extent of their "thinking outside the box." Best-selling author and public policy professor Richard Florida labels this group "the Creative Class" and argues it has already displaced the old bourgeoisie as "the new dominant class in society" (2002: xxvii). Ray and Anderson, similarly, identify a vast and rapidly expanding social group they refer to as "Cultural Creatives," with a "whole new worldview" (2000: 4) that is transforming the "deep structure" of American culture. In these works, written in generally optimistic prose for a lay audience, the Creative Class emerges as a kind of apolitical, quasi-spiritual movement with the implied power to change the world for the better.

While more theoretically oriented social critics have tended to shy away from such pie-in-the-sky proclamations, their work also treats the current cultural emphasis on creativity as new and fundamentally transformative. Marxists like Lazzarato (1996) and Hardt and Negri (2001) see a profound restructuring of the very concept of work around forms of "immaterial" or "intellectual labor." The demands of capitalist production, they argue, have shifted away from the manufacture of actual goods toward the production of information and entertainment. As physical manufacture is outsourced to the developing world, already developed nations in Europe, North America, and Asia concentrate their energies on marketing, branding, and the production of "affect" (see Hardt and Negri 2001), those sentiments and associations that fuel further consumption. The "Third World," in other words, makes consumer goods, while "the First World" produces the "consumer subjects" who desire and purchase those goods. Transnational companies, these days, sell the very idea of consumption. They hawk images and emotions, immaterial objects that require scads of "creative" individuals to produce them. As a consequence, "a new 'mass intellectuality' has come into being" (Lazzarato 1996: 134), in which creativity is experienced as a social compulsion, an authoritarian discourse. "One *has* to express oneself," (1996: 135) claims Lazzarato. The health of the economy depends on it.

The DIY ethos, as discussed in this book, is closely related to this emergent authoritarian discourse. It imposes similar demands on its subscribers, and constructs similar mandates. I make no effort in this book to separate the DIY ethos and the creative ethos as two distinct entities. No doubt they share a similar logic and sensibility, if they are not, in fact, the very same thing. Today, in our interconnected immaterial economy, creativity is the driver of production. It is our most valued asset, the possession of which distinguishes the "creators" from the "manufacturers," the "First World" from the "Third." And no longer is it the domain of the elite few, either, the strangely dressed bohemian set cut off from mainstream society. Today, the stiffest corporate executive—whether in Jakarta or the Silicon Valley—thinks of himself as a creative renegade, strives to "think outside the box," and diverge from the herd (Frank 2000). In a world where economic growth depends on the rapid production of new ideas, creativity has become conceptually linked with freedom, selfhood (Boellstorff 2008: 211), and even citizenship.

The DIY ethos is not, then, regardless of what some self-aggrandizing statements from punk rock zine writers might suggest, anti-capitalist sentiment writ large. The spirit of thinking independently, of pursuing one's passions for their own sake and going out and doing something on one's own terms rather than attempting to work "through the system," are thoroughly compatible with the needs of today's market. Campbell (1987), Frank (1997), and Heath and Potter (2005), in fact, have each argued that the logic of the counterculture, with its emphasis on individualism, creative expression, and hedonistic consumption has always been, in essence, one and the same as the logic of late capitalism. I am not sure I am ready to go quite that far. There are times, as this book will demonstrate, that the DIY ethos seems very much at odds with the cultural logic of late capitalism. As Moore (2010), Martin-Iverson (2008), and Duncombe (1997) have argued, DIY is often felt as an impulse toward de-alienation (Duncombe 1997), a cry of protest against the dehumanizing tendencies of contemporary corporate culture. It may use the master's tools (i.e., entrepreneurship, market exchange, etc.), but it longs desperately to move beyond them, even if it lacks a clear conception of where that "beyond" might be.

I do, however, agree with the sentiments of Boellstorff (2008), McRobbie (2004), Comaroff and Comaroff (2001), and others, that the impulse inspiring contemporary creative production, whether DIY or otherwise, maintains a variety of complex linkages to the social, economic, and cultural restructuring of global capitalism that cultural critics are inclined, these days, to gloss as "neoliberalism." I also agree with Frank and Heath and Potter that the actual practice of DIY production, no matter how countercultural DIYers imagine it to be, poses no structural threat to the smooth running of a free market capitalist economy. Instead, DIY fuels entrepreneurship, contributes to economic growth, provides sources of income and labor to youth, as well as useful training in business and management skills, and, of course, increases the total number of goods available on the market. In other words, the activities of DIY production further the ends of global capitalism, even when DIYers themselves stand against those ends.

The picture of the DIY ethos presented in this book, then, is never so cut-and-dry as pro- or anti-capitalist. DIY's relationship with capitalism, I will demonstrate, is far too fraught and inconsistent to be so easily simplified. At times it appears to challenge the status quo, at times it appears to be it. And it has been that way for a very long time.

Origins of the Term "DIY"

Historian Steven Gelber suggests that the phrase "do-it-yourself" may have first appeared in a 1912 Garrett Winslow article on home decoration in the American magazine *Suburban Life* (Gelber 1997). It introduced the term as a cost-saving measure, a way to cut back in hard times, and while it may have added something new to the American lexicon, it hardly introduced a new idea. Penny pinching was an American institution by the time of the Puritans. But the article, and the sentiment it promoted, seemed to Gelber to represent the beginning of something else, a shifting cultural attitude accompanying larger changes in the American way of life.

By the end of the nineteenth century, Gelber notes, home ownership had firmly taken root as one of the primary measures of social status and personal achievement in the United States. The Industrial Revolution thoroughly underway, more

Americans than ever owned homes, and many began to see their homes as their castles, their own personal barricaded retreats from factory life. The home was a space of leisure, insulated from the realties of work and the cold materialism of the market. Consequently, working on one's house was gradually being reconfigured in public consciousness from a task performed out of necessity—and a decidedly déclassé one at that—to a "labor of love," a form of work that blurred the very distinction between labor and leisure, carried out by one's own hands on a timeline of one's own choosing (Gelber 1997). There was, then, an incipient revolutionary sentiment in the impulse toward home improvement, an implicit critique of the work ethic embedded in the ordinary activities of domestic life.

Carolyn Goldstein, a curator at the National Building Museum and a historian of home economics, says that such home improvement projects "began to assume a self-conscious character and to play an active role in American culture" (Goldstein 1998: 15) around 1900, as mass-circulation magazines played in to this emergent handyman ethos and began featuring articles on home remodeling and repair. This, of course, was one of DIY's first internal contradictions: its autonomous spirit was itself, at least in part, mass-produced.

It was not, however, until the 1930s that home improvement really took off. After the stock market crash of 1929, an out of work population began to take solace in around-the-house tasks as a way to "participate in the work ethic" (Goldstein 1998: 17) without formal employment. "Hobbies" became all the rage as magazines touted the pleasures of doing-it-yourself as a fun, fulfilling activity for one's spare—or all too abundantly free—time. Then, in the wake of the Great Depression, government loan programs enabled a broad swath of the American population to purchase a home for the first time. In 1934, the federal government also began to guarantee home improvement loans of up to US$2,000, further encouraging the home-improvement trend, as well as inspiring a slew of new marketing campaigns to entice homeowners to buy tools, materials, and how-to-guides.

World War II continued this trend, as large numbers of American men gained hands-on building and repairing experience overseas, and women began to assume the factory jobs once held by men. Tool shops and home materials supply stores, once catering exclusively to professionals, opened up to the general public and shifted their marketing emphasis to a new demographic. By the 1970s, notes Goldstein, "undertaking repair and remodeling work on one's own had become so commonplace that even some of the most challenging home-improvement projects could be accomplished by amateurs" (Goldstein 1998: 52). The feminist movement of the 1960s and 1970s, combined with rigorous marketing campaigns targeting both men and women, helped expand the home-improvement trend beyond the narrow confines of chauvinist culture, and DIY assumed its place as a key symbolic activity of American independence.

Today, Home Depot, America's leading supplier of home-improvement goods and tools, claims more than 2,193 big box stores throughout the United States,

Canada, Mexico, and China. Ace hardware has some 4,600 stores, and operates in 70 countries outside the United States, including Indonesia. An expansive repertoire of magazines and how-to books supply helpful tips on how to get the biggest bang for one's home improvement buck, and a growing number of cable television channels, including TLC, HGTV, and its sister networks DIY and Discovery Home, have made renovation into mass entertainment. Home improvement is now a US$300 billion business in the United States alone, making it one of the United States's leading retail industries. Whether DIY home improvement's market success compromises its capacity to serve as a meaningful alternative to the alienation of modern capitalist life is an open question, but there can be no doubt that its symbolic promise of autonomy has become an American obsession, one we have worked hard to export to just about everywhere else.

Beyond Home Improvement

Across the Atlantic Ocean in the United Kingdom, the home improvement phenomenon had a big impact, as well, strengthening the cultural associations between domestic labor and symbolic independence, and inspiring legions of British homeowners, particularly men, to take on tasks once reserved for trained professionals. But the anti-alienation sentiment such "domestic masculinity" (Gelber 1997) obliquely represented was already a hundred years old by the time it was first applied to around-the-house tasks. In the UK, the Industrial Revolution produced its adversaries right from the start, most famously, perhaps, in the form of the Luddites, the rebel band of weavers who launched a crusade against the machines that threatened their livelihood at the end of the eighteenth century (Sale 1995). As mechanical production gradually replaced handcraft and other, more individualized modes of manufacture, art historians, social critics, and disgruntled artisans alike bemoaned not only the coal-blackened buildings, the air thick with soot, the meager living conditions allotted the working poor, but also the loss of human dignity intrinsic to industrial techniques. "In handcraft and manufacture," wrote Karl Marx in 1867 of the English workplace, articulating a common sentiment of the time, "the workman makes use of a tool, in the factory, the machine makes use of him" (Marx [1867] 2009: 75).

In nineteenth-century England, industrial production was often seen as degrading, alienating, and unfulfilling, a menial, mindless form of labor carried out by those with little power to do otherwise. As such, a variety of public intellectuals began to long out loud for an earlier era, when objects were made by hand and instilled with some greater presence of meaning. The art historian John Ruskin waxed poetic about the Gothic period of architecture, when builders united "fact with design" and instilled their work with a kind of "truthfulness" (Ruskin 2009: 143) utterly lacking from mass manufacture. Craft advocate, curator, and all-around renaissance man William Morris lamented the epoch of "the automatic machine which supersedes hand-labour" (Morris 2009: 150), turning men into little more than machines themselves. His solution: a revival of older, slower, and more personalized techniques. The "utilitarian ugliness" of modern life (Morris 2009: 151) must be countered by the intricate deliberateness of the handcrafted.

Morris and Ruskin were incredibly influential proponents of what came to be known as "The Arts and Crafts Movement," an early politicization of handicraft that would resonate with crafters for well over a century, and which continues to resonate with DIYers today (Gauntlett 2011). This longing for a simpler time is a theme that would be repeated again and again in British and, later, American and European cultural movements, from the free-festivals of the hippy 1960s to the "traveler" caravans of the mid-1990s (see McKay 1996).

It was punk rock, however, arising from the post-industrial metropolises of the United States and the UK in the mid-1970s, that would most stridently hoist the banner of DIY, popularizing the term for a new generation, and forging a conceptual template of DIY that is still very much in use today. Punk helped define what DIY is and should be for countless youth in places as far afield as Sweden and Indonesia (see chapter 2), and as such, it warrants some consideration here.

At its most radical, punk advocated seizing the very means of production, enacting the long-dormant promise of Marxist revolution. At its more mundane, it pushed a sort of militant amateurism, stripping rock of its virtuoso pretenses and replacing it with an anyone-can-do-it simplicity. Although punk, like any other variety of music, has had more than its share of bouts with genre purism, attempts by various parties, both inside and outside of the scene, to conscribe and limit what gets to be called "punk," the sheer variety of styles associated with it over the last four decades foils any attempt to finally describe, or circumscribe, its sound. Moreover, punk was never merely a sound. It was a fashion, a style of publishing, and a lifestyle choice. As such, punk describes less a genre than a "general sensibility" (Moore 2010: 2). The first incipient punk bands—depending on who you ask, The New York Dolls, The Ramones, Patti Smith, Television, or going back even further, The Stooges, MC5, and The Velvet Underground—forged a scene out of a deeply felt, if obliquely expressed, populist sentiment—the idea that anyone could form a band, whether they had talent or not, whether they were beautiful or not, that taking the stage and belting out a tune was no longer the exclusive reserve of well-polished music industry decoys. The message: *you* could do this, too. *You* could be us.

The idea of early punk was to challenge the very formula of music industry success. It was fervently anti-hierarchical, even ignoring the division between performers and audience during live events (Laing 1985). Audience members would climb up on stage. Bands would propel themselves into the crowd. Scanning a room before a performance, it was almost impossible to tell who was a performer and who was not. Everyone was dressed down, in dirty blue jeans and faded black T-shirts. When glamour and glitter did enter into early punk performance, it entered in the form of parody (Hebdige 1979; Laing 1985), The New York Dolls' rough-and-tumble drag or Debbie Harry's mock-vacant pout. Punk was anti-glamour, spectacle expunged and exposed.

Spectacle for its own sake did, however, eventually become a punk rock mainstay, a fact the public at large has never quite been able to forget. What most Brits and Americans remember about 1970s punk was its brash image; its cut-up and reassembled aesthetic; its shocking artificiality; giant, multi-colored coifs; and incongruent fascist paraphernalia famously chronicled by Dick Hebdige in *Subculture: The Meaning of Style*.

Punk historians like to trace this development—or perhaps *blame* this development—on Malcolm McLaren, The Sex Pistols' own Lou Perlman,[1] a Svengali figure who assembled the legendary London punk band as an updated Situationist advertisement for his King's Road clothing store and fashion label SEX, which he co-owned with girlfriend, fashion designer, and Sex Pistols personal stylist Vivienne Westwood (Marcus 1989). McLaren and Westwood capitalized on punk as a self-aggrandizing agit-prop statement for nothing in particular, a vague but iconoclastic image that made nihilism into a brand identity. It is not surprising, then, that it was in the wake of the Pistols' commercial success that punks themselves began to pronounce the death of punk rock (Laing 1985: 106). It would be the first of many subsequent deaths and resurrections.

The Pistols' meteoric rise to fame, their outlandish antics on stage and television, and their personification of the nihilistic, anarchistic persona that came to define the popular representation of punk have been recounted so many times as to hardly warrant further discussion here. Suffice it to say, The Sex Pistols would become the media image of punk and something of a detachable archetype. But as a collection of stylized misfits put together by McLaren and Westwood as punk rock's first boy band, who signed their first record deal with the major label EMI (before subsequently being dumped by them and signed by the then-boutique label Virgin),[2] The Sex Pistols were hardly the DIY ideal of today. The same could be said of many of their British (and American) contemporaries, including The Damned, The Clash, and Siouxsie and the Banshees (or The Ramones, Television, and Blondie on the other side of the Atlantic), all of which released their records on subsidiaries of major labels or with smaller independent labels with established relationships with the majors (O'Connor 2008: 7). Instead, early British punk seemed hell-bent on imposing their own brand of bratty rock 'n' roll rebellion on a mass audience. Cooperation with corporations was simply the fastest path to public notoriety.

It wasn't really until after punk—or rather, after its first death and resurrection—that punk music took on an explicit, clearly articulated DIY character. This was largely a result of a small, but vocal, faction of the punk community attempting to redefine what punk was and could be after its mass commercialization (Laing 1985; Reynolds 2004; O'Connor 2008). There was a general consensus among this punk vanguard that the rapid descent into spectacle and excess that punk experienced early on was at least in part a product of the music industry's profit incentive. "Real" punk, that is, punk with true revolutionary potential, undiluted by crass capitalism, would have to come from record labels independent of that system.

Independent labels, of course, had already been around for decades (Reynolds 2004). Detroit's Motown Records began as an independent label, as did influential labels like Sun and Ha, and back in the 1950s, Reynolds (2004) notes, about half of American rock 'n' roll and R&B hits were released by independents. But it was punk bands like the Manchester four-piece The Buzzcocks who were "first to make a real polemical *point* about independence" (Reynolds 2004: 26, italics in original). The Buzzcocks' 1977 EP *Spiral Scratch,* released on their own label New Hormones, inspired thousands of aspiring bands to stop courting record deals from major labels and just release their stuff for themselves already.

The Buzzocks' East London contemporaries, Desperate Bicycles, took DIY recording a step further (Laing 1985; Reynolds 2004). For them, DIY was no less than the "overthrow of the establishment music industry through people seizing the means of production, making their own entertainment, and selling it to other creative and autonomous spirits" (Reynolds 2004: 31). And quality control did not have to be an obstacle to self-release. Desperate Bicycles borrowed their style from a cut-and-paste lineage stretching back through Situationism and Dada to pioneer the sloppy, scrappy, Xeroxed aesthetic that would become the default look of punk rock album covers—and T-shirts, posters, and other music merchandise—for years to come. In the newly established era of readily available copy machines, it was an utterly achievable aesthetic, as anti-elitist and un-slick as an aesthetic can get. In doing so, Desperate Bicycles helped pave the way for bands like Crass, The Slits, and The Pop Group, for whom having one's own label was as critical as having a band at all. They established the basic format and precedent for independent outfits like Rough Trade, SST, Alternative Tentacles, Epitaph, and Dischord. For these groups and labels, independence was the only non-exploitative route to music-making (Laing 1985; O'Connor 2008). Signing with the majors was a brand of indentured servitude.

The move toward indie labels may have happened relatively late in the game, but there was, nonetheless, a sentiment in early punk of skill as surplus that inspired countless other bands to get in on the game, and which became a basic tenet of the DIY ethos for decades to come. What mattered in punk was style and attitude, not well-honed musical chops. If you could afford—or at least steal or borrow—an electric guitar and a set of drums, you had all you needed to form a band. The old excuses for not taking part in musical expression were breaking down. In punk rock's brand of populism, anyone who could get on the stage *should* get on the stage. And anyone who didn't was a model of mainstream mediocrity.

Punk's DIY ethos was also glaringly evident in its fashion sensibility. Inspired by the early work of designer Vivienne Westwood, British punks in the mid 1970s pioneered what is now standard punk practice, altering their own garments with scissors, safety pins, and permanent markers, constructing new ones out of found or recycled materials. In fact, for many non-musicians, fashion became the entryway into punk cultural production. "While some innovations in visual style," notes Laing, "came from the early bands, later shifts came equally from off-stage and outside the auditorium. It was here the do-it-yourself part of the punk ethos spread productively to the audience" (Laing 1985: 91). Punk fans would rip up school uniforms and pin them back together, cover their jackets with buttons, badges, and Sharpie-drawn art, elevate their hair into gravity-defying styles with craft glue and egg whites. They would repurpose dog collars as must-have fashion accessories, and scrawl profanities over the prints of their T-shirts. In punk, personalization was an absolute must. To do anything other than reconfigure one's clothes was a tacit admission of one's consumer conformity. "True punks made their own outfits," writes Laing, explaining the common attitude of the times, "the 'posers' merely bought theirs" (Laing 1985: 124).

The Meaning of "Indie"

The indie scene in Indonesia is in many ways a direct descendent of punk rock, inheriting much of its attitude and aesthetic. The pioneers of the scene (see chapter 2) saw themselves as part of an international punk underground, self-consciously appropriating punk rock's brand of militant amateurism as their own, and employing it as a loudspeaker of political dissent. Its current sensibility, however, evident in the fashions and sounds it so rapidly produces, came to Indonesia through a later cultural expression, the lighter, less aggressive post-punk reiteration of the DIY ethos most commonly known as "indie rock."

The term "indie," anthropologist Wendy Fonarow notes, is not just a derivative of independence; it is a diminutive of "independence" (Fonarow 2006: 45). It is independence in an oversize cardigan sweater and a pair of granny glasses, independence garbed in the protectionist tropes of an imaginary, deeply Anglicized childhood. Indie, she explains, describes a style of production and distribution outside mainstream commercial channels. It could, in theory, refer to any number of sounds or styles, but in practice, it has had far more specific connotations, referring to those "harmonic pop sounds" (2006: 39) associated with British bands like Primal Scream and The Stone Roses, melodic, guitar-heavy, jangly rock composed with "clever and/ or sensitive lyrics," (Hesmondhalgh 1999: 38) and a commitment to simplicity and austerity. It is music that avoids guitar solos and the showier trappings of mainstream rock, music stripped down and simplistic enough not to depend heavily on skill to be played, but which, nonetheless, displays a range of references to obscure musical movements broad enough to impress the dourest of used-record store employees (Hesmondhalgh 1999; Bannister 2006).

It is hard to determine a clear starting point for what has come to be known as "indie rock." Its ties with punk rock have never been fully severed, and many bands and labels were already using the term "indie" prior to indie rock being recognized as a movement in its own right. In the United States, up until the mid-1990s, indie was largely known as "college rock," further testifying to its upper-middle-class credentials (Hesmondhalgh 1999). It is often discussed as the musical accompaniment to "Generation X" (Oakes 2009; Moore 2010), those young adults coming of age in the recession of the early 1990s—the first generation of white middle-class Americans, notes Ortner (1998), who expected to have a lower standard of living than did their parents. College rock was music for the overeducated and underemployed. It was rooted in a feeling of being uprooted, a widespread cynicism toward commercial culture and the trappings of bourgeois life, and a certain economic fatalism that gave bands and labels the courage to pursue noncommercial ventures. After all, went the common sentiment, if we fail, what difference will it make? It's either this or work at the Gap, and I don't think they're hiring, anyway.

College rock had its own radio stations, generally run by universities, and its own pop charts, listed, among other places, on the back page of *Rolling Stone* magazine. It had no clearly defined genre parameters, but tended to feature those white rock bands with a vaguely punk lineage—The Replacements, Hüsker Dü, Dinosaur Jr.— and little hope of mainstream radio play. It was then re-classified under the more generic umbrella term "alternative rock" when bands like REM, Smashing Pumpkins, and Jane's Addiction proved to have broader commercial potential, making significant forays into the Top-40 charts.

In the UK, on the other hand, indie was used as a descriptive moniker from the mid-1980s onwards, largely among industry insiders and journalists (Wendy Fonarow, personal communication, 2011). It referred, ostensibly, to the independent status of a band's record label, but also to something of its general sensibility, a preferencing of earlier aesthetics of pop rooted in the folksier, less improvisational genres of garage and psychedelic rock. As in the United States, it was a largely white, middle-class phenomenon, rooted in a nostalgia for an imagined, pre-corporate past (Hesmondhalgh 1999; Fonarow 2006), when there was still some aspect of everyday life as of yet outside the commodity system. In the UK, it could have been The Smiths or The Stone Roses who deserve to be called the first genuine indie rock bands, groups with a throwback 1960s sound and a fey, bookish disposition. In the United States, the title probably goes to Beat Happening, the Olympia, Washington-based band fronted by college radio station deejay, K Records founder, and man-about-town Calvin Johnson.

Calvin Johnson was one of the first cult figures of American indie rock. An oddball music fan, with admittedly little musical talent of his own, a distinctive, occasionally gender-bending fashion sense—involving a crew cut, thick belts, too-tight T-shirts, and undersized jeans—and a penchant for the cute, cloying aesthetics that would eventually become a key component of indie identity worldwide, Johnson helped define what the indie movement looked and sounded like through much of the 1980s and 1990s (Azerrad 2001; Reynolds 2004; Oakes 2009). His home-recorded, cassette-based record label, K Records, brought a variety of international pop acts to American audiences. His little kid, stick figure scrawls of cover art helped launch the "cute core" turn in punk. His contributions to the zine *Sub-Pop*, particularly his decision to include local, and sometimes national, music acts on a cassette inside, helped make it an international name, going on to take on a second life as the record label that brought the world "grunge." Kurt Cobain, the deceased lead singer of Nirvana, even had a "K" tattooed on his arm to demonstrate his allegiance and gratitude toward Calvin Johnson.

Kurt Cobain had a profound impact on Calvin Johnson, too, but not perhaps, in the way one might anticipate. When Nirvana's *Nevermind* became one of the best selling albums of the 1990s, the Olympia-based scene out of which Beat Happening emerged had to reconfigure itself to maintain its outsider identity (Azerrad 2001; Moore 2007; Oakes 2009). Olympia scenesters screamed corporate co-optation, and one of indie's many self-restylings transpired. In fact, Johnson's brand of college rock bands began to make self-conscious use of the borrowed moniker "indie" in the early 1990s, largely as a means of distancing themselves from the commercial giant that "alternative rock" had become. Indie was an alternative to alternative with an aesthetic sensibility to match. Where alternative was abrasive and loud, indie tended to be quiet and melodic. Where alternative played up its working-class "lumberjack roots" (Azerrad 2001; Reynolds 2004), indie was far more comfortable in scholarly garb.

The American indie scene has since moved on to other buzz spots, but the legacy of Olympia lives on. It helped define the smart, homespun, geeky fashion sense so long characteristic of indie, what Oakes describes as "thrift-store librarian chic" (Oakes 2009: 122). It rejected the masculinist aesthetics of contemporary alternative rock, the abrasive sound and image of punk, and delved in to a kind of retro-progressive reworking of awkward American childhood.

Indie, however, was never strictly a musical movement. Like punk, it expanded into the realms of fashion, film, publication, and any number of other media-related ventures, uniting its participants behind a common ethos of taking part and making happen. Indie, one could argue, took over the helms of DIY when punk was looking the other way. It became its biggest advocate and its biggest success story to date. Or perhaps more accurately, punk itself, at least the variety of punk continuing to operate on the fringes of cultural production, became subsumed under the umbrella of indie, one of many sub-categories of a larger cultural movement. Indie has, then, in recent years, taken on "a more global kind of definition" (Oakes 2009: xiv). It has become shorthand for any variety of cultural production operating outside the reach of the cultural industries. In a sense, indie is a bourgeois takeover of punk, a middle-classification of DIY. Its adherence to an anti-capitalist rhetoric is just as defined as earlier movements, but it phrases these sentiments in the erudite vernacular of overqualified coffeeshop baristas.

This is not to say that indie is intentionally elitist. On the contrary, indie discourse is perhaps the most self-consciously egalitarian of the genres to emerge from punk rock. That which has been granted the distinction of indie (often not without controversy) has no doubt gone through a wide variety of trends, spawning an immense variety of obscure sub-genres and producing its own distinctive brand of subcultural snobbery; but at its best, indie represents a commitment to cultural democracy, to everyone's right to have their voice heard and their creativity acknowledged. "Indie is not just about DIY," writes Oakes, "though DIY remains its central tenet. It's about serving your community, self-actualization via creativity, and it's about empowerment, all of which occur as a result of DIY" (Oakes 2009: xiii). For many, the indie scene provides a supportive community of like-minded creators, a safe place to express, and an infrastructural apparatus of alternative distribution for those outside of established commercial media companies.

Indie Diffusion and Digital Age Ubiquity

Indie is a much more diverse field these days than it used to be. Acts like New York's TV on the Radio; London's M.I.A.; Mexico City's Rodrigo y Gabriela; Johannesburg, South Africa's Blk Jks; and Jakarta, Indonesia's White Shoes & the Couples Company infuse non-Western, often African and Latin musical elements (not to mention actual people of color), into the once glaringly white, Anglo-Saxon genre. And even among all-white bands, the sound has been considerably "ethnicized." Performers like Animal Collective, Yo La Tengo, Sufjan Stevens, tUnE-yArDs, Caribou, Beirut, Gang Gang Dance, and Yeasayer have ditched the old, restrictive insistence on the guitar, bass, and drums four-piece in preference for more eclectic instrumentations that include everything from keyboards and computers to sitars, trombones, and maracas. Indie, in other words, has gone foraging for new inspirations. It is multifarious, eclectic, reaching its tentacles into every possible direction, and absorbing influences from dozens of musical styles as it expands to a worldwide phenomenon.

Indie can do that, of course, because it has blown up big. Sometime toward the end of the 1990s, following in the wake of grunge, alternative rock and college rock, indie became commercially viable, the newest coolest thing in a pop cultural industry that feeds on novelty and change. It showed up first in the precious indie films playing in small theaters across the United States and Europe—films, that is, already infused with a similar sensibility, and which drew considerable attention as they began winning Academy Awards in the early 2000s—then television commercials for Volkswagons and iPods, and teen film franchises like the *Twilight Saga* (Newman 2009). Sometime in the early 2000s it became clear, indie was not an alternative to rock anymore; it was the new face of rock, with scant few examples of the older, more bombastic, long-haired alt rock groups left standing. These days, alternative rock feels like a dinosaur. Even the mainstream audience has little use for it, as Canadian band Nickleback recently discovered when their bid to play an NFL halftime show was fervently rejected by Detroit Lions fans.

In part, notes Hesmondhalgh, this is a consequence of increasing cooperation between indie labels and the majors, in addition to collaboration between music labels and other kinds of corporations. For a variety of reasons, including the shrinking presence of radio and the decline of album sales—usually blamed on the Internet—bands and labels began to capitalize on such partnerships in order to increase their pool of potential customers. No one, after all, wants to have to keep their day job, and bands began to suspect that old-fashioned notions like "selling out" were keeping them from mattering on the global stage (Hesmondhalgh 1999; Newman 2009). Cynicism about the possibility of true autonomy became widespread, and many indie scenesters began to see little difference between indie production and the other, more conspicuously commercial variety, to believe "that no strict division between authentic alternatives and 'corporate scumbags' will hold" (Newman 2009: 21).

But perhaps the single biggest contributor to indie's coming out to the light of day has been the Internet. Stories of indie Internet successes are so commonplace as to have become their own cliché, rags-to-riches tales of obscure underground artists like Lilly Allen or Arctic Monkeys using MySpace to launch themselves into public consciousness, and perhaps land a major record deal in the process. DIY, here, appears as the Horatio Alger myth of the Internet era.

No doubt the Internet has in many ways been a boon to the expanding indie scene, in the United States, Europe, and certainly in Indonesia. Open-source and download-able recording software have made DIY music production easier than ever. Indie music labels can now convert themselves into netlabels with almost no overhead cost, thereby eliminating middlemen. Web blogs, with their built-in templates have become a free alternative to designing and printing physical zines. Social networking websites like MySpace, Friendster, and Facebook have become a nearly effortless means of promoting one's products.

Long-time indie scene participant and zine writer Kaya Oakes sums up this positive influence of the Internet this way: "Not only did every indie writer, artist, or band have a Web site and a blog," she says, "we were all networking online and in person and constantly providing one another with ideas for staying solvent, distributing our work, and in some cases hooking up and starting relationships with one another" (Oakes 2009: 15). The Internet, in other words, expanded the size and efficacy of indie even further. At least initially, it enlarged and enriched the indie community. People didn't have to *know* each other in any significant "real world" way to help each other out, and barriers to cross-border communication were breaking down overnight. Indie scenes popped up in what may have once seemed like the least likely of places, China, Spain, Brazil, the Philippines, even in pockets of the Middle East.

But indie's self-identity was breaking down, too. If social solidarity is maintained, at least in part, by social differentiation, by having an in-group and an out-group, the Internet made it increasingly difficult to identify the boundaries of either one. Without any steadfast distinction between indie labels and commercial labels, indie sounds and mainstream aesthetics, virtually anything and everything could now lay claim to indie status. Simply put, indie's "subcultural capital" (Thornton 1996) has undergone massive inflation. Being indie is easier today than it used to be, both in the sense of easier to access and easier to identify with without fear of retribution. And when we commit less of ourselves to something, it stands to reason that we are likely to be less committed to it. Perhaps this is why when Oakes asked her UC Berkeley writing class what "indie" meant in 2007, she received a room full of blank stares, until one young woman sardonically quipped, "Indie's just hipsters in skinny jeans. That's all it is anymore" (Oakes 2009: 194).

Hipsters, an International Cultural Affliction

In the early 2000s, "the hipster" emerged as the contemporary popular representation of indie, a scruffy, style-over-substance aesthete, who knows how to pose and party, but has little interest in the political ramifications of DIY. In this folk depiction, the hipster is the cheapening of indie culture, what happens when indie goes mainstream. Whereas the classic indie kid of the 1980s and 1990s was idealistic and optimistic, the hipster, in this line of thinking, is ironic and cynical. Whereas the indie kid was deeply committed to his style as a unique representation of his identity, the hipster merely plays with his, adopting indie as a temporary mask, a fleeting affiliation. And whereas the modest indie kid hides behind a mop of hair and a calculated slouch, the garish hipster flaunts his ironic moustache and bicep-exposing muscle shirt on narcissistic websites like Last Night's Party and The Cobra Snake.

By the time I moved to Los Angeles in 2002 to pursue a PhD in anthropology, "hipster" and "indie" were terms used almost synonymously. Any distinction between the two categories had been lost. Television infotainment shows like *Access Hollywood* and *Extra* began referring to trend-setting Hollywood celebrities like Ryan Gosling, Jared Leto, Natalie Portman, and especially Zooey Deschanel and Chloe Sevigny as hipsters. *The LA Times* and *The New York Times* ran frequent profiles on prominent hipster clubs and trends. This, to me, was a profound reversal of role. Once labeled as freaks, geeks, and outsiders, indie was the new in-crowd. And so, rising starlets dressed in signature indie style, Hollywood actresses dated drummers from prominent indie rock bands, and suddenly labeling a fashion line, film, or music group as "indie" lent it an instant cachet, a credibility marker (Newman 2009), meaning, in essence, that it was quirky and kind of pretentious, but still pretty good.

Of course, all changes in status come with a price, and when indie became hip it lost something of its ideological innocence. It stopped, or at least, so the common accusation goes, believing in its own political potential, and succumbed to what its members increasingly saw as the inevitable fate of all subcultures, co-optation. "Notions of anti-commercial authenticity," notes Moore, "proved to be increasingly outmoded in a post-Fordist economy" (Moore 2010: 127), an economy that sucks up youth cultural trends into a massive, constantly spewing meat grinder of new products. For the hipster, authenticity is simply impossible. Indie is style, and style is all we can ever really achieve anyway.

But who is the hipster, really? Is it, as Greif (2010) suggests, the dominant class dressed in the subcultural garb of the subordinate? Is it the bourgeois gentrifier pushing out the urban poor so he can live out his bohemian fantasies (Greif 2010; Clayton 2010)? Or is it even a meaningful subject position at all? Is the hipster an actual identity to cultivate and live through, or just a postmodern bogeyman (Greif 2010: xvi) representing, to those with stake in depicting and deriding him, all that is wrong with this moment in transnational consumer culture?

It is worth pointing out that hipster is an identity openly embraced by almost exactly no one. It is, instead, nearly always a pejorative and distancing term (Greif 2010: 8). Hipsters are those other, less-conscious subcultural practitioners, the ones getting it "wrong." As Greif writes, "The hipster is by definition the person who does not create real art. If he or she produced real art, he could no longer be a hipster" (Greif 2010: 12). The hipster is, then, the faker, that ostensibly artsy person who hangs out at art events looking cool rather than doing anything meaningful of his own. He is the very antithesis of a DIYer. In fact, I would suggest, he is the DIYer's straw man (Clayton 2010: 30). He is the metaphorical infiltrator of indie culture, the constant threat of corporate pollution. Before the term "hipster" made a resurgence within indie scenes internationally, there was "the poser" and "the trendy," and before those there were the "part-time punks" and the "hangers on," and before those any number of other varieties of conceptual others serving a similar, border-patrolling function.

This doesn't mean the hipster does not exist, though. It just means he does not exist as a singular, self-professed, or embodied identity type. The hipster as scapegoat is a convenient fiction. But the hipster as sensibility has a far more prolific social life. Few people may be willing to fess up to being a hipster these days, but that doesn't mean those same people do not exhibit any hipster characteristics or recognize such characteristics in others. The hipster, rather, represents a set of traits, attitudes, and stylistic significations increasingly common in the digital age, ones we may not fess up to publically, but nonetheless experience and live through. It is that stylistic promiscuity, that slipperiness and lack of commitment, that knee-jerk ironic attitude that so many of us take so very much for granted. The concept of the hipster, then, retains some significant utility for diagnosing and comprehending certain trends in international style. It represents, I argue in this book, a digital age recalculation of what it means to be "outside" of corporate capitalism. The hipster, I suggest in chapter 4, is a new articulation of the DIY ethos for an era of media interpenetration, an era where a genuine outside is no longer possible.

The appearance of the hipster, then, whether at clubs, in blogs, zines, or popular representation, does not signify the end of "real" indie culture, as so many indie scenesters fear, the crumbling of the DIY ethos and the weakening of its attendant values. On the contrary, the hipster represents the adaptation of indie culture to changing cultural circumstances and the endurance of DIY values in the face of potential cooptation, commercialization, and superficializition.

Indie Flows and Disjunctures

As indie style has become more and more deeply entrenched in commercial culture—an economy, whether real or imagined, of cheap hipsterdom—DIYers worldwide have tended to respond in one of two ways: First, they have embraced the hip persona outright (even while railing publically against hipsters), adopting its modality of slippery selfhood, its ethic of cynical awareness, and its irony-infused aesthetic as a means of moving easily between a commitment to subcultural values and a fascination with the worst commercial culture has to offer. Hip, in this sense, is a way to have one's cake and eat it, too (Luvaas 2006). In Indonesia, I will demonstrate, this is one of the primary strategies of contemporary DIYers. In fact, Indonesian DIYers never knew indie before hip. It was hip before it ever reached them, and that, of course, was part of its appeal.

Second, DIYers have consciously veered away from anything too strongly associated with hip in the popular imaginary, turning to modes of production seemingly outside of its domain. Among a certain faction of the indie scene in the United States and the UK, particularly among those now entering their early to mid-thirties, those, in other words, who experienced the commodification of 1990s and 2000s indie culture as something of a personal loss, this has often meant turning to media about as far from hip as humanly possible, things like handicraft, beekeeping, and urban farming—activities, in other words, which seem more "hippy" than "hipster." Indie has launched its own "back to the land" movement. And yet, as Stevens (2009) has argued, even the indie craft scene maintains something of a hipster approach to production, employing the postmodern practice of the remix to instill folksy craft projects with parodic and satirical content.

And how could it be otherwise? Indie, with its aestheticized nostalgia for childhood and eras past, its continual remixing of sounds and styles, has never really resisted the logic of late capitalism, that postmodern tendency to flatten all of history into a single depthless moment (Jameson 1992), despite its numerous flirtations with modernist austerity. Even punk, its ideological forbearer, resisted outside efforts to pin it down or instill it with meaning. These are movements that continually shift their orientation, their content, even their articulated motivations. They have always, to some degree, adopted a hip positionality.

The hipsterization of indie, then, is not a simple case of corporate cooptation. DIY production has always maintained a complicated relationship with capitalism, pushing away with one hand what it pulls to it with the other. American home improvers sought autonomy from the marketplace by purchasing parts and tools and fueling a global industry of box stores and how-to guides. Punk's pioneer bands were marketed and distributed by major record companies, promoted as a novelty for mass amusement. Even William Morris, the idealistic, avowedly socialist, founder of the Arts and Crafts Movement spent most of his career selling trinkets to rich people, a fate not unfamiliar to DIYers today.

The hipsterization of DIY, then, may be less a selling-out of DIY to the tenements of global capitalism than a coming to awareness of its own longstanding complicity with it. It is, in a sense, an embracing of DIY's own internal contradictions. Hip DIY is DIY without the naïve idealism that has infused modes of DIY production since at least the Arts and Crafts Movement of the mid-nineteenth century. It is DIY without an inflated sense of its own purpose.

But that does not mean that DIY is no longer idealistic, or that it contains within it no potential threat to capitalism as usual. As this extended study of Indonesian indie culture will testify, contemporary DIY style lives and multiplies through the interstices of market and meaning, self and sociality, those flows and disjunctures that construct the contemporary experience of global capitalism. DIY, I hope to demonstrate, is an ethos both of and against capitalism—the state institutions that support it and the corporate actors who enact it. It is never a simple or singular choice between the two.

I begin this work with a brief history of the people and politics of Indonesia, a history that, any way you tell it, reads like the cut-and-pasted collage of an inveterate DIYer. It is in this chapter where I lay much of the groundwork for the rest of the book, the economic and cultural dynamics that give Indonesian DIY its own idiosyncratic character. I then move on to the in-depth ethnographic case study that will animate the rest of the book.

–1–

Indonesia, Republik DIY

Cutting and Pasting a Nation

Since gaining independence from the Dutch in 1949, the sprawling island nation of Indonesia has been, and continues to be, a decidedly tenuous union. Spread across some 17,000 islands in the South Pacific, the Indian Ocean, and the South China Sea, Indonesia is a country of incredible cultural, regional, and biological diversity. Its 233 million people, divided into more than two hundred distinct ethnic groups, practice an immense assortment of religions, from Hinduism to Protestantism and animism, and speak several hundred languages, some as linguistically far apart as are English and Mandarin. Islam might be the majority religion, with around eighty-eight percent of Indonesians claiming it on their identity cards, but this designation masks the plurality of perspectives that constitute Indonesian thinking, or even Indonesian Islamic thinking, from the highly syncretic, Muslim mysticism of the Javanese majority to the hardline "modernism" of Acehnese boarding schools.

Indonesia's dense tropical rain forests, meanwhile, are home to an almost unmatched diversity of species. Indonesia's oceans have a greater variety of marine life than anywhere else on the planet. Its unique geology boasts some of the world's most abundant supplies of crude oil, copper, gold, and tin. This abundance of natural resources, combined with a strategic location, right in the middle of maritime trade routes between mainland Asia, India, the Pacific Islands, and the Middle East, have made the Indonesian archipelago an attractive plot of land to a variety of pirates, usurpers, and colonizers. The islands making up today's Indonesia have been claimed by numerous states, from the Hindu Srivijaya kingdom (roughly 500 C.E.–1300) to the great Muslim empire of Sultan Agung (early to mid-1600s), each of which have left their mark on the architecture, languages, and cultural traditions of the archipelago.

It was spices, however, that first made the archipelago attractive to Europeans, who began making frequent expeditions to the region in the fifteenth century. The eastern end of the archipelago, known today as the Moluccas, were the mythical "Spice Islands" that Christopher Columbus was intending to reach when he crashed into the New World instead. The British and the Portuguese laid claim on pieces of the Southeast Asian archipelago early on, but it was the Dutch, through the world's first multinational corporation (Vickers 2005; Li 2007), the Dutch East India

Company (VOC), who succeeded in dominating the bulk of the region for European control, laying claim to the Spice Islands in 1602, and controlling the spice trade in the region from then on. By the early twentieth century, the Dutch had taken dominion over nearly all of the territory constituting today's Indonesia. Indonesia, thus, has been implicated in the global political and economic system for centuries, its diverse, cosmopolitan population subject to more than its share of conquests and land grabs.

Not surprisingly, then, when the revolutionary leader and first president Sukarno announced on August 17, 1945, just two days after the Japanese unconditional surrender to Allied Forces in World War II, that these greatly diverse peoples, whose only shared tradition was a long legacy of colonial exploitation, were now all part of the same newly liberated nation-state, his audience took it with a healthy dose of salt. They had, after all, heard similar claims before, and not so long before, either. When the Japanese landed on Indonesian shores in 1942, a few months after bombing Pearl Harbor, they had claimed to be freeing Indonesians from the stranglehold of Dutch imperialism. But like the Dutch, and a dozen empires before them, the Japanese had treated the archipelago as a treasure trove of natural resources. In particular, they were drawn to its oil, a massive subterranean supply they would use to help fuel their own war efforts. And they saw Indonesia as an inexpensive source of labor, as well, for agricultural production, for manufacturing, and for occupying the trenches of a rapidly expanding world war. The Japanese attempted to cast the local population as characters in a larger narrative of emancipation from the Western world, of joining in a grand unification of Asia (Vickers 2005). They were not, however, prepared to treat them as equals.

The Japanese had some early success at forging the former colonies of the Netherlands into a well-oiled human war machine. Many young people were militarized under the Japanese regime, eagerly trained in combat and defense, and convinced of Asian supremacy by their Japanese occupiers, as well as the urgency of action against the global imperialist giants (Anderson 1972; Vickers 2005). Many more experienced a groundswell of nationalism, as the Japanese encouraged locals to feel pride in their ethnic and regional roots, and even allowed political agitators like Sukarno and Mohammad Hatta to tour the country spreading the message of revolution, just so long as that revolution wasn't turned against them. At first, recalls novelist Pramoedya Ananta Toer, many local people "were in awe of the Japanese. The Japanese had severely dented the glory of the white man's realm both in mainland Asia and throughout the archipelago" (as cited in Vickers 2005: 87). Many locals wanted to be part of their story. But the Japanese's ulterior motives showed through soon enough, as many Indonesians received even lower wages, fewer rations, and less respect than under the Dutch.

Few tears were shed when the Japanese finally withdrew from the archipelago at the end of World War II. There was little good will left for them. But there was even less good will left for the Dutch, who attempted to reassert themselves as the imperial authority of the archipelago, backed up by the might of Allied Forces once the Japanese surrendered. They were met, not surprisingly, with stark opposition. Nationalism had already taken roots too deeply in the colony. A coalition of loosely aligned revolutionary youth made their move, and Sukarno, sometimes against his own will, was thrust forward as their leader. He declared independence from his Jakarta residence, while kidnapped by associates of Menteng 31, a hardline independence group. Years of bloody battle ensued, with tens of thousands of local people giving their lives for independence, sometimes wielding little more than talismans and ritual swords against the far-better armed Dutch and Allied Forces, and out of the bloodbath, thus, was born Indonesia.

The world community finally recognized Indonesia as an independent nation in 1949, four years after independence was declared. As a condition of their independence, brokered by the United States, Indonesia agreed to assume the considerable debt the Dutch had amassed during their reign as the colonial authority. It helped set up Indonesia for the "third world" status it has suffered from since. It was a tall price to pay for independence, but one the revolutionary leaders were willing to take on for their dream of a sovereign nation.

This does not mean that all the citizens of the newborn nation-state saw things in this light. The notion that state authority would now be transferred from the hands of the Dutch to an administrative center in Java, led by Javanese revolutionaries, and controlled through a bureaucratic infrastructure established by the Netherlands, was for some a hard pill to swallow. It felt, frankly, a lot like a continuation of colonialism as usual. To many, the new Indonesian nation seemed a shallow façade, an official gloss that justified the exploitative interests of the newly empowered Javanese. As a result, there have been numerous prolonged struggles for independence spanning the archipelago since 1949. Only one of these, the struggle for Timor Leste (formerly East Timor), has ended with emancipation. Others, like the ones in West Papua and Aceh, still wage on. From the beginning, then, the Indonesian government has realized that the only way to maintain national unity, to stabilize the nation's boundaries and solidify its assets, was to convince the diverse members of the nascent nation-state that they were indeed all Indonesians.

In this chapter, I survey some of the efforts of the Indonesian government to cut and paste together a unified, Indonesian national culture out of the myriad regional traditions of the archipelago—traditions, it warrants pointing out, that were themselves already similarly syncretic, cobbled together through a long history of conquest and trade. I portray, in other words, an interesting continuity between the cut-and-paste DIY practices discussed in later chapters of this book and the larger projects of nation-building and economic development that have been a mainstay of Indonesian life since gaining independence in the late 1940s. Indonesian DIY and national development, I hope to show, are inextricably linked, informing one another and sharing something of a common logic, even when they serve as imagined opposites.

This is not to say that DIY and development are the same thing. Far from it. Development projects as laid out by the Indonesian government have often actively thwarted efforts by Indonesians to create and produce on their own terms. Like DIY's relationship with capitalism more generally, the relationship here is more fraught and complicated than a simple either/or. The DIY ethos is both a continuation and a rupture in development thinking, a historically specific reworking of a larger, and longer running, cultural theme.

The Indonesian state, after all, has preferred central management to radical democratization, a model of leadership Geertz (1981) and others (see Pemberton 1994; Baulch 2007) have referred to as the doctrine of the "exemplary center," where the provinces were to always look to the capital of Jakarta for their example of how to think and behave. The first two presidents, Sukarno and Suharto, implemented an essentially paternalistic mode of government, where father knows best, and the great family of the nation would be wise to follow his lead. As we shall see, then, whatever steps the state has taken to enable Indonesians to live more empowered and less alienated lives, it has also stifled and suppressed through decades of authoritarian rule. Autonomy has continually been held up as a shared mythology for Indonesians, a promise of the revolution and an ideal of Indonesian development, but it is one that is never quite allowed to materialize. The state, rather, has long seen fit to dominate and discipline the terms of cultural production. Anything outside their control, at least prior to the fall of Suharto in 1998, has been read as a threat, pure and simple, both to national unity and state sovereignty. DIY, in this context, emerges both as the failed promise of revolution and an internalization of national development thinking. It is a contemporary remix of an old theme, a nationalistic number with a new transnational beat. Or more accurately, Indonesian DIY is a remix of a remix of a remix.

The National Remix

Article 32 of Indonesia's constitution asserts the necessity of developing an inclusive, "supra-ethnic national Indonesian identity" (Chandler et al. 1987: 422), which expresses "the personality and vitality of the entire people of Indonesia" (Foulcher 1990: 301). Its basis would be the existing cultural traditions of the diverse people of the archipelago, and yet, it had to be generalizable, to contain moral, ideological, and aesthetic dimensions that could apply equally to all of Indonesia's people, no matter how different. At the same time, this supra-ethnic culture had to exclude a conceptual "outside" (Heryanto 1990: 290), justifying national boundaries and rendering natural and inevitable the current territorial configuration. The new national culture, in other words, was to establish and reinforce an Indonesia-wide "imagined community" (Anderson 1983), a shared fiction of common bond and common cause, made real and reinforced through constant repetition in the institutions encountered through everyday life. A vast bureaucracy "extending from Jakarta to the remotest villages through offices of the Department of Education and Culture" set out to shape a single national narrative and to situate local cultural groups within it (Sutton 2002: 21).

The goal of the Indonesian government's massive culture-building project was not simply to intellectually convince diverse Indonesians of their essential "Indonesianness," but to impose the notion on their very understanding of reality. In fact, as Pemberton has pointed out about the New Order government, who ruled Indonesia between 1966 and 1998, once Sukarno was removed from power, the Indonesian state has taken great pains to erase any evidence of its role in culture-building. "New Order Indonesia," wrote Pemberton, "seems to present itself as an ideal absence in which nothing, as it were, happens" (Pemberton 1994: 4). Through a diverse range of events and institutions, the Indonesian government has sought to make the national culture a fundamental aspect of experience, an undeniable part of who Indonesians are and how they think of themselves. It is useful, then, to think of Indonesian national culture as a "hegemony," as cultural theorist Raymond Williams defined it, "a practical consciousness," or "a saturation of the whole process of living that defines the boundaries of 'simple experience and common sense'" (Williams 1977: 110). It is a culture which "also has to be seen as the lived dominance and subordination" (Williams 1977: 110) of diverse members of Indonesian society.

This does not mean, however, that the Indonesian culture-building project has been wholly successful. On the contrary, it is continually "resisted, limited, altered, and challenged" (Williams 1977: 112) by the people on which it is imposed. I argue in chapter 6, in fact, that Indonesian indie music constitutes one such reworking. DIY streetwear (see chapter 5) no doubt constitutes another. Indonesian cultural hegemony, thus, must be understood as a process, not an end product, an ongoing struggle between competing notions of self and society. As such, state hegemony must be continually updated, modified, and renewed (Williams 1977) in order to be maintained. And the primary means through which the Indonesian state has done this is through a process of constant appropriation, of sucking up all that is foreign to it within Indonesia's borders as part of its own self-constitution. Indonesian literary figures have often described the Indonesian government as a *dalang*, a traditional Javanese shadow puppeteer, manipulating events from behind a screen. It could just as easily be described as a DJ or a studio engineer, spinning a massive cultural remix out of parts sampled from hundreds of different cultures and movements.

It should come as no surprise, then, that the official state motto of Indonesia is "*Bhinnéka Tunggal Ika*," a hackneyed, oft-repeated mantra that translates roughly as "Unity in Diversity." "Indonesian citizenship," Atkinson writes, "is constructed pluralistically" (Atkinson 2003: 135). It is not, however, constructed haphazardly or indifferently. Cultural difference is only allowed "so long as it is difference within, not distance from, certain nationally defined parameters" (Atkinson 2003: 135).

As anthropologist Anna Tsing has written, "[T]o be a legitimate expression of ethnic identity, local culture must become harmless, officially sanctioned 'entertainment'" (Tsing 1993: 246). The state incorporates only "safe," superficial aspects of ethnic distinction into its official cultural canon. Only those performative markers of difference, such as ethnic "costumes" (Rutherford 1996), folk dances (Kuipers

1998), and handicrafts (Adams 1998), which in no way threaten the idea of national unity (Foulcher 1990; Heryanto 1990; Pemberton 1994), are put on public display or forged into official representations of Indonesian culture. Everything else is banned, suppressed, or otherwise censored. The Indonesian state, thus, approaches diversity as a sort of trans-cultural pageant (Pemberton 1994; Rutherford 1996), a parade of surface-level differentiations that merely support the state's claim to represent a broad spectrum of peoples. It is this performative aspect of national culture that Pemberton refers to as "Mini-ization," the disacknowledgment of real difference through the display of an innocuous cultural pastiche (Pemberton 1994). Cultural idiosyncrasies are thereby reduced to a spectacle of empty visual signifiers.

Perhaps the place where mini-ization is at its most deliberate and ostentatious is in the massive ethnic theme park on the outskirts of Jakarta from which mini-ization derives its name, *Taman Mini Indonesia Indah* (the Beautiful Indonesia-in-Miniature Theme Park). Taman Mini, as it is more commonly called, is laid out around an 8.4-hectare pond built as a replica of the Indonesian archipelago. It includes a series of miniaturized "ancient monuments," a giant hotel and shopping center, extensive recreation facilities, a revolving theater, a man-made waterfall, and an immense amphitheater for cultural performances. Its crowning achievement, however, was the set of twenty-six one-hectare plots assigned to each of Indonesia's provinces. Each plot contains a house, built in the "genuine customary architectural style" (Pemberton 1994: 152) of each province's population. And each province, of course, is simplified substantially, reduced to one cultural representation, that of its most "distinctive" or flamboyant ethnic group. At Taman Mini, culture is made entertaining, accessible, and fun for the whole family. It is Disney-fied, remade as an amusing wonderland of unthreatening difference (Anderson 1990; Pemberton 1994).

Institutionalizing the Nation

In chapters 5 and 6, and again in the Conclusion, I describe a DIY tendency toward pastiche of this sort strongly evident in the products of the Indonesian indie scene. Among indie designers and musicians, transnational youth subcultures from death metal to dubstep exist side by side as decontextualized—one might say mini-ized—signifiers of a vague, global sensibility. Both the Indonesian government and the lifestyle armies of contemporary DIYers appropriate assiduously, re-making other peoples' cultural products into their own. But where DIYers appropriate as a means of challenging and undoing the imbalanced power relationships in which they find themselves, the Indonesian government samples to subordinate. Their project of culture-building may be a sort of grand, national remix, making use of the preferred form of production for millions of DIYers worldwide, but it is not, by any means, itself a DIY project. It is not the Indonesian people, after all, who make the official culture of today's Indonesia. It is the government who forges it out of the people's collective past efforts. The government hoards culture and alienates it from its original producers. It museumifies it, suffocates it of its living tradition. Rather than "do-it-yourself," this is closer to "don't do anything rash, and if you insist on doing something, let us decide what it means for you." "Let us define the terms of who you are and what you can be." While often bearing the rhetoric of pride and empowerment, the practice of such national appropriation often results in the opposite: objectification and exploitation.

Take, for example, the instance of *tongkonan*, intricately carved longhouses, common among the elite of the Toraja people in South Sulawesi. These ostentatious abodes of the Toraja aristocracy have long attracted tourist attention. Miniature renditions are sold at gift shops (Volkman 1990; Adams 1998) and on display at Taman Mini. Tongkonan motifs cover T-shirts, postcards, and posters. Today, the image of the tongkonan, one of many visual signifiers of Indonesia's rich, collective heritage, covers the back of the 5,000 rupiah bank note. It has been rendered state property, and by extension, an aspect of Indonesian national culture. Detached from local significance and incorporated into the realm of pan-Indonesian cultural property, objects like the tongkonan reflect an emergent Indonesian self-image. Cultural attributes are flattened, miniaturized, and mass distributed. Potentially threatening difference is domesticated (Rutherford 1996: 586) and rendered harmless.

The performing arts have been a particularly important source of pan-Indonesian symbolism (Keeler 1987; Hatley 1990; Rutherford 1996; Adams 1998; Sutton 2002). Cultural performances and festivals are a staple of Indonesian state pageantry. Important government officials pay prestigious Javanese puppeteers (*dalang*) to perform elaborate, nine-hour shadow plays (*wayang kulit*) for state functions (Keeler 1987). Biak *wor* dance and music troops are invited all the way from West Papua (Indonesia's easternmost province, some five hours by plane from Java) to perform for the day at Taman Mini in Jakarta (Rutherford 1996).

But no Indonesian institution has played a more formative role in the establishment of a common Indonesian cultural identity than has the educational system. It is in public schools, Siegel notes, "where the sentiments of nationalism are centered" (Siegel 1986: 139). The Indonesian school system, thus, is highly centralized and standardized, employing identical textbooks, class structures, and instructional curriculum. Children are required to wear uniforms. Teachers are expected to convey a fixed set of ideas. In the words of Anderson, "the government schools formed a colossal, highly rationalized, tightly centralized hierarchy, structurally analogous to the state bureaucracy itself" (Anderson 1983: 121). And the homogeny of schools presents a highly effective medium for imparting shared cultural values. Schools, apart from teaching the fundamentals of arithmetic, Indonesian grammar, science, and (even) religion, attempt to instill in pupils the moral convictions of "good Indonesian citizens." It is in school where children learn the geography and national boundaries of the Indonesian nation, and it is in school where the official state ideology of *Pancasila* is introduced, explained, and reinforced.

Understanding Pancasila is critical to a comprehension of the terms and conditions of full Indonesian citizenship. Composed of five "universal" principles (the belief in one supreme God, a just and civilized humanitarianism, Indonesian national unity, democracy through consultation and consensus, and social justice for all Indonesian people), the state ideology of Pancasila was developed by Sukarno, the first president, back in 1945, shortly after he proclaimed independence, and it was subsequently included in the Indonesian constitution (Kitley 2000: 396). Its tenets are posted in classrooms, memorized, and repeated by students, and made the subject of essays, school plays, even classroom sing-a-longs.

Another fundamental component of Indonesia's public education curriculum, and indeed a major theme of Indonesian movies, television shows, and literature, is the recounting of the history of the Indonesian revolution. The Indonesian revolution is the focal point of Indonesian official history, largely because it is during this tumultuous period between Sukarno and Hatta's declaration of independence in 1945 and the defeat of the Dutch in 1949 when early nationalists "first began to think of themselves as Indonesians" (Chandler et al. 1987: 422). In the common struggle against Dutch imperialism, Indonesian nationalism was born. Or, at least, so the story goes. But this "official" history of the Indonesian revolution is by no means a neutral account of indisputable events. "National historiography, or the narrativizing of nationhood, can never be a politically innocent act" (Atkinson 2003: 136). It always involves selectively attributing significance to some actors and events and not to others (Atkinson 2003: 136). It involves composing out of a fragmented series of events occurring among different people in different parts of the archipelago, a single storyline of common struggle (Hoskins 1987; Henley 1993; Atkinson 2003).

Perhaps, however, the most important role Indonesia's public educational system has played in the formation and elaboration of an Indonesian national culture has been its teaching of Bahasa Indonesia, the official national language of Indonesia. In a nation of several hundred regional languages, establishing a common language was a necessary precondition for effective and lasting rule. It is the speaking of the national language, above all, which defines a resident of the archipelago as "Indonesian" (Keane 1997; Siegel 1997; Kuipers 2003).

Bahasa Indonesia is not the language of a particular ethnic group in Indonesia. It is not a "real" language at all, "that is, a language with a culture attached" (Siegel 1997: 31). Rather, it is a lingua franca, a trade language, which developed between Southeast Asian merchants and traders from Southern India, the Middle East, and elsewhere over the course of hundreds of years. As such, it contains elements from a number of languages, including Hindi, Sanskrit, Farsi, and Javanese, just as local cultural practices contain such elements. It is a language which, as Siegel writes, developed "in the middle, between the speakers" (Siegel 1997: 16) rather than among them. It was also loosely tied to colonial structures (Siegel 1997: 26). The Dutch East India Company (VOC), and later, the Dutch colonial administration, used an incipient form of Bahasa Indonesia (then known as "Melayu") to govern and conduct business with local people in the terrain of the "East Indies." The use of the language, then, has long been tied to structures of power. To speak in Bahasa Indonesia, as Siegel (1997) argues, means reformulating one's thoughts in the language of the state. No wonder, then, that so many Indonesian indie bands have chosen to sing in English instead (see Chapter 6).

Disseminating (and Complicating) the Message

It is, however, the mass media, more than any other single institution, where the struggle over Indonesia's self-conception most conspicuously ensues, played out in spectacular displays of state power and local resistance. The mass media has become nearly synonymous with the "modern," and it has from the beginning played a major role in Indonesia's construction of a national culture.

Inheriting an established network of relay stations from the Dutch, one of Sukarno's first acts as Indonesia's president was to create a national radio network, Radio Republik Indonesia (RRI) (Sen and Hill 2000). RRI was to become the communicational frontline of the revolution. Then, when Indonesia gained its independence, radio assumed a missionizing function, bringing its gospel of nationalism and development to the furthest reaches of the archipelago. It was, as Sen and Hill note, "used extensively in education, especially political education," including preparing the electorate for the first general elections in 1955 (Sen and Hill 2000: 82). But the media was also seen as potentially dangerous. It could carry subversive messages or corruptive Western influence, which, the government thought, could threaten the very cultural fabric of the new Indonesian society. Sukarno, and his successor Suharto, thus kept a tight grip on media content. In 1946, before even achieving independence, Sukarno established the Ministry of Information, an ironically named government agency whose job was to monitor and censor anything on air or in the press which threatened national unity, implied instability, or challenged the official state ideology of Pancasila (Kitley 2000; Sen and Hill 2000). Over time, the state governed the media more through the threat of censorship, than through censorship itself (Sen and Hill 2000). Filmmakers, television producers, radio DJs, and news reporters had a deeply instilled sense of what was acceptable for air and what was not. The principle rule was to simply avoid depictions of social disorder and conflict. And if conflict was depicted, it must be resolved before the end of a production (Heider 1991; Kitley 2000). Hence, the archetypal plot line for television or film during the New Order regime was to move from order to disorder to the restoration of order (Heider 1991; Sen and Hill 2000: 150). It was the job of the media to maintain the illusion that everything was running smoothly at all times, that everyone was getting along just fine, and that nothing was really happening (Pemberton 1994: 4).

When Suharto took power in 1965, he set out to make the new technology of television one of the principle mediums of the "national culture project" (Kitley

2000: 3). He founded Televisi Republik Indonesia (TVRI), the first, and until the early 1990s, only television station in Indonesia. In 1976, he ordered the launch of the Palapa television satellite, the fourth such national television satellite in the world, in order to widen the reach of the official state message. Relay stations were erected across the archipelago, and Suharto even had television sets delivered to the heads of villages in remote parts of the country. Suharto's intention was to reach as many people as possible, including the illiterate, who would be unable to develop a national consciousness through reading newspapers and other printed publications (Kitley 2000: 24). Television "was devised to be both the channel and the manifestation, the nightly dramatization of a shared cultural identity" (Kitley 2000: 47).

It should be strongly emphasized, however, that the government's hold over the media has never been complete, and it was through those gaps between the New Order regime's iron fist that DIY culture first slipped into Indonesia, first through punk and underground metal, and later through indie rock. Short wave radios, for instance, have for decades ensured that relatively well-off Indonesians could access foreign media sources. Satellite television dishes, likewise, became available in Indonesia in the early 1980s, and by the mid-1990s, they had spread like mushrooms across the archipelago, sprouting first on the rooftops of the rich, and gradually to those of even the lower middle class. Today, satellite dishes are nearly as common as the rooftops that house them, and the government's ability to determine what they pick up is extremely limited. Moreover, urban elites, making frequent trips to neighboring Singapore and Malaysia, have never had much trouble moving cultural goods across borders, and the streets of city centers across the archipelago have long sold unlicensed, sometimes smuggled in, copies of popular cassettes, CDs, and VCDs with minimal police interference. Many of the bands that inspired the early Indonesian indie scene, thus, were ones that never played on state radio or television, ones that were never even sold in local, "legitimate" music stores.

Plus, state censorship of Indonesian media content has only ever reached so deep. Accustomed to years of government monitoring, filmmakers, newscasters, and above all, musicians, have long since learned how to subtly encode subversive messages into their products without getting caught. Heryanto (1990) speaks of a "shadow language" that grew out of media censorship; a way of communicating covert messages though poeticized speech. Rock musicians, in particular, have long known how to walk the fine line between government appeasement and social commentary. Rock superstar Iwan Fals, for instance, sometimes called the Bob Dylan of Indonesia, frequently sings about corruption, collusion, and nepotism, but stops just short of accusing specific members of the government of misconduct. His lyrics, furthermore, are always just ambiguous enough to enable regime-friendly readings. Early indie bands, meanwhile, were able to bypass censors in two ways: first, through producing their albums outside the major recording industry and second, by singing in English (Wallach 2003). DIYers, in other words, shielded themselves from a state crackdown by keeping their distribution small and their message inaccessible. As the New Order government assumed most Indonesians did not understand English, nor have access to or interest in the low-fidelity recordings of DIY bands, they tended simply to look the other way.

Then, in the mid-1990s, the government, acknowledging its waning authority over the airwaves, began to switch tactics from limiting media content to simply regulating it. They opened up television to private industry, and where there was once only one permitted station, now there were five. The government then opened up the television and music markets to outside investors, and soon, international stations including MTV Asia, StarTV, CNN, and HBO were available in millions of Indonesian households (Kitley 2000). Multinational record labels like Sony-BMG and Columbia, meanwhile, were setting up shop in the capital city of Jakarta, signing Indonesian artists and cultivating a massive local pop music market. Now, national networks and record labels had to compete with the internationals, and the effect was profound. Popular music became more diverse, polished, and commercial. Soap operas (*sinetron*) and "infotainment," cheap to produce but sensationalist in content, became the most popular shows on television. And with international news coverage available, local news sources had to expand their coverage in order to compete. It was no longer possible for the government simply to feed news to local stations (Sen and Hill 2000).

The Internet, of course, complicated factors even further. In Indonesian cities across the nation, local entrepreneurs began setting up Internet cafes in around 1996, making the World Wide Web accessible to a wide variety of Indonesians. Gradually, the younger generation of urban middle class developed the feeling that they could say virtually anything they wanted with impunity and anonymity (Sen and Hill 2000: 210). Plus, they could access media content from anywhere in the world, whether the government deemed it appropriate for them or not. Information was more freely available than ever before, and so were a range of new musical and stylistic inspirations.

The Indonesian media, then, has been a site of struggle for decades, of attempted state hegemony and ongoing acts of resistance, of multiple parties with different interests and varying degrees of access to power battling for prominence. In this sense, the media is a projection of social conflicts within Indonesian society at large. It is not a coherent reflection of a single national culture, but a nexus of differing agendas, conflicting values, and opposing visions of Indonesian modernity. Few institutions, notes Hefner, have played a larger role in the contest of meanings than the media (Hefner 1997). As such, it should come as no surprise that it is media, in the forms of music, magazines, and fashion, that have asserted themselves as the central preoccupations of DIY practice.

Developing the Nation

Not everyone in Indonesia, though, has access to the mass media, not to mention the public educational system that trains Indonesians to be good and respectable citizens. Seventy percent of the Indonesian population continues to live in rural areas, many without electricity or access to running water, let alone satellite television and the Internet. The Indonesian quest to become a modern nation has left many on the margins, and many others in the shameful position of disappointing government efforts toward modernity and progress. Inability to speak the national language, lack of membership in one of the officially recognized world religions, and lack of a formal education have stigmatized large populations of people across Indonesia (Tsing 1993; Atkinson 1996). It is this stubborn reality, incongruent with Indonesia's self-concept as a modern, industrializing nation, which has fueled Indonesian national efforts toward development (*pembangunan*).

Development has been a consistent component of Indonesian state rhetoric since the nation's very inception (Foulcher 1990; Heryanto 1990; Anderson 1983; Atkinson 1996; Brenner 1999; Li 1999; Kitley 2000; Tsing 2003), continuing a theme begun years before by Dutch colonists (Li 2007). The term *pembangunan* is frequently employed in official documents, appears on billboards advertising government initiatives, in television campaigns, and government-approved textbooks. It is virtually ubiquitous as a national theme. Though seldom defined, "development" ostensibly refers to the ideal of a distinctly Indonesian modernity, where all Indonesians have access to basic resources, participate in the Indonesian democracy, and adhere to the tenets of Pancasila. It also has something to do with personal accountability and autonomy, a trait glossed by government rhetoric as *kemandirian*, or standing on one's own two feet (Vickers 2005). The ideal developed Indonesia would be a nation of responsible, ethical, and self-managing citizens (Li 2007; Rudnyckyj 2010), whose labors serve productive functions for Indonesia as a whole, expand the Indonesian economy, and bring prestige and respectability to the "third world" country. Indonesia in this vision would be a nation, in other words, of something like DIYers, self-initiators making their own fortunes through socially and morally responsible activities. Or at least, it would be a nation of DIYers stripped of critical intent, DIYers anxious to go along with the government program, rather than wandering too far on their own paths.

What development is not, however, is Western-style individualism, a fact the Indonesian government has reiterated time and time again as part of official national rhetoric. Individualism, as Sukarno laid out in no uncertain terms in dozens of his famous speeches, is the selfishness of a consumer society, the collapsing of social obligation into solipsism and greed. Indonesia strives toward something else, a more distinctly "Asian" brand of standing on one's own two feet. *Kemandirian* is a project of mutual uplift, one we can all only accomplish together. Here again, the collectivist orientation of the DIY ethos seems strangely conducive to governmental goals. And yet, the Indonesian government has also repeatedly cracked down on movements toward collective autonomy, whether organized labor or socialist activism. Collectivist projects must always take place on the state's own terms.

Government concerns with development have led to a variety of state projects, including the transmigration of Javanese from the overpopulated island of Java to remote, less "developed" regions of the country—in the apparent hope that such transmigrants would impart their "superior" cultural practices upon the local population, the building of public facilities in run-down or "primitive" communities, the relocation of "backward" groups to more central areas, and the organization of hundreds of self-help style workshops, designed to impart on Indonesians the go-getter values of the citizen of the modern world (Li 1999; 2007; see also Rudnyckyj 2010). According to Li, the rationale for this kind of development follows "a general logic of governmentality" (Li 1999: 196). It is more than simply a humanitarian mission; it is a civilizing effort, a means of bringing Indonesia's diverse population under the fold of state control. It is, Li writes, "a project to normalize bodies, subjectivities, and communities and discipline them to the nth degree. It is a complete attempt at social engineering, governmentality in gross form" (Li 1999: 301). It is also, she explains, a goal thoroughly commensurate with another, more recent state agenda, one that ideologically aligns Indonesia with much of the industrial and industrializing world: the goal of establishing a relatively free market economy. A free market, after all, depends on a developed infrastructure. It depends on training and experience. And most importantly, it depends on modernized, self-motivated individuals, capable of harnessing for themselves the bountiful natural and human resources of the archipelago. Li summarizes the scope of this agenda with one simple term: neoliberalism.

Neoliberal Interventions

A couple of points are probably necessary at this juncture to avoid misunderstanding about the view of neoliberalism presented here. First, although I use the term "neoliberalism" in this chapter, and throughout the rest of the book, to describe the latest, deregulation-obsessed phase of global capitalism, I do so with a good deal of reservation. In my field of anthropology, the term has become so commonplace as to have lost much of its analytic utility. Attachment to it has led scholars to perform some increasingly daring theoretical acrobatics to make it work as a descriptive feature of diverse national economies with varying degrees and types of government involvement. Ong, for instance, chooses to refer to neoliberalism as it manifests throughout the globe only with a "small 'n'" (Ong 2006: 3). Expressions of neoliberal structuration, she argues, are as varied as the economic and cultural milieus in which they appear and always operate as part of a larger cultural "assemblage" (Deleuze and Guattari 1987; Rudnyckyj 2009) or "cluster" (Ong 2006: 3), along with such other factors as governmental state-building projects, religious practice, and regional traditions. This is an important caveat, to be sure. But it begs the question as to whether neoliberalism is really the correct theoretical tool for the job in the first place. Like

Stewart (2007), I am quite skeptical of the ability of terms like "neoliberalism," "late capitalism," "globalization," or even "the DIY ethos" to capture actual, lived experience. They are, at best, useful fictions or imperfect metaphors for far more complex (and far less tangible) processes. Nonetheless, there is quite compelling evidence that as an economic paradigm, the ideology summed up by anthropologists, sociologists, and other critics of global capitalism as "neoliberalism" has been "hegemonic as a mode of discourse" (Harvey 2005: 3) for the last several decades, particularly in Western countries and Latin America, and more recently in Indonesia. At least in these limited contexts, it is a crucial cultural force to reckon with. As such, I use "neoliberalism" here not so much to describe a clear economic reality as a force of structuration, what Stewart describes as a "scene of immanent force" (2007: 1), operating in tandem with numerous other competing forces. It is a sort of organized will imposing its sensibility in numerous locations with varying results, or rather, it is the amalgam of numerous, competing wills patterned into a cultural formation.

Li (2007) has presented compelling evidence that the philosophy of neoliberalism, at least in an incipient form, drove many of the decisions of governance in the Dutch East Indies. The VOC, after all, was in some sense the world's first multinational corporation (Vickers 2005; Li 2007). Its goal in occupying the region was always first and foremost profit. But although the Dutch, too, were quite concerned with development, educating a select set of upper-class Indonesians, teaching industrial and agricultural techniques to the native population, and pursuing essentially a laissez-faire model of governance (making use of existing social hierarchies to rule and intervening as little as possible in local, cultural affairs), it lacked the later drive of the Indonesian government to forge Indonesia into a developed nation. The VOC had no intention of putting Indonesians on a level playing field with Dutch colonists. Nor did it seek to forge Indonesians into modern, capitalist subjects. It was left to the New Order regime to devise such a plan.

Indonesia's push toward neoliberalism began in earnest with an alleged coup in 1965. Although a great deal of mystery continues to surround the events of this coup—largely as the result of government efforts to suppress information about it—what is known is that on September 30, 1965, six generals in the Indonesian armed forces were assassinated by unknown assailants in an apparent attempt to wrestle power away from President Sukarno, the once revolutionary general, who led the Indonesian resistance against Dutch occupation. Suharto, a top-ranking general in the armed forces, then seized the reigns of government, ostensibly to restore stability and order. There continues to be a great deal of speculation about the role Suharto played in the coup itself.

Now in power, the Suharto-led "New Order" government sought to legitimize its leadership and squelch any perceived opposition by blaming the coup on the Indonesian Communist Party (PKI). The new government spread fierce anti-communist rhetoric, and the armed forces launched a ruthless campaign to systematically eliminate the "communist threat" from the archipelago. Supplied with a list of left-wing "agitators" by the American CIA, the military carried out mass executions of suspected communists and communist sympathizers, and within weeks, had managed to organize large numbers of civilian vigilantes to do the same. Over the course of the next year, hundreds of thousands of Indonesian citizens were brutally slaughtered, and Suharto firmly established his status as the sovereign head of the troubled nation.

Under the advice of a UC Berkeley-trained cadre of economic advisors (known, not-so-affectionately as "the Berkeley Mafia"), and with very little opposition from the left still standing, Suharto began to implement sweeping economic reforms and turn the course of the Southeast Asian nation away from public ownership and toward something approximating free market capitalism. The centerpiece of the New Order government's economic strategy was to open up Indonesia's natural resources to development and exploitation by international timber and gold mining firms (Tsing 2005; Gellert 2008). Indonesia became one of the world's foremost destinations for transnational capital investment. Thousands of people were displaced from the rainforests of Kalimantan and Irian Jaya, while Jakarta capitalists, most of whom had strong ties to the New Order regime, grew rich off the misfortune of others.

This was not, however, strict "neoliberalism" in the sense in which the term is used today. Suharto's government continued to subsidize a variety of industries, and the officials and politicians in his employ were infamous for their cronyism and nepotism. Suharto's own children were some of the greatest recipients of foreign investment and some of the biggest profiteers in the new economic climate. Furthermore, entrenched "discourses of Indonesian nationalism, Asian difference, and, of course, Indonesia's great nationalized oil and timber wealth" (Nevins and Peluso 2008: 10), kept the emergent neoliberal tide from swelling too quickly into a free market tsunami.

Gradually, however, the economic circumstances of the vast island nation began to change. Throughout the 1980s and 1990s, pressure from ASEAN, the World Bank, and the international financial community pushed Indonesia substantially further in the direction of the free market, as did internal pressure from Indonesia's corporate sector. Ultimately, however, in keeping with Naomi Klein's thesis that neoliberalism feeds on catastrophe (Klein 2007), it took the Asian financial crisis of the late 1990s to bring Indonesia (more or less) thoroughly into the free market fold. As a condition for massive financial bailout from the International Monetary Fund (IMF), Indonesia wrote ten "Letters of Intent" over the period of eighteen months regarding the implementation of economic deregulation policies, antitrust legislation, and the privatization of industry (Neilson 1999). Gradually, these intentions became policies, and as a consequence, the once closely guarded doors to global commerce were thrown wide open.

What sealed the deal, however, on Indonesia's embrace of neoliberal economics was the fall of the New Order government. After months of fervent, sometimes violent, protests by fed-up student activists and a range of dissatisfied citizens, many of whom were active participants in the Indonesian indie scene, Suharto stepped down from power in May of 1998, ushering in a period of intense social, political, and economic reform widely known as *Reformasi*.

The social consequences of Reformasi, and particularly the emphasis on deregulation and (relatively) free trade within it, are difficult to overestimate. Outside investment fueled a massive expansion in Indonesia's industrial sector and a comparable restructuring of social and economic power. In 1980, only two percent of the value of the nation's exports came from manufactured goods, but by 1999, they already accounted for fifty-four percent (Nevins and Peluso 2008: 8). Something like an Indonesian proletariat began to emerge to meet manufacturing demands, a social sector of lower-rung factory workers, largely from rural and poorer backgrounds, who migrated to the cities to make the sneakers and track suits for transnational companies like Nike and the Gap. A large professional and managerial sector also began to emerge in tandem with this proletariat, as members of the older merchant class and civil service sought to take advantage of new opportunities and establish a more prominent place for themselves within a rapidly changing economic infrastructure.

This group of urban professionals, widely referred to as the "new middle class" (*kelas menengah baru*), has become the deregulated economy's intellectual labor pool, an expansive sector of the relatively elite, who have begun developing a "style of life" (Weber 1978) quite in keeping with similar socio-economic formations worldwide. And in order to maintain this lifestyle, the new middle class has become a major lobbying force in the push toward increased economic deregulation.

No doubt the advent of what is essentially neoliberal capitalism has been deeply traumatic for many Indonesian citizens. The economic policies of the Indonesian state have long been implicated in military violence, forced displacement, and the decisions of government to pursue international contracts at the expense of local projects. The manufacturing sector continues to live and work under conditions that can only be described as bleak, eking out a meager income in hot, over-crowded factories and making their homes in dilapidated, densely-populated shanty towns in parts of Jakarta that fail to live up to government expectations of progress and development.

Nonetheless, a substantial portion of Indonesia's population, that is, the new middle class, has benefited in a number of ways from economic deregulation, or at least had benefited from it, prior to the recession of the late 1990s, and it is no surprise, then, that they were such staunch advocates of its expansion. The relatively open economy created well-paying private sector jobs for many young educated urbanites, whose families had previously gotten by on modest government salaries and the sparse profits of small businesses. The relatively free market also made goods and services, like skate clothes, rock T-shirts, and imported music, available to the elite few who could afford them at a rate unimaginable ten or so years previous. Life had substantially changed in a relatively short period of time. Young people had all sorts of consumer goods they had never had before, goods that linked them to broader youth cultural movements, that helped them feel like part of something larger than themselves, larger, in fact, than even the established national and cultural boundaries of Indonesia. It is here that government projects of development, rooted in nationalist politics, and middle-class projects of identity formation, increasingly grounded in DIY practices of self-expression, begin to part ways.

The New Middle Class

"Class" is no doubt a problematic term for discussing the social and cultural configurations of today's Indonesia. There is little agreement among Indonesianist scholars about where divisions between classes lie. After all, the language of "class" itself emerged out of late-eighteenth-century France and England during the Industrial Revolution (Lamont and Fournier 1992; Joyce 1995; Lustig 2004) and is largely associated with two nineteenth-century German thinkers, Marx and Engels. As such, Lev (1990), Tanter and Young (1990), and others are right to question its applicability to the Indonesian context. Prior to Dutch occupation, there was no such thing as an Indonesian class system, merely a diverse collection of radically different social organizations, from relatively egalitarian tribes to rigidly hierarchical feudal states. The Dutch colonial regime exploited existing social inequalities, regional tensions, and internal hierarchies, often solidifying in the process loosely defined systems of stratification. It also put into place the framework for a massive civil service that remains one of the central organizing features of the Indonesian nation-state to this day.

Nevertheless, "class" is a significant component of contemporary Indonesian political and economic discourse—and for good reason. The last several decades of neoliberal economic reform have seen the emergence of social configurations that, although perhaps not precisely the same in structure as similar formations in the United States and Europe, bear enough resemblance to class groups to warrant a similar theoretical treatment.

The term "middle class" has been particularly contentious, as those individuals typically characterized as middle class in newspaper accounts and government rhetoric include a broad range of occupations, income levels, and political attitudes. Lev, then, prefers to use the term "middle groups" rather than the all-encompassing "middle class" to describe "a dynamic bunch growing in the space between two polarized classes," (Lev 1990: 27) that is, the peasant and working-class majority and the tiny, urban elite. Robison, along similar lines, has suggested conceiving of Indonesia's middle class as a series of divisions, including the "new rich," the "petty bourgeoisie," and the "lower-middle classes," comprised of civil servants and low-level white collar workers (Robison 1996).

Common to both these classificatory schemes is the notion that the middle class is a diverse, differently situated social grouping, a "multiplicity of formations" (Aronowitz 2003: 11), rather than a single coherent unit. It describes a range of Indonesians from differing backgrounds who occupy a common position of "in the middle." This includes urban professionals, living on the 25th-floor of luxury apartment complexes towering above Jakarta, just as much as it includes the dormitory-dwelling hipsters who reside in the pages of this book. Liechty suggests, in discussion of the case of Nepal, conceiving of the middle class as a group distinguished by its "shared project of locating oneself in a new and legitimate space between two devalued poles" (Liechty 2003: 67). I sympathize with this agenda and borrow a good deal from Liechty's conception here. I would, however, go a step further and suggest that the middle class is not in fact *united* by a single project at all, but, rather, *divided* by a series of related projects conducted by those who occupy an uncertain middle ground in Indonesian society. Most Indonesianists see the rise of fundamentalist Islam among Indonesian youth as essentially a middle-class phenomenon, just as they tend to describe the rise of a hedonistic nightclub lifestyle or the expansion of the environmentalist movement as distinctly middle-class (see Tsing 2005).

For me, being in the middle is the defining feature of middle-classness in Indonesia today, as it is in many other parts of the world. It is an existential and ontological orientation as much as it is an economic condition or a sociological category, an orientation of stuckness and betweenness that goes a long way in explaining the distinctly middle-class character of so many forms of contemporary DIY expression that will be explored later in this book. DIY seems to promise a way out of this stuck position, a way of connecting beyond class distinctions, national borders, and the officially sanctioned boundaries of Indonesian culture. It is inextricably embedded in a class politics it seeks to both erase and overcome. DIY is thrust forward by its proponents as a democratization of access, an undermining of the old position of the bourgeoisie in favor of a new field of cultural production in which the means of production are more evenly distributed, both among class groups and across national boundaries. Nonetheless, like Indonesia's larger project of development, it is very much an incomplete democratization, a democratization still encapsulated within an evolving, but extant, class hierarchy. The fact remains that some people have more access to DIY means of production than others, and some people are in a better position to have their DIY products received, appreciated, and understood by others, and as long as this continues to be the case, DIY itself will continue to contribute to class-based differences, just as projects of development have disproportionately benefited an elite few. DIY, then, both resists and reinforces the emergent class system, just as it resists and reinforces government projects of national and economic development.

DIY as a Rupture and Continuity in Development Thinking

I argue in the next chapter that it was the temporary loss of the newly established stature of the emergent middle class in the midst of the Asian financial crisis of the late 1990s that first triggered Indonesia's DIY movement. But this eventuality, as the current chapter demonstrates, has to be understood as fundamentally framed by an ongoing set of discourses and practices surrounding nationhood, class, and economic development. The DIY ethos, after all, made sense to those Indonesians who adopted it as their own, in large part because it fit so neatly into those ideals of national modernity imparted upon them from an early age. It was a model of Indonesianness opposed to the stark individuality of the West, and a model of development rooted in an ideology opposed to consumerism and greed. Plus, it held the added bonus of at least seeming to simultaneously oppose such mainstream Indonesian values. To those who adopted it, DIY was reckless and expressive, thoroughly disapproving of the idle conformity of national or regional tradition. It was driven forward by the restless energy of youth. DIY, then, was both a continuity and a rupture. It helped place the young and middle class in their hard-earned position of distinctly modern, and yet it did so through the aesthetics of rebellion and resistance, the anti-bourgeois pretentions of the urban bohemian.

And young Indonesians' adoption of cut and paste as a practice of cultural production always had an heir of familiarity about it as well. DIYers' own identity as Indonesians had been produced through just such a process, and their own cultural backgrounds, defined by centuries of interaction, imposition, and exchange, were themselves built out of such a synthesis. Appropriating the images and ideas circulating through the global mediascape (Appadurai 1996) as part of the very process of production was as logical and common-sensical as any practice could be. It was, after all, just how things are done. Indonesia, with its legacy of colonialism extending back well over a millennium, is as cut-and-paste of a country as they come. Being Indonesian has always been about bringing the "outside" inside, assembling the multiple, the various, and the incongruent into a single, syncretic whole. The rest of this book will focus on young Indonesian DIYers' efforts to do just that, forging, in the process, a new, revitalized version of Indonesian national culture, no longer attached to colonialism or the efforts of the Indonesian state to dominate cultural expression.

–2–

DIY Capitalism: Class, Crisis, and the Rise of Indie Indonesia

It's not just a fashion, it's Indonesian creative movement!!

—From a Flier for KICKfest 2011

Riotic Times

For Dadan Ketu, punk rock has always held the promise of autonomy—from state, from tradition, from a culture, he says, "that until then had stagnated." When he first discovered it back in the mid-1990s in his hometown of Bandung, West Java, he thought, "Ok, this is my music." It was unapologetically abrasive and loud, some-times even outright unlistenable, and had an attitude of rebellious activism that seemed to fit with the times. Those were the last days of Suharto's thirty-two-year authoritarian regime. Kids were rioting in the streets.[1] Universities were buzzing with demonstrations. Change was brewing up beneath the surface. It needed a big, boisterous soundtrack to help shake off the dirt.

Of course, it wasn't easy to get a hold of punk rock back in Indonesia in those days (see Sen and Hill 2000; Baulch 2007; Wallach 2008a). Record stores didn't carry it. Radio didn't play it. Strict government oversight, an entrenched culture of self-censorship and a dearth of private television stations led to the continual recy-cling of more sanitized sounds (Yampolsky 1989; Kitley 2000; Sen and Hill 2000). In this context, a well-worn cassette of Crass, Suicidal Tendencies, or the Blind Pigs was like a small token of personal liberation for Ketu. Even owning it was a slight act of subversion. Ketu had to send for his music from international mail-order cata-log, or sometimes even trade directly with foreign bands. It was a slow, drawn-out process, but it made him feel like he was part of an international secret society, a global music underground. When he and his friends managed to get hold of new stuff, they made each other copies and circulated their finds throughout the budding network of Indonesian punk fans. Ketu started playing in a band himself around that time and getting to know other people in bands, dressing "punk"—which at the time meant beat-up, Levi's 501-style jeans (usually knock-off), black band T-shirts, and a pair of black and white Chuck Taylor Converse All-Stars—and hanging out with the hordes of other punk kids in front of the Bandung Indah Plaza (BIP) shopping mall. That was before the staff of BIP started placing large potted plants and unfriendly signs on the steps to discourage loiterers.

Those days, Ketu explains, people just did not know what to make of kids like him. They stared, even shouted things at them, and it was really hard for punk bands to get gigs. Most potential sponsors, like high schools, cigarette companies, and other commercial exhibitors, wanted nothing to do with them, so they organized their own events, renting out sporting arenas and concert halls, sometimes with thirty or more bands pooling their resources to make it happen. The resulting concerts, Ketu recalls, were sheer chaos. Some seven thousand kids would gather at a single event. Metalheads, punks, even would-be "skinheads," with swastika patches on their knock-off flight jackets, uneasily occupied the same space. People would shout insults at bands like "fuck straight-edge!" or "metal sucks!" and fights broke out all the time. A few people even died. But at least, stuff was happening, says Ketu, and for the thousands of youth attending those gigs, they were a breath of fresh—albeit smoke- and alcohol-saturated—air.

Ketu and his other band friends gradually evolved into a more organized collective, joining a number of similar collectives operating among their larger network of peers, who together became known as the Indonesian "underground." Later, they would be redubbed the "youth independent" or simply the "indie" scene. They put together a number of concerts and began to make a decent amount of money off them, too, so they decided to use the money to make an album featuring some of the acts playing at those gigs. They called it "Bandung's Burning," in reference to the seminal UK punk song "London's Burning" by The Clash, and it, too, was a relative success, sold hand-to-hand at gigs and other events. They had saved a fair amount of money at this point, but weren't exactly sure what to do with it. "Finally," Ketu tells me, "we decided, alright then, let's open up a kiosk" (*Udahlah, kita bikin kios*). They set up in the parking lot behind the BIP mall, where they sold their own bands' merchandise, and those of other acts from Jakarta, Surabaya, and elsewhere in Indonesia, whom Ketu had met touring the country. They even included some international acts Ketu had begun trading with by mail. They also began producing their own zine, called *Submissive Riot*, which they sold at the kiosk along with other local zines like Arian Arifin's *Tigbelas* (*Thirteen*) and Wendi Putranto's *Brainwashed*. Uttu (2006), a long time observer of and participant in the scene, claims *Submissive Riot* was the first Indonesian zine to explicitly link music with politics.

After a series of discussions between them, Ketu's punk rock collective settled on the name "Riotic" for the shop. It's not that they advocated riots, Ketu explains. "Riotic" just sounded cool, and more importantly, it sounded punk rock. To Ketu, that meant something specific. It meant taking culture into your own hands, becoming an active participant in the riotous social transformation Indonesia was undergoing—not just sitting back and watching the struggle.

Today, Riotic has a shop on Jalan Dago in northern Bandung. It is one of a number of similar shops along the main street, including Arena Experience, Blankwear, and Barbel, and it is where I first met Ketu in the early part of 2007, cruising the streets on the back of a motorbike with my self-appointed tour guide nicknamed "Megadeath," a man whose awesome name was more than matched by his unrivaled knowledge of the scene and truly original fashion sense—faded, early 1980s heavy metal band T-shirts, tight jeans, and a perpetual puffy white faux fur jacket. Riotic is a small shop, no bigger than the average two-star hotel room, with rows of black T-shirts lining the walls and a glass display case full of cassettes, CDs, badges, pins, and other merchandise for a variety of local bands. It is no doubt a humble spot to serve as one of the best-known vendors of Indonesian independent music, and it is credited, along with a skate and imported music shop called Reverse, with being the first genuine distro (independent distribution outlet) in Indonesia.

The indie scene has changed a lot since Riotic started out. It is bigger, for one thing, and much more inclusive, with punks, metalheads, knob tweakers, and twee poppers all banded together for a common, though sometimes rather vaguely defined, cause. Unlike some comparable scenes in the United States and Europe, the indie scene in Indonesia has stopped reading its members' sub-categorical taste preferences as unbreachable divides. The scene these days describes itself as a family,

Figure 2 A row of distros on Jalan Sultan Agung, Bandung.

a tight-knit community of like-minded youth. What ties it together, claims Ketu, is not so much half-understood "alternative" styles imported from elsewhere—as was perhaps the case in the 1990s as they were getting started—but a common commitment to community participation and DIY-style production. Through lots of work by lots of people, the Indonesian indie scene has become a cooperative network of thousands of bands and brands extending throughout the Indonesian archipelago.

But more than an ideologically driven collective, the network of DIY practitioners that comprise today's Indonesian indie scene has become something else, something about which "old-school" Bandung punks like Ketu feel more than a little ambivalent. It has become an industry, a vast and profitable collection of small music, fashion, and publication enterprises, with some individual companies, such as Unkl347 in Bandung and Satellite Castle in Jakarta, bringing in as much as US$120,000 per month. DIY production is now big business in Indonesia, and its biggest names are often touted in the popular press as the cutting edge of Indonesia's emergent "creative economy" (see Florida 2002; McRobbie 2004; Hesmondhalgh 2007; Banet-Weiser and Sturken 2010). They have become the new face of Indonesian economic development, the poster children of post-New Order *pembangunan*. The kids behind this business prefer to see themselves as rebels, activists, and anti-establishment types, far outside the mainstream of Indonesian culture, but it has become clearer and clearer that the indie business model is hardly a threat to Indonesia's emergent neoliberal economy. There is, after all, another term that economists use to describe DIY practitioners like Ketu: entrepreneurs.

In a deregulated Indonesia, with a burgeoning media and advertising industry, where production is increasingly immaterial in nature (Lazzarato 1996; Hardt and Negri 2001; Hesmondhalgh 2007;), DIYers like Ketu emerge as something like "agents of the neoliberal order" (McRobbie 2004: 194), advocates of a developing transnational value system rooted in late capitalistic practice. This is not an uncritical endorsement of neoliberal capitalism. Nor is it merely the latest phase in Indonesia's long quest for development. Indonesia's indie kids are as anti-authoritarian and anti-corporate as the next indie scenester, and as anti-individualist as the propaganda pamphlets against encroaching Westernization put out by the Indonesian government circa the 1960s and 1970s. Indie scenesters help each other out, pool their resources, downplay the importance of profit in their community, and do whatever they can to build a far-less alienating and atomizing local version of global capitalism. It would be grossly inaccurate, then, to describe their alignment with the ends of global capital and government initiatives as the imposition of a new cultural order from on high. The DIY ethos they espouse and enact is as built from below as it is borrowed from abroad, a set of strategic responses to changing social, economic, and political circumstances. Capitalism it most certainly is, but this is DIY capitalism, grassroots capitalism. If it is neoliberalism, it is neoliberalism cut-and-pasted, remixed, and reassembled, neoliberalism sampled and re-engineered into the grand remix of Indonesian culture.

In this chapter, I explore the political and economic factors that contributed to the growth of DIY production in Indonesia and delineate the various linkages between Indonesia's social and economic restructuring and the indie scene's DIY ethos. My intention here is to demonstrate just how actively involved Indonesian youth are in appropriating and repurposing the tools of global capitalist production, rather than depict them as hapless dupes of state projects and corporate interests. In doing so, I hope to show that capitalist expansion today is not the kind of succumbing to inevitability, or passive embracing of a hegemonic ideology, so feared by left-wing academics, not to mention Indonesian Islamic groups. It is a continual working through, a "negotiation," as anthropologists are inclined to call it. Indonesian youth are not just shaped by global capitalism; they are, in no small way, helping shape it themselves.

Out of the Ashes of *Krismon*

Sociologist Ryan Moore (2010) has made the compelling case that the American youth music movements of the last several decades were born out of social and economic crises brought about, in large part, by the growth of the neoliberal ideology. In 1970s New York, for instance, withdrawal of government support for the arts—combined with economic recession, weakening labor laws, a disappearing social welfare system, and the conglomeration of the media industries—led to working-class disenfranchisement, art school cynicism, and widespread disgust with mainstream commercial culture, the perfect cocktail, in other words, for a dissident aesthetic movement like punk rock. New York punk bands like Television, The New York Dolls, and The Ramones emerged as a collective blast of sonic alienation. This was rebellion set to music, protest without any of the Age of Aquarius utopianism of the 1960s counterculture, nihilism with a beat.

Indonesia's indie scene emerged in similar circumstances, at the end of an authoritarian regime and in the middle of deep economic recession. It had a similar rhetoric of alienation and despair, a similar sonic and aesthetic sensibility. But what it seemed to be missing was some kind of clearly articulated rage against the capitalist machine. Certainly, there were moments of this, with groups like Homicide and Jeruji attacking corporate capitalism in stark, angry lyrics. But it is just as easy to make the case that from its very inception, Indonesia's indie scene promoted consumer culture (Barendregt and Zanten 2002; Baulch 2007), or at least its own niche market within consumer culture (see Frank 1997), as much if not more actively than the large corporations toward which it posed itself in opposition. This was a movement that saw consumption—of punk rock, of metal, of British indie pop, and all their stylistic accoutrements—as an active form of rebellion, a mode of resistance against the Suharto status quo. And when fans formed bands and labels of their own, they advocated capitalism as a method as much as a target. As Azerrad has claimed of American indie record labels in the early 1980s, "In true capitalist tradition, entrepreneurs recognized a need, however small, and catered to it" (Azerrad 2001: 6). Indonesian DIY also catered to a specific market, the young, middle-class, and disenfranchised. And it was born less out of revolt against corporations per se than a middle-class identity crisis, of the haves discovering they no longer had all that much.

Or at least, that was the story told to me by W. Satrio Adjie, founder of the early indie clothing label and distro No Label Stuff. Adjie spent most of the 1990s skateboarding and listening to punk and hardcore music, had gotten used to a relatively chichi lifestyle of fast food chains and coffee shops, imported music and designer clothes. He and some friends of his, including Arief Maskom, a professional skateboarder and the founder of Ouval Research, another early distro, formed a hardcore band called Full of Hate, and he played bass. They did pretty well, developed a following in the Bandung underground, along with other mainstays like Puppen and Koil, and staked a good deal of who they were in an image of being cutting edge and alternative. To Adjie and his friends, that meant slate gray, black, or navy-blue boarding shorts with puffy, bold-colored Vans on one's feet. It meant boxy, oversize T-shirts advertising surf and skate brands like Volcom, Juice, and Stüssy, and baseball caps turned slightly askew. They adorned themselves, in other words, in the international uniform of late 1980s skate culture. For them, skatewear was a kind of declaration of personal independence.

And then the Asian financial crisis hit. The value of the Thai currency dropped and sent shock waves throughout East and Southeast Asia. All of a sudden, Adjie and his friends couldn't afford any of that stuff anymore. The expansion of the middle-class in the 1980s and 1990s had established a set of lifestyle practices and consumer patterns for kids like Adjie and Maskom (Heryanto 1999; Kompas 1999; *The Jakarta Post* 1999; Priyono 1999) that were simply unsustainable once the value of the *rupiah* dropped. Their hard-earned status as the cool kids was in jeopardy. So Adjie and his friends came up with a possible solution. If they could not afford the over-priced rock and skate paraphernalia to which they had become so accustomed, then *baiklah* (fine), they would just have to make it for themselves. In Adjie's words:

> It happened at first with my friends, my buddies, and me. We used to skateboard together [and] play in a band together. Then at some point, at the time of the monetary [crisis], tried to make a clothing line, just to satisfy our needs, really. Just our needs as young people … I borrowed a sewing machine from my mom, an old sewing machine. I borrowed my mom's garage, too, and started production there. It was all truly Do-It-Yourself (*Benar-benar Do-It-Yourself lah*).[2]

For Adjie, as with a number of skate and music fans of the time, DIY was first a matter of "necessity," a way to stay current when the requirements of youth culture were moving out of reach. They could no longer afford to buy imported skate and music merchandise, so they made their own, using their moms' old sewing machines along with improvised silkscreens composed of scrap wood and cloth. It was later that DIY became an ideal in and of itself. That, Adjie and others have told me, they got from the various discourses circulating through zines and online magazines about punk and indie movements happening elsewhere. It was an ideal imported after the fact. The music came first. The fashion came second. Then, when DIY was already a common practice, it was canonized as a common ideal. DIY became the ideological flag of the emergent indie scene. Creative production, no matter how ragtag or small, became central to the scene's identity. It became the way indie kids distinguished themselves from the dreaded "mainstream" (Thornton 1996), a mode of distinction (Bourdieu 1984) from the old economic order of the Suharto era, and a medium of connection, uniting them with a transnational community of like-minded DIYers.

The DIY ethos of Adjie, Maskom, and Ketu advocated taking the initiative in difficult times, taking advantage of circumstances, rather than letting those circumstances get the better of them. It was, in other words, a highly adaptive stance to take considering the Asian financial crisis—one that just so happened to correspond with an economic shift toward deregulation—and had such youth been advised by economists about how to respond to the recession, I am fairly certain they would have used similar rhetoric to that circulating in the embryonic indie scene.

Adjie and his friends were entrepreneurs, the ideal type of neoliberal classificatory schema, enterprising free agents launching new businesses in response to perceived market needs (Bourdieu 1998; Harvey 2005; Freeman 2007). Nonetheless, when they started their clothing line, Adjie and his friends had no intention of turning it into a business. It did not even occur to them at the time that they might be able to do so, Adjie told me. Their very name, "No Label Stuff," was a reference to the fact that they were *not* a clothing label at all, "just a bunch of kids making stuff" for their own purposes. They gave their clothing away to friends for a number of months, and only began charging for their products when demand started getting out of hand, and even then, they only charged enough to cover their costs. Capital growth was never the point of DIY.

No Label Stuff began selling their shirts at concerts and other events, then at kiosks such as Riotic and distros such as Reverse. Eventually, they opened up their own shop out of a friend's house, before expanding, moving a couple more times, and ending up at their current location on Jalan Trunojoyo, the indie scene's closest thing to a pedestrian mall in central Bandung. Their reasoning was: if we turn a profit off this stuff, then we can make clothing full-time. Making clothing full-time, in turn, will strengthen our connection to the larger DIY underground. In other words, the business supported the creative practice, not the other way around.

The Rise and Fall of the New Middle Class

Ahmad Marin's experience was quite similar to Adjie's. He came from a comfortably upper-middle-class background, a line of prominent members of the military, with two parents working as botanists and a grandfather serving as a major in the armed forces in Bogor, a wealthy city just outside Jakarta. Throughout most of Suharto's rule, Marin explained, being a financial success meant having ties to the regime, and his family did. They used those ties to establish a transportation company. They drove expensive cars and led a relatively luxurious lifestyle.

In 1978, Marin and family moved to Bandung and took residence in a family home, an Old Dutch colonial house on Jalan Setiabudi, now one of the major streets in northern Bandung, famous for its factory outlets and high-end cafes, but back then it was just a sleepy neighborhood up in the hills. Marin went to junior high (SMP) and high school (SMA) in Bandung, then on to university, where he majored in economics. His real interests, though, were in art, design, and music, but he didn't get into the art program at ITB (The Bandung Institute of Technology), so he settled for a background in something more practical. "I had a dream in 1997 or 1998," Marin told me in well-studied English, as we chatted in the coffeeshop that was set up in front of his colonial house, "of becoming a bank employee, working in Jakarta, falling in love. That was the youngster dream in that era, I think ... Be a very [rich] man so you can get a Mercedes." He did, in fact, work for a bank for a time, but when the monetary crisis hit, that particular dream fell apart. His family lost their business and most of their money. Most of the banks in Indonesia went bankrupt, including the bank where he worked. Marin had to look for something else to do.

Fortunately, he already knew what he was interested in. Marin had been designing clothes in an amateur sort of way since 1994, and he had been going to punk and indie gigs for a while. Most of his friends, Ketu, Adjie, and Maskom among them, were artists, designers, and musicians. Bandung had become one of the centers of protest and demonstration against the Suharto regime, and Marin got caught up in this activism, as well. The people he was hanging out with were itching to start something new, something more meaningful. So they divided their time between protesting the New Order government, hitting the hot new night spots popping up in Bandung, and producing fashion and music inspired by the wealth of media that had begun to be available to them.

In 1998, Marin set up Monik House, the distro outlet of his clothing line Monik/Celtic, in his parents' Dutch colonial home. His parents had already moved back to Bogor to work at its famous botanical gardens, and no one else in the family seemed to care at all what he did with the place. He knew it was a risky venture and did not have any expectations about profit, but that didn't matter to him. Times were tough. He was an educated middle-class twenty-something, but like the members of Generation X in the United States described by Ortner (1998), Marin found himself in a situation where he simply could not live the lifestyle he had grown used to. Having suffered from the "educational inflation" (Bourdieu 1984) inevitable when a university degree has become commonplace and not enough jobs are available for graduates, Marin lost faith in the Indonesian state mantra of *pembangunan*, and gave up the dream of luxury and excess that had fueled his career moves for so long.

Marin is a believer, however, in doing what you like (*yang senang aja*). "If you like something and you enjoy it," he said to me, "the vision will follow." It is hardly a revolutionary ideology, and, of course, is the kind of sentiment only maintainable by the already financially secure. He pronounced for me a familiar philosophy of "following your dreams" and pursuing your own desires regardless of the personal sacrifices it might entail, which is just what he did. Marin followed the example of some friends of his—Ketu over at Riotic and Adjie over at No Label Stuff—and set up a distro to sell his own designs. Monik/Celtic, the label he established, is now one of Indonesia's best-known clothing lines. It has even succeeded in selling its products overseas in Malaysia and Singapore. Now it is working on the U.S. and European markets.

Ironically, however, it is Marin's temporary disavowal of material interests that led to his financial success. His willingness to postpone economic ambitions for more immediate creative pursuits, to incur substantial financial risk for the sake of personal passions, is what enabled him to establish his fashion label in the first place. A number of theorists of neoliberalism have suggested that flexibility and the valorization of risk are, in fact, the key traits required for success under the conditions of contemporary capitalism (Beck 1992; Martin 1994; Ong 1999; Comaroff and Comaroff 2001; Harvey 2005; Elliot and Lemert 2006). Weber's Protestant ethic, of dutiful saving and considered investment (Weber 1930), is no longer the most appropriate ethos for the age. Instead, the slippery economic conditions of modern life reward those individuals willing to endure periods of poverty for the sake of postponed achievement (Bauman 1998).

As Lloyd has suggested, "it may be the bohemian ethic, not the Protestant ethic, that is best adapted to new realities" (Lloyd 2006: 236). Marin's cultivated "bohemian" (Lloyd 2006) disdain for the bourgeois lifestyle of bank employees proved to be quite utilitarian, given the realities of *Krismon* (the Asian financial crisis). Under the unsteady financial circumstances of a modern capitalist economy, the old ethos of working hard, saving steadily, and conforming to the social conventions of the company man are giving way to a new ethos of doing what you love, taking risks, and expressing yourself in a "non-conformist" manner. This is what Comaroff and Comaroff (2001), Mankekar (2008), and others have in mind by "the culture of neoliberalism," and what McRobbie (2004) and Banet-Weiser and Sturken (2010) mean by "creative entrepreneurship."

But whether Marin, Adjie, and Ketu's adoption of neoliberal values was a kind of grassroots response to economic crisis or a further inculcation into an increasingly hegemonic culture of neoliberalism, the practices they conducted were clearly in line with larger economic trends in Indonesia. Indonesian indie kids have moved toward neoliberal values as Indonesia itself has moved further and further toward the free market.

Bandung, Fashion Capitol of Indonesia

It is no accident that this kind of indie experimentation happened first in Bandung. The West Javanese city has a well-earned reputation for innovation and entrepreneurship. It has been an important liaison between Indonesia and the West for a long time. In Dutch colonial days, it was essentially a European city, nicknamed *Parijs van Java* (the Paris of Java) for its opulent colonial architecture. Its high altitude and relatively cool temperatures made it an ideal site for colonial officials to settle, and it quickly became an important center of manufacture, trade, and European-style education. This status continued when the Dutch finally admitted defeat to Republican forces and acknowledged Indonesian independence in 1949. The Bandung Institute of Technology (ITB) was established there in 1959 as one of Indonesia's premier institutions of higher learning, and to this day it retains its position as one of the top two universities in the country. It is also the pioneer institution for a variety of communicational technologies, and Indonesia's first experiments with laying an Internet infrastructure happened there, as well.

The famed Asian-African Conference was held in Bandung in 1955 as a meeting of new countries hoping to cooperate economically and unite in opposition to the neocolonial efforts of the United States and the Soviet Union. The conference helped maintain Bandung's status as an important cultural outpost in Southeast Asia, as did the popularity of the city as a destination for high-profile foreign travelers, including, as many Bandung natives proudly told me, Charlie Chaplin. Plus, the proximity of Bandung to the capital city of Jakarta (three hours by train, two by car) and its comfortable mountain climate have made Bandung a top weekend destination for Jakartans seeking to escape the smog, the heat, and the bustle of big city life. A thriving hotel, restaurant, and tourist industry has made Bandung one of the easiest places in Indonesia to score sushi and Starbucks, and has lent Bandung's residents a kind of savvy for global culture that often takes years to reach the rest of Indonesia.

Moreover, Bandung's long status as a center of trade and manufacturing, as well as its weekend influx of tourists from Jakarta, has led to the steady growth of a cottage clothing industry. By the 1990s, Bandung had become one of the centers of the Indonesian fashion world. It was home to hundreds of garment factories (or, sweatshops, if you prefer), and an even greater number of "factory outlets" (FOs) lining the main streets, packing in roving crowds of weekend shoppers from Jakarta. These were places that produced large volumes of goods at cheap prices, often under contract to transnational companies such as Ralph Lauren, Penguin, Hugo Boss, and The Gap. The infrastructure for an indie fashion industry was firmly in place, long before kids like Marin and Adjie began taking advantage of it.

It was easy enough for budding DIY fashion labels to purchase used silkscreens from apparel production houses moving to heat transfer technology for printing on fabric. And that's what the DIY labels did early on. Getting them to manufacture their goods, however, a tactic increasingly common as the scene developed, took some negotiating. No Label Stuff, Monik/Celtic, and other budding distro labels simply were not doing the volume of business of transnational companies. In fact, they were catering to a decidedly niche market, mainly their friends and other kids like them, and had no intention of doing large runs of their prints, merely a few dozen of each. The prevailing standard was to do no more than seventy editions of a single design, and then send these designs to distros in some ten different cities. They wanted to be outsiders to the fashion world, the avant garde of youth style, in a word "indie," not just another manufacturer of trendy garments. Limited editions were a way of resisting mass production, lending each individual clothing item something of the "aura" of a work of art (Benjamin 1955).

The solution they came up with was to pool their resources. Brands like No Label Stuff and Monik/Celtic would put in orders together with other distros, sharing the costs of a minimum production order of, say, 300 T-shirts. The owners of these distros were friends, anyway. They didn't see themselves as being in competition with each other. If they were in competition with anyone, it was the factory outlets, along with the department stores, and big-name foreign brands that cluttered the fashion magazines. And what they were competing for wasn't so much profit as the right to determine the dominant meaning of youth culture (Bourdieu 1993). The distros positioned themselves as the anti-factory outlets, the voice of creative expression in a field of "mindless conformity." They advocated clothing as self-affirmation, clothing as lifestyle, clothing as community, not just clothing as another identifying feature of a well-polished bourgeoisie.

Of course, the dependence of indie labels on established production houses begs the question of just how DIY Indonesian indie fashion really is these days. Putting together one's own label, manufacturing one's own goods, and selling them at distros can involve dozens of laborers and intermediaries, many of whose contributions go almost entirely overlooked when credit is claimed over individual contributions to production. Although some larger labels now have the resources to produce their goods in-house and the occasional small label still sews and silkscreens their own stuff, the vast majority of labels today rely on existing clothing manufacturers to produce their garments and print their designs. The ready availability of inexpensive clothing manufacturers, who established their services to meet the needs of a national and international clothing industry, has made it inefficient and uneconomical for would-be DIYers to spend their time and money hand-crafting their own goods. It has also given Indonesian indie scenesters, frankly, a leg up on many comparable streetwear scenes in other countries. So indie designers outsource their labors and spend their energies on the more creative side of the industry. The nuts and bolts of production happen elsewhere, in other peoples' hands.

Viewed in this light, DIY fashion ends up looking a whole lot like the old-fashioned apparel industry. They make use of the same infrastructure, employ the same laborers, and take all the credit for production. As in the classic Marxist formulation, garment manufacturers become alienated from the products of their labor and are relegated to the debased position of anonymous seamstress or nameless silk-screener. Their production houses reap the bulk of the profit from the deals they make with distros and the distinction between bourgeoisie and proletariat remains firmly in place. The only practical difference, in this case, between the production of indie fashion and the production of commercial fashion is their relative scale, the number of garments they request from their outside vendors.

The indie scene has, however, taken a number of steps to minimize the built-in hierarchy between designer and manufacturer, immaterial and material laborer. Some companies, such as Unkl347 in Bandung or Triggers Syndicate in Yogyakarta, employ silkscreeners and even garment manufacturers from within the scene. Production is carried out on site, rather than farmed out to others. The Bandung heavy metal group Burgerkill, for instance, has established a silkscreen studio for its own and other indie metal acts' merchandise in the home of its guitarist Ebenz. Members of the band take an active part in printing the designs, and everyone involved with production hangs out in the same places and sees themselves as part of the same community. This is not, unfortunately, the norm of labels claiming DIY status. The commercial clothing industry made indie fashion possible in Bandung, but indie designers and distro labels are still exploring ways to ultimately become independent of it.

Figure 3   Silkscreening the old-fashioned way at Burgerkill Studios, Bandung.

The Distro Community

No doubt, then, the Bandung indie scene remains dependent on the established commercial clothing industry for the production of its goods. But if you ask its participants, its greatest resource has always been friends. It is friends who sell and distribute each other's products, friends who actively promote by word of mouth the quality of each other's designs. Distros, goes the party line, stick together, help each other out, and pull each other up. This may not be the way of things for all the new crops of distros popping up in every back corner of Indonesia, but for established, "old-time" institutions like No Label Stuff, Riotic, or Monik/Celtic, "supporting the community" (i.e., the other members of the indie scene) is a matter of pride, and a decisive source of their business success. In the indie scene, *gotong royong*, village-level cooperation, is alive and well.

As Dede Anonim, founder and co-owner of Anonim Wardrobe[3] told me, "In Bandung, there is no competition between distros. It's more like family." This is no doubt an exaggeration. As the number of distros in Bandung has entered into the hundreds, competition has become quite intense between at least certain sectors of them, but it does capture something of the ideal scene members subscribe to and actively work to maintain.

Like Adjie before her, Dede never really had any intention of starting a distro. When she opened Anonim in 1999, the word "distro" wasn't even in her vocabulary. She wasn't a scenester, didn't play in a band, didn't skate, and didn't design clothing. But she did like American rock music a lot, and above all, Hollywood films. She collects movies and television shows on DVD, files them in alphabetical order, composes lists of her current selection, which she loans out to friends (such as my partner Jessica and me). She imagined herself opening a shop selling imported VCDs, DVDs, and band merchandise, using something like the model Reverse had already established. She had recently graduated with a degree in psychology that, given the ailing economy, was practically useless, but she figured, no matter how rough the economy gets, people will want to watch movies. The problem was that with costs of shipping rising ever higher, and with the Indonesian currency worth less and less, she simply could not afford to import these items. So she chose another tack instead, stocking music and clothing produced locally.

To start her business, Dede invited a couple of local-label clothing manufacturers to consign their products to her shop, Monik/Celtic and No Label Stuff among the first, but these days they seek her out. Anonim thereby helped establish the standard model of inter-distro and clothing label business: *sistem penitipan* (the consignment system). Clothing labels ask distros to display their clothes at no cost. If they sell, distros share the profit with the label (generally 50%). If they don't sell, they don't get anything. But they don't lose anything either. It reduces the risk for both parties and enables individual distros to experiment with a variety of brands.

Having one's clothes consigned at Anonim Wardrobe has become a marker of a label's success. Many labels, like Adjie's No Label Stuff, went on to establish their own distros only after achieving success there and at other local shops. Anonim carries more than a hundred local brands. Their selection is one of the best in Indonesia. Jakarta celebrities visit Dede's store when they're in town. Bandung teenagers flock there on weekends and weekday evenings. In 2007, they even had a new shop, big and warehouse-like, with deep yellow walls and flamingo-pink counters, where I spent a good deal of time, reclining on the black leather couch, watching customers and chatting with employees. "*Kayak FO*," Dede said to me, chuckling the first time I visited the new spot, "like a factory outlet."

But no matter how big they get, Anonim has maintained its status as a scene mainstay through strict adherence to scene ideals. Although they are "business-minded" in the brands they choose to sell—Dede even used a survey at one point to determine which brands were in her customers' radar, and invited those listed to sell at her store—Anonim is well-known in the scene as a distro with integrity, a "pure" distro to use the term in common parlance (*distro yang pure*). They are a big supporter of *komunitasnya* (the indie community) and maintain positive ties with a number of other distros.

Despite her initial intention of selling imported music and movies, Dede now, quite consciously, sells only local goods, and only those active in the indie scene and with a reputation of being "authentic" indie labels. Dede tells me that they often advise customers to visit other distros when Anonim doesn't carry exactly what the customer is looking for, and they stock fliers, advertisements, and event announcements for a variety of other shops. They look out for the other distros in Bandung, she says, and the other distros do the same for them. It is part of maintaining a family feel to the scene, she explains, keeping competition to a minimum, and fostering the larger indie community. For Dede, Anonim is not just a business; it is a social project.

The Entanglement of Work and Leisure

Dede is not the only one who sees it that way. Dendy Darman, the charismatic founder of Unkl347, insists that his company is more a "creative collective" than a business. Unkl347 operates out of a warehouse in southern Bandung. It is surrounded by garbage dumps and military bases, and is the kind of place you would have to know about to find. It has the feel of a New York industrial space reclaimed by artists. Pictures of Dendy and crew on surf expeditions line the walls. Music blasts. There are two communal offices, where employees, many of whom are independent contractors, lounge around with laptops out, surfing the Internet, chatting with other employees, or taking part in impromptu jam sessions on the company's drum set, bass, guitar, or DJ turntables.

I used to hang out at Unkl347 as if it were a café, and plenty of other people did, too. On my first visit there, several of Bandung's prominent indie rock stars stopped by and worked out the melody of Michael Jackson's "Billie Jean" in the main office. Unkl347 feels like a social club, a leisurely environment for tinkering with designs, bouncing ideas off of others, or just hanging out (*nongkrong aja*).

This doesn't mean profit is irrelevant to them, though. Unkl347, according to Dendy, brings in between 700 million to 1 billion rupiah per month (roughly US$75,000–120,000), a near fortune by Indonesian standards. They sell their goods in Singapore, Malaysia, even Australia, and keep a small army of designers at hand to make sure they maintain their edge as one of Indonesia's most innovative clothing companies.

But that is not what keeps them designing. Dendy sees his company as first, a community of designers and musicians, and second, as an example for other distros. Its status as a business comes in a distant third. They show the young folks how it's done, Dendy explains, how to stay "true to their roots," while making a healthy profit. Plenty of other distros see Unkl347 this way, as well. Dendy is known in the scene as "Uncle D," and it is easy to see why. He's a heavy-set guy in his early 30s, with longish black hair and a scraggly goatee. He has an infectious smile and a friendly, avuncular demeanor. His status as something of a godfather of the Bandung scene is the inspiration behind his company's latest name change. They have been through several, from 347boardrider co., named after the address of the Jalan Dago home he and his early partners were living in when they set up shop, to simply 347, then Eat347 (playing on the fact that "347" looks something like the letters "EAT" if you squint just right), then just Eat, and finally to Unkl347, when a disagreement between designers led the company to split into two. Eat, the other half of the company, had a shop right next door to Unkl347 in 2007, and they continued to maintain positive ties and promote each other (though some of his company's designs, including such slogans as "Eat Division" and "Eat will tear us apart" make subtle jabs at his neighbor).[4] They may not agree with each other on design issues, but they still have the same ideology of DIY and community support, and the rivalry between them seldom ventures beyond a kind of harmless ribbing.

Dendy and his friends were avid surfers and skateboarders when they founded Unkl347, and the original concept was very much a surf and skatewear theme, inspired by American and Australian labels like Ocean Pacific and Rusty. Their T-shirts were simple, plain, printed in bold greens, blues, yellows, and reds, with simple designs, often making use of their own "bowl" logo that mimicked those of other board-based clothing brands. Like Adjie of No Label Stuff, Dendy was a middle-class kid, no longer able to afford expensive surf clothes, but deeply invested in the "coolness" they bestowed upon him. He had left his hometown of Makassar, Sulawesi, to attend ITB, but ended up going to a much cheaper school (unbeknown to his father at the time), and using the rest of the money his father sent him each year to surf, instead. Going into business with his friends was in part a way to further support the habit and in part just another way to have fun. They didn't take it all that seriously. They worked when they wanted to, and played when they wanted to, and it became increasingly difficult to tell the difference.

As the company progressed, 347's designs became more and more eclectic, leaving behind the surf emphasis for a range of motifs that spanned from parodies of larger brands to tributes to British pop bands. Their range was omnivorous, expansive, a possibility brought about by the company's commitment to cut and paste as a design strategy. Unkl347 became enthusiastic supporters of Indonesia's "design revolution." What started as a game took on the feel of mission.

The secret to their success, however, may have had less to do with their designs than with two other factors: their shrewd business acumen and their construction of not just a label but an entire "media assemblage" (Liechty 2003), a collection of products that promote, cross reference, and are in constant dialogue with one another. Dendy knew from the beginning that if 347 were to survive, they had to find ways to promote themselves. So they sponsored concerts and "endorsed" bands, advertised in local publications, and put on events. Perhaps their biggest promotional innovation, however, was in establishing their own zine, *Ripple*. In the beginning, it was essentially just a cheap advertisement for their clothing line, Xeroxed at a local copy shop, but it also featured a few articles about surfing and the like and some solicited ad spots for Australian surf brands such as Rusty. Issues came out sporadically and were only a few pages in length. Their first issue was a thin six-pager, including the cover. By 2001, though, the magazine was coming out semi-regularly, was substantially thicker, and had attached to it a staff that was a veritable who's who of today's indie scene, with Satria N.B. (better known as "Iyo"), the long-time manager of and now singer for indie pop band Pure Saturday, serving as editor-in-chief; David Tarigan, the founder of Jakarta's Aksara Records as music and art editor; and Dendy himself as chief executive. The coverage had expanded to include skateboarding, music, and lifestyle themes, articles about local bands, up-and-coming brands, and tattoo artists. Other distros, like Anonim Wardrobe and No Label Stuff, had begun to use their pages to advertise, as well.

Then, David Tarigan, borrowing a move from Calvin Johnson and *Sub Pop*, had the idea of including a cassette with the magazine. A bunch of Iyo's friends got together, made a recording of their music, and *Ripple* gave away the album for free with the 3,500 rupiah they charged for the magazine itself. That one decision changed everything, Iyo recalls. *Ripple* transitioned from an extended ad for a surf-wear company into a genuine lifestyle magazine in its own right. Issues got bigger and thicker, as the scope of their content expanded. Publication became more frequent. All sorts of people involved in the Bandung underground got involved: zine writers, musicians, skateboarders, tattoo artists, clothing designers. *Ripple* became the venue through which the scene most publicly articulated who it was and what it was all about.

After a couple of years, *Ripple* officially split from 347 and became its own distinct entity. By 2007 it was a relatively big publication, producing 8–10,000 copies a month, with a PDF version available online for free, but it still felt like a family affair.[5] At their office, located in Iyo's home in Bandung, music blasted. Little kids ran around. There was almost nothing to identify it as a business place at all, except the few scattered computers and printers.

Ripple gradually positioned itself as the premier publication for indie scenesters, a key resource for youth to turn to in evaluating trends and becoming actively engaged in indie production themselves. *Ripple* were among the scene's strongest voices articulating the DIY ethos, with whole issues devoted to starting one's own label and distributing one's own zine. Readers were incited to get involved and become active, not just buy the latest album and support the coolest brand. By 2006, they no longer charged for their magazine, with their financial support provided by a variety of local distros and clothing labels who advertise in their pages, and had become a vivid example of the connectivity between the producers involved in the indie scene.

Figure 4 *Ripple* magazine #41, The "Indonesian Independent Culture Issue."

Unkl347, in addition to launching *Ripple*, has also branched out into other forms of media. Like many distros in Bandung and elsewhere, they sell the cassettes and CDs of local bands, often friends of Dendy and other employees, as well as international acts such as Tiger Milk, Cherry Tree, and Club 8, who they have managed to connect with online. They continually sponsor music, skateboarding, and art events in Bandung, and established DISTANCE in 2002, Bandung's first outdoor rave series. Their parties, several of which I have attended, are multi-media events in their own right, with DJs and VJs, skate art and Polaroid photography exhibitions, and heavily made-up girls in matching 347 T-shirts and short shorts serving hors d'oeuvres on circular trays and posing for photographs with guests. They also set up their own music label, called Flatspills, and a "cinematic lab," distributed through their shops as well as through the wider distro network.

Indie Diffusion

When I lived there in 2007, Bandung had long since established itself as the undisputed center of Indonesia's indie scene, with Unkl347, Monik/Celtic, Riotic, No Label Stuff, and Anonim leading the pack as some of its most recognizable brand names. The area around Jalan Sultan Agung and Jalan Trunojoyo, just north of downtown, had become Bandung's equivalent to San Francisco's Haight and Ashbury or London's Kings Road, the place to go to buy too-tight T-shirts, studded belts, and other assorted accoutrements of teen angst. People came from all over the archipelago to shop there. Unkl347 was located there, as was No Label Stuff, Cosmic, Evil, d'Loops, Airplane Systm, Screamous, and the new Monik Woods outpost for Monik/Celtic. But DIY fashion was by no means confined to Bandung. Rather, the Bandung scene had become the example young designers and musicians from all over the rest of the archipelago turned to for inspiration, their cooperative business model touted as *the* distro ideal.

Diana Slackers, herself a Bandung native, has played a significant role in spreading the DIY ethos of the indie scene beyond the city limits of Bandung. Only twenty-five years old when I met her, she had already established the city of Yogyakarta's biggest and longest-running distro, Slackers, a two-story monster of a store, hang-out space, and design studio, full of distro-label T-shirts, backpacks, jackets, CDs, and shoes.

Diana describes herself as "just an ordinary girl" who was lucky enough to come across a group of people with a similar attitude, lifestyle, and way of thinking to her own. She moved to Yogyakarta from Bandung to attend university after completing high school, and that's when, she says, she began "looking for [her]self through community." Eventually, she told me, she decided she wanted to "*mengaktualizasi diri*" (actualize herself) through more active participation in the scene, and that led to the development of the idea of Slackers. She started by designing clothes, and then began producing her own clothing label. The idea behind it, she says, was to bring the Bandung indie ideal to Yogyakarta.

Diana says she was attracted to design because she wanted to bring out and create what was inside her thoughts. It was a need she felt, an itch she had to scratch. She had always liked music, but "didn't have any skill," was in a band as a vocalist briefly but didn't want to devote herself to something she "couldn't do to the maximum," so she concentrated her energies on a clothing line, instead. At first she had no intention of starting a distro, she told me, rephrasing a now familiar sentiment. She just wanted to do something that was her own creation. But when her clothing line had gained a substantial reputation, she and her then-boyfriend (now husband), Okko, decided it was time to open a distro of their own. She, like many of the distro owners I know, described the transition from labor of love to marketable enterprise as a kind of natural evolution, a process so subtle and gradual, it was hardly noticeable while it happened.

There were already a few distros in Yogyakarta when Slackers started, but none like the ones out of Bandung. They were small stands on the side of the road, in the style of Riotic's early days, and Diana hoped to provide Yogyakarta with a better model of distro innovation. They set up the distro in Okko's grandfather's house, a modest home on Ring Road Utara on the outskirts of town. They simply could not afford to rent a place of their own, and his grandfather was generous enough to give them something to work with. At first it occupied only the front room, but by 2006 it had already taken over the whole house, music blasting from speakers, large flat panel screens broadcasting MTV. It is like a checker-boarded youth culture theme park.

Diana settled on the name "Slackers" for the distro after reading about adolescent character types in some pop-psychology book she read in college. It was listed as the youth type that just wants to have fun. She didn't really know what it meant beyond that, she says, and hadn't even heard of the Richard Linklater film *Slacker*, often cited as the key filmic text of America's Generation X. To her, slackers are not lazy kids or social rejects. They are not just youth afflicted with modern malaise. They are people who prioritize fun, who strive to always be happy, and opt out of the rat race for something more meaningful. In other words, they are people who epitomize the DIY ethos. Slackers like her friends and her, Diana says, are not afraid to work hard. They simply want their work to have meaning.

Diana, like Dede Anonim, describes Slackers as a community as much as a retail outlet, a collection of "kids who crave freedom from authority and pursue things because they are passionate about them," not because they need to or desire financial reward. Almost all of her employees are in bands. Some have their own clothing labels, zines, and fashion blogs. "We just believe in ourselves" (*kita percaya diri aja*), she said. "We don't need to be successful to be inspired."

Her employees have all become close personal friends of hers, and they spend a great deal of time together outside of work, going to each others' houses, eating barbecued chicken at the popular *warung* (food stall) Bale. Since they support her with their labor, Diana tries to return the favor by helping them develop their talent as designers, writers, or musicians. She supplies them with clothes to wear on stage, encourages them to participate in designing clothes for the label, even puts on an annual show featuring her store's bands alongside national and sometimes even international acts. She describes the Slackers style as "rebel," which in practice means a good deal of black and designs featuring skulls and bones, but to Diana, it also means not trying to be the same as other people. "We have to be willing to stand out," she says, "to be different."

Diana ended our formal interview telling me that many people believe that much of the initial idealism behind distros has disappeared, lost in commercial transactions that equate quality with marketability. Diana, however, doesn't think so. She thinks that people's willingness to pay for items she has created demonstrates their valuing of those products, and more importantly, the ideals and self-expression behind them. She doesn't see capitalism as incompatible with idealism. Money, she claims, simply enables the indie scene to progress even further. It provides the support necessary to fund acts of creativity. The difference, she told me, between a successful distro and a mainstream company is the continued desire of distros to support one another. Big distros like hers continue to support the community of kids around them, and if they don't, they lose their distro status. The crucial thing we have to remember, she concluded, is "don't ever forget our community" (*jangan pernah lupa komunitas kita*).

Neoliberalism Revisited

Distros and clothing labels like No Label Stuff, Unkl347, Monik/Celtic, Anonim, Riotic, and Slackers are powerful examples of DIY capitalism, grass-roots cooperative economics. In a sense, the Indonesian indie scene is the vanguard of neoliberal cultural infiltration into Indonesia. It promotes an entrepreneurial ethic that sees personal ambition as nearly a moral imperative, one that actively emphasizes acts of creation as a means of personal salvation. There is no question, then, that it does not make sense to see DIY—as many members of the Indonesian indie scene certainly do—as an "alternative" to commercialization or an antidote to global capitalism. Their style of indie production never escapes from being capitalist in orientation. It provides wage labor to hundreds of young people, makes use of commercial factories, perpetuates the same system of production, and upholds its old hierarchies and inequities. That does not, however, mean it blindly reiterates the rationality of neoliberalism. It has, for one, replaced the emphasis on rational individualism described by Harvey (2005) and others as critical to neoliberal philosophy with a decidedly more social model, and reinserted the importance of the group over the pursuit of profit.

Resistance to neoliberalism in Southeast Asia, claim Nevins and Peluso in their introduction to a recent book on the subject, "is often about resurrecting the 'social'"

(Nevins and Peluso 2008: 4). The Indonesian indie scene is an excellent example of this. Yet both "resistance" and "resurrection" seem somehow inadequate terms for describing the practice. The social was always a precondition for indie scenesters' participation in the neoliberal economy, a given. It was never up for elimination in the first place. When members of the Indonesian indie scene went into business, they adapted the culture of neoliberalism to their needs. They did not merely adapt to it. The end result, a local manifestation of a global capitalist project, a unique assemblage of cut-and-pasted neoliberal cultural values and autochthonous modes of sociality, may look more or less the same as any similar satellite of the neoliberal empire (Hardt and Negri 2001), but it does not feel the same. It has its own texture, its own idiosyncratic rhythm, its own infectious community-driven optimism that insists idealism and market principles can exist side-by-side. After spending months in indie businesses, factories, and exhibition halls, I can attest that it is hard not to get caught up in this optimism, to not begin to believe that youth with a vision, even if that vision is for sale, can somehow change the very course of Indonesian history.

—3—

DIY in DIY (Daerah Istimewa Yogyakarta): Everyday Production in the Indonesian Indie Scene

All the industries in Bandung emerged out of hanging out at first. The pioneers (of the indie scene) emerged out of the hangout spots … And it's still like that to this day.

—Ahmad Marin, co-owner Monik/Celtic and FFWD Records.

Nongkrong Aja

Since the late 1990s, distros have become some of the most active sites of youth cultural production in Indonesia, assuming a more and more prominent position in the world of fashion, music, and publishing, while maintaining a small-scale, grass-roots orientation. They are a bold illustration of the DIY ethos put into practice, kids getting together and making stuff, then selling and distributing it through their own peer networks, without direct investment or mediation from larger corporate, state, or financial interests. They are one possible template of what DIY production can be, and at least in certain corners of the world, has already become, a mode of *creative collectivist capitalism* built from the ground up by engaged and empowered teenagers and twenty-somethings. It is easy to picture these shops and production houses, then, as a flurry of activity, a hothouse of new trends and ideas, constantly buzzing with the chaos and energy of youth. That is not at all what a typical distro feels like.

Showing up on an average weekday, you would probably find a shop nearly empty of customers, with several bored-looking employees standing around or texting on cellphones, and a couple of designers and musicians hanging out in the backroom staring at a computer screen, perhaps tweaking a design, or more likely, blasting some new Panda Bear MP3 they read about on Pitchfork.com. Day-to-day life at a distro is decidedly prosaic. Hands down, the most common activity that takes place there is *nongkrong aja,* or just hanging out.

In this chapter, I describe the daily activities of distro life, the ordinary, one might say, mundane practices that constitute the lived reality of DIY cultural production in the Indonesian indie scene. I chronicle the cast of characters and typical routines of a single distro, where I spent a good deal of time in the city of Yogyakarta, Central

Java, a now-defunct music and clothing shop called Reddoor. Although distros come in all shapes and sizes, and my description of Reddoor by no means sums up the experience of all distro communities, let alone all sites of DIY cultural production worldwide, it does provide one vivid example of the irreducible specificities of time and space in which DIY is embedded. I am not attempting to construct a universal theory of DIY production here, simply suggesting that in order to understand DIY, what it means and how it works in specific instances and contexts, we must look at processes of production at the ground level, in moments, of course, when production is actively occurring, but also, and perhaps most importantly, during its downtimes, where it brews beneath the surface.

Hanging out, I argue in this chapter, is not an idle waste of time for the young people of Reddoor, a symptom of the general malaise of a jaded generation. It is not the lazy space between active creative moments, but an important creative activity in its own right, one that mediates all other forms of production and consumption for participants. Hanging out is where ideas are generated, group sensibilities forged, and collective interpretations developed. And what is being produced most readily through hanging out is a particular cultural attitude, defining a specific moment in Indonesian and, indeed, global capitalist history, an attitude I have been calling the DIY ethos. In-person sociality, then, remains a critical component of DIY practice, despite the oft-discussed digital age reconfigurations of time and space. I will begin this chapter with a brief introduction to Yogyakarta, then launch in to my more detailed description of Reddoor Distro.

Dareah Istimewa Yogyakarta (DIY)

The Special District of Yogyakarta (Daerah Istimewa Yogyakarta), appropriately abbreviated as "DIY," is an urban area of around three million people in south-central Java, but as soon as you leave the main streets, it feels more like a collection of villages, sewn together into a labyrinthine tapestry of muddy alleyways and back roads. It is a noisy, bustling amalgam of *kampung* (villages, or village-like neighborhoods), teeming with motorbikes and over-crowded minibuses. It is a bigger city than Bandung, some seven hours away by train, but it feels smaller, more isolated, more cut off from the centers of production. Traffic is not quite as bad, the streets aren't quite as packed with people, and residents move at an observably slower pace. This despite the fact that Yogyakarta is a major educational center, a city of students (*kota pelajar*) with more than a hundred institutions of higher learning that serve some twenty-five percent of Indonesia's total university population. Yogyakarta's schools, including Universitas Gadjah Mada, one of Indonesia's premier state universities, where I spent the first semester of a study abroad back in 1996, attract students from all over Indonesia, leading informants of mine to often quip that Yogyakarta is "*kayak Indonesia kecil*" (like a miniature Indonesia).

Yogyakarta, or "Yoyga" as it is more commonly called, is best known in the tourist literature, and anthropological literature for that matter, as the "cultural center of Java" (Taylor et al. 1997), the *kota budaya* (city of culture), where "fine dancing was still practiced and where the sonorous music of the gamelan floated through the night's tranquility" (Mulder 1996: 24). It holds a similar mythical status in the Indonesian popular imagination, as well, as a tradition-heavy stronghold of all that is Javanese, and despite all evidence to the contrary, was repeatedly described to me as I traveled to other cities in the archipelago as a sleepy, relaxed (*santai*) town, still steeped in the old ways. Carefully selected imagery of exotic *wayang* dancers, shadow puppets, *gamelan,* and old men in traditional court garb woo visitors from far and wide. The reputation of Yogyakarta as an artistic and cultural center, as well as its proximity to Borobudur and Prambanan (ancient Buddhist and Hindu monuments, respectively) has made Yogyakarta the second-most tourist-visited region of Indonesia, after Bali.

It also, however, deserves to be recognized as a longstanding outpost of Indonesia's avant garde, a center of youth culture and political activism, artistic experimentation and creative expression. Yogya's Institut Seni Indonesia (The Art Institute of Indonesia) is widely considered the best art school in the country, and creatively inclined youth are drawn there from all over the archipelago. Many of them are involved in the larger indie scene. Organizations like Indonesia Visual Arts Archive (formerly Cemeti), Lembaga Indonesia Perancis (The French Indonesian Foundation), The House of Natural Fiber new media arts laboratory, and the Kedai Kebun Forum work tirelessly to maintain Yogya's cutting-edge reputation.

In the international press, however, Yogyakarta is probably best known these days as a disaster-prone region, home to more than its share of earthquakes and volcanic eruptions. As the disasters of 2006 and the more recent eruptions of 2011 testify, it probably deserves this reputation. On May 27, 2006, four months before I left for Indonesia, Yogyakarta was struck by a 6.3 magnitude earthquake. Some 5,782 people were killed, 36,299 injured, and nearly 600,000 left homeless. An estimated 300,000 houses were destroyed, innumerable buildings damaged, and as the casualties were counted and the destruction surveyed, another threat appeared, literally on the horizon. Mount Merapi, the volcano perched precariously over the northern suburbs of the city, had begun belting out steam and lava with an intensity it had not shown in years. The world watched, holding its breath, for an even harsher blow to hit Yogyakarta's already frazzled population.

I was holding my breath, too. I had friends in Yogya and a year's worth of experiences there from my time as an exchange student in 1996, and I faced the very real possibility that my planned fieldsite simply would not be there when I arrived. As it turned out, this fear was unwarranted. Merapi spewed out plenty of lava and ash, but never erupted with the ferocity expected. And although large portions of the southern part of the city, particularly in the district of Bantul, were decimated by the earthquake, damage was barely visible in the northern part of the city where I spent most of my time. The earthquake did, however, have a long-term impact on the emotional landscape of the city. Although my research informants, mostly college students and recent graduates from elsewhere, were primarily unaffected by the physical damage that occurred, many of them discussed psychological scars. As Ekil, a coffeeshop barista and distro attendant I met early into my research, told me, he was mostly affected *dalam hati* (in his heart). Although it had not displaced him or his family, it had left him stinging with a sense of just how tenuous and uncertain life can be. He worried about all the *nakal* (bad) things he had done in his life, and had yet to repent for. He worried he would never get a chance to make something of himself.

Ekil didn't undergo any profound personal transformation as a result of the earthquake, or even, he admitted to me, adjust his behavior all that much, but still, it lingered in his mind as a menacing presence. And this seems to be how many of my informants experienced the natural disasters that afflicted Yogyakarta and the rest of the archipelago, as haunting possibilities, lending a sense of immediacy and urgency to everyday life.

Nevertheless, I was shocked by how little the sense of impending doom entered into the everyday experience of my informants. For my first couple of months in town, conversations came up about the earthquake fairly frequently. People would point out cracks in walls, share anecdotes about their personal experiences. But references to it grew more and more rare, so that by the time I left, I had to remind myself that the earthquake had ever even happened. For a long time, life in Indonesia has been relatively unpredictable. Dramatic change has been incorporated into the very fabric of ordinary experience. Several months of benefit concerts, visits from politicians, and heightened activity by foreign non-profits gradually gave way to a reign of incongruous normalcy.

Behind the Reddoor

For months, Reddoor Distro was my home base in Yogyakarta. It was the place I started and ended my evenings, my default fieldsite when no special events were taking place. Most of the people I knew in Yogyakarta, whether bands, designers, zine writers, artists, or filmmakers, I knew through Reddoor. The community that gathered there, a collection of college students and recent graduates in their late teens to late twenties, were among my best informants and best friends in Indonesia.

It did not start out that way, though. It took me weeks to gain a foothold into Reddoor Distro, not because the kids who worked and hung out there were particularly closed off to me—they were without exception warm and welcoming—but because I, frankly, was intimidated by them. I knew them by reputation long before I knew them. And when I first saw them, I recognized them immediately as a familiar type, one I took for granted in my East Hollywood neighborhood, but had never expected to see here. They bore all the requisite signifiers, the right combination of the casual and the fussy, the trendy and the ironic: tailored corduroy or denim jeans, baggy on top and tapered down to the ankle, sometimes with patterned boxer shorts peeping out from beneath, or a thick-white belt hugging the waste line, tight T-shirts in solid colors with bold text printed across them, and sleeves cut high up on the arm to show off bicep tattoos. They wore cardigans and V-neck sweaters, sometimes argyle, sometimes plaid, but always referencing an Anglophile style characteristic of designer brands, such as Ben Sherman or Burberry. On top of those were cheap but tailored canvas sports coats and military jackets, even the occasional woven neck scarf dangling down toward the waist—garments, in other words, that seemed better suited to a different climate, a whole other part of the world, as if the seasons, too, had been cut-and-pasted onto the archipelago. On their shoulders were permanently affixed canvas messenger bags and side satchels (though never a backpack or a purse), as if they had just arrived from school, or were off to a café to theorize on revolution. On men, hair was cut into faux-hawks and fashion mullets, or worn long and scraggly, sometimes as a moptop, sometimes with the Britpop earlocks of Oasis lead singer Liam Gallagher, and sometimes simply long and rocker-like with no obvious stylistic interventions. Other times, it was covered over with a newsboy cap or a trucker hat, a woven beanie or a fedora. On women, there were Louise Brooks bobs, pixie cuts, and shoulder-length Zooey Deschannels, bangs cut blunt as if to deflect the light. And on both men and women, thick-framed glasses abounded, some in pointed at the sides, retro 1960s granny style, others large and square, taking up nearly half the face. These, in other words, were the hipsters of the Yogyakarta indie scene, too hip even to admit that's what they were.

According to Yudhi, owner and designer for Groovy Distro, a mile or so away, Reddoor was a gathering place for kids with lots of potential (*anak yang berpotensi*), a creative hotspot. Like Unkl347 in Bandung, it is something of a creative collective, a space where young aspiring cultural producers of various sorts get together and motivate one another. It was also a great place to get drunk, and kids got drunk on the sidewalk out front of Reddoor more or less every night.

Situated in the northern section of Yogyakarta along the drainage ditch known as Selokan Mataram, and just across the street from Universitas Gadjah Mada, Reddoor was in a small red building with a large tinted window, filled most of the year with a collage of Xeroxed pictures of Reddoor regulars holding up heart-warmingly ironic signs that read "I ♥ mom." Empty walls on either side sported graffiti and the marks of local taggers, most significantly a stenciled tag Reddoor gave itself, a pyramid with an eye, like the Masonic symbol on the U.S. dollar bill. A bulletin board on the eastern side of the shop featured posters and fliers for upcoming concerts and distro-related events. Next to it was a red pipe leading to the ceiling and a false, red metal fire-extinguisher compartment mislabeled "Hydrant." The door leading in to the store was, as one might expect, painted red.

Inside, Reddoor was done up in a local approximation of artsy urban chic, fake exposed piping and wires on the ceiling, red metal pulleys mounted on the walls to hold up racks of T-shirts and jackets. A couch leaned against the main window with a newspaper and magazine rack next to it for customers, employees, and hangers-on to laze about on in the middle of a scorching hot Yogya day. At the northeastern end of the shop was a makeshift dressing room where a customer could pull a fabric shower curtain around them to try on clothes. Just west of that was a doorway into the back room, followed by a counter with a computer on it and a glass display case filled with buttons with cutesy slogans, stickers, bracelets and other music and cloth-ing paraphernalia. On one side of the counter was a magazine rack featuring older editions of *Ripple,* and other, hard-to-find (in Indonesia) imported magazines from the United States and the UK, including *NME* and, occasionally, *Maximumrocknroll* and *Alternative Press.* Behind the counter was a rack of music CDs and cassettes, all of local bands.

During the day, the most active part of the shop was behind the scenes, in the back storage room where redundant employees and their friends hung out, tinkered with the shared computer, and reclined on a beat-up black sofa. This is where much of the design of Reddoor's products was done, sometimes communally with everyone contributing small pieces, but mostly individually with those people hanging out constantly offering up their opinions. Design was sporadic, intermittent. It followed no regular schedule.

The Reddoor Kids

Regulars at Reddoor are testimony to just how diverse Indonesia's indie scene is and provide a complicated picture of the people, aesthetics, and tastes that constitute this emergent social formation. I will introduce a few of them individually, to give the reader a sense of the social milieu that made up the Reddoor experience.

Adegreden (or Ade) was the manager of Reddoor as well as the designer for the in-house clothing label FireFighter Fight! (see chapter 6). Growing up in a strict Muslim household in Pekanbaru in the Riau region of Sumatra, he was currently a student of interior design in his final year at ISI, Indonesia's top-ranked program in that field. In fact, this was something like his fourth final year in the program—a common pattern for Yogya students, who find other, better things to do than finish their *skripsi* (senior thesis or project) in a timely manner. He was also something of a father figure to the Reddoor crowd. A few years older than many of the other scene members (twenty-six at the time), Ade took responsibility over the welfare of others, and my own, making sure everyone had rides to events, everyone got home alright, and no one did anything too self-destructive during long nights of binge drinking and sidewalk socializing. He was also a very sharp dresser, with a personal style that borrowed heavily from indie, punk, and gothic fashions. His typical outfit was a pair of black, cotton trousers, tapered in the standard scenester style (tight at the

Figure 5   Inside Nimco Distro, Yogyakarta.

ankle, looser at the waist), typically with a wallet chain or a spiked belt, sometimes with the legs tucked into a pair of twenty-eye Converse All-Stars or imitation Doctor Martin boots. He wore T-shirts he had designed himself, or other Reddoor-related products; hooded sweatshirts, for instance, or canvas blazers or faux military jackets with buttons and badges of bands and brands adorning the sides. He had his hair configured in a number of styles over the course of the year, from a simple shaved head to a faux-hawk and a classic skater cut, bangs hanging just past his eyes. His style, to put it simply, was restless, and yet confined to certain generic parameters, always shifting subtly from week to week between parallel subcultural expressions.

Pipu was Ade's girlfriend (*pacar*) and an active participant in the indie scene in her own right. Born in Yogyakarta, but raised alternately there and in Kalimantan, she personifies the middle-class mobility characteristic of the indie scene. She was a first-year student of architecture at Universitas Islam Indonesia (The Indonesian Islamic University) at the time of this study, and due to her striking personal appearance and severe fashion sense (borrowing most evidently from Japanese gothic Lolita and British punk rock and mod), was sometimes a model for local distro clothing labels. She had a short, a-lined bob, with bangs cut asymmetrically across her forehead; wore short denim, pleather, and schoolgirl skirts, sometimes with safety pins adorning the sides and a large studded belt across the waist; thick cotton tights in black, fishnet, or bold stripes, all seemingly incongruous with the heat; a variety of boots extending from just past her ankle up to her thighs; and an assortment of tops, from simple tanks to ruffled blouses, typically with short sleeves. She had a collection of blazers, trench coats, and military-style jackets to top off her outfits, all with heavily cinched waists to emphasize the thinness of her frame. Several months before the end of my fieldwork, she and Ade went on to open up their own distro, Pipuangpu, and much of the Reddoor crowd followed them there, leaving Reddoor an empty shell of what it once was.

Agnes was a student at Atma Jaya University in something like economics or management, which she chose more for the sake of her parents' peace of mind than her own personal fulfillment. Born and raised by a Christian, ethnically Batak (from Northern Sumatra) family in the oil-rich town of Balikpapan, Kalimantan, she was currently dating another Reddoor regular, Vata, also from Kalimantan. With a more corpulent figure than the rail-thin norm of the Reddoor kids and a talkative, jocular disposition, Agnes had been dubbed *Bunda,* Javanese for "mother," by the Reddoor kids and assumed something of a matronly role within the community. Her outfits were simple and unfussy, involving regular cut jeans or mid-length black cotton skirts, T-shirts and hooded sweatjackets, a pulled back ponytail, and only occasionally a fancier element, a tailored blazer or military coat, perhaps, or a polka-dotted dress. She's also a great conversationalist and kept me entertained many nights with stories from her hometown in Kalimantan, parables of undead practitioners of the black arts who eat the soft spots out of infants' foreheads to procure the power to propel their detachable heads as fireballs through the night sky.

The members of the band Nervous, including Alfonso (vocals), Aga (drums), and Novan (bass), as well as Novan's girlfriend Bolot, were a big part of the Reddoor experience. One, or all of the band members were there nearly every night (except the band's guitarist, Doni, whom I barely knew). Although not technically employees, they behaved like them, lounging around in the back of the store, using the shared computer, even occasionally ringing someone up at the cash register if no one else was available. Before every gig, they would gather at Reddoor to dress themselves up in cardigan sweaters, slacks, and sports coats.

Alfonso (Fonso) is Agnes's brother and, hence, also from Kalimantan. He was introduced to the Reddoor crowd by his sister, and found himself recruited into Nervous as the keyboard player and backup vocalist. When the other members kicked out the existing vocalist, he climbed the ranks to lead singer and guitarist, a role he carried out in his characteristic austere fashion. With his permanent black-frame glasses, large enough to cover most of the upper part of his face, locally made cotton sports coat, and remarkable ability to endure rather thick, scratchy sweaters through the tropical heat, Fonso had something of the status of a scene poet, and contributed a philosophical, moody atmosphere to late-night conversations.

Aga, from Ade's region of Sumatra, was sometimes referred to, in an ironic reference to prefabricated "boy band" personality types, as "the good-looking" (*cakep*) one in Nervous. He's a sharp dresser with a penchant for argyle and pinstripes, derby hats and ties, clunky black dress shoes, and clean pleated slacks, wore a straight-from-the-salon variation on a Beatles moptop, and was an avowed, and quite obvious anglophile, who plays soccer several times a week and listens primarily to gloomy indie rock. He's an easy guy to get along with and is very social. I once ran into him ill and curled up on a couch at a party, looking like hell (though still well dressed in a shirt and tie). I asked him why he didn't just go home, and he told me "*sendirian di sana*" (it's lonely there).

Novan, also the bassist in another successful, major label alternative rock band, Captain Jack, is from Kalimantan, and had a kind of scruffy but sweet demeanor that allowed him to move easily between several distro communities in the larger Yogyakarta independent scene. He had a much more casual personal style than did the other members of the band, usually sporting a Reddoor or a Captain Jack T-shirt (or no shirt at all), a pair of dirty skinny jeans, and a stylized mohawk, often hanging limply on his head. He always seemed like he was on his way to somewhere else and spoke in a fast-paced mumble it took me months to comprehend. He was also just beginning to master the fine art of opening a beer bottle with his teeth by the time I went home. His first few efforts left him bloody, with chipped incisors.

Bolot, Novan's girlfriend and near-constant companion at the time, was anything but a stereotypical band groupie. Rather, a student in Universitas Gadjah Mada's prestigious Fisipol (Social Science and Politics) program, she was a brazen, outgoing woman in her early twenties who contributed an energy of intensity and enthusiasm to the Reddoor crowd. Whereas Pipu personified the distro version of stylized feminine severity, Bolot maintained a more dressed-down, tomboy look, with short, permanently disheveled hair and thick-frame granny glasses, skinny jeans and trim T-shirts, and simple V-neck sweaters. She was one of the most outgoing of the Reddoor kids and one of my favorite people to be around.

But Ito, for me, was perhaps the definitive contributor to the Reddoor mood. A guitarist and vocalist for two well-respected Yogyakarta indie bands, diSko and Anggisluka, as well as an aspiring filmmaker and painter, Ito was born in Germany to diplomat parents, but raised primarily in Jakarta. He came to Yogyakarta some eight years previous to study economics at UGM (Universitas Gadjah Mada), but discovered that music was more his thing. Ito was one of the people who first made me feel at home at Reddoor, engaging me in long discussions about music, between sips of Bintang beer. He's an attention glutton and was also stubbornly unstylish for a Reddoor regular, a fact that led to many nights of pre-show making-up by Pipu, Bolot, and others, who painted his nails, outlined his eyes, and teased his scraggly, longish hair to near comical dimensions. His typical look was little more than a T-shirt, typically untailored (rather unusual for a Reddoor kid), a pair of corduroy jeans and Converse All-Stars, and possibly a button-down cardigan. It's the kind of look that crosses boundaries easily between scenes, an uncommitted look, relentlessly casual, and nearly always more or less appropriate.

Rezka, in contrast, was all cool poise and stylish composure. He, like Ade, had his own clothing line, Boor, and held a reputation for being something of the scene "playboy." One of the elite few Reddoor kids who actually grew up in Yogyakarta (along with Bolot), he had a steady stream of short-term girlfriends he would bring by the shop on his motorbike before dropping them off at their *kost* (boarding house) and coming back to *ngobrol* (chat). Nearly every month I knew him, he had a brand new tattoo to show off, ranging from an elaborate Japanese-inspired demon and hell-fire scene on his upper arm to the ironic "good boy" printed across his back. Rezka was fond of newsboy caps, fedoras, and occasional nods to classier, vintage styles of dress, but his day-to-day wear was decidedly more casual: skinny jeans, T-shirts, and blazers, often his own design. He wore a number of thin black rubber bracelets on both wrists, along with a watch, the occasional ring or necklace, and a frequent scarf around his neck. Toward the end of my stay, he started to take to a trim, rather dapper moustache. I could never tell if he meant it to read as ironic or not. Rezka was also the first person I met at Reddoor, confidently strolling over to meet me one night as I browsed through T-shirts and jackets.

That night, he, Ade, and several other guys took me to a nightclub opening called "Caesar Babes" at Plaza Ambarrukmo, the newest mall in town. We swigged Jack Daniels and some variety of locally brewed *lapen* (grain liquor mixed with various herbs and flavorings) in plastic bags in the back of an SUV in the parking lot before heading inside, where all twelve of us were on the VIP list for free entrance. Ade had connections. That night, the only night I ever saw Ade dance—and on top of a bar, for that matter—was my first, blurry introduction to the Reddoor crowd, a drunken, instant initiation into scene membership.

The Distro as Elective Community

For a number of months after that night, I became something of an honorary Red-door kid, assuming my role as the resident *bule* (white person, literally "albino") in the group, and providing an easy conversational topic when people ran out of other things to talk about. But I was by no means the odd man out in an other-wise homogenous community. I may have come the furthest to hang out at Reddoor, but I was one of many immigrants there. The Reddoor kids, as should be evident from my descriptions, come from all over Indonesia. They stem from many ethnic backgrounds (including Javanese, Sundanese, Melayu, Dayak, Batak, Balinese, and Makassarese), speak a variety of first languages, and have several different religions printed onto their identity cards. Although all of them fit roughly into the category of "middle-class," their actual economic circumstances vary profoundly. Some, such as Vata, are children of civil servants, whose pay is roughly US$200 a month, more than the average in Indonesia, but not much more; while others, such as Agnes and Fonso, have parents employed by international oil companies, and make substantially more. This is not, then, an inevitable grouping of people, forced by circumstance and geographic proximity to share a common identity. Rather, it is an *elective community,* a community of choice, made possible by the ever-increasing mobility of Indonesia's middle class.

Recent work in youth cultural studies have emphasized the fluid and part-time nature of the "network socialities" (Weinzierl and Muggleton 2004: 12) that populate the contemporary world, the ways in which young people tend to form temporary alliances organized around common aesthetics (Maffesoli 1996; Polhemus 1996; Thornton 1996; Muggleton 2000;) rather than shared locality or ethnic identity. Thornton, in her influential work *Club Cultures,* for instance, proposes the term "taste cultures" to describe such groupings, who "congregate on the basis of their shared taste in music, their consumption of common media and, most importantly, their preference for people with similar tastes to themselves" (Thornton 1996: 3). Thornton does not discount class as an important structuring component of taste cultures, but it is not the single factor that brings them together. Club kids in the UK, for instance, come from all walks of life, and those on the higher rungs of the socioeconomic ladder, she claims, often downplay their own backgrounds, even take on some of the accents and affectations of the working class. Taste cultures, she goes on to say, often intentionally obfuscate class origins, resisting "the trappings of the parent class" (Thornton 1996: 12) in favor of internally defined group tastes.

In a sense, the Reddoor kids, as well as any number of other communities forming around distros, constitute such a "taste culture." They are often temporary groupings from a variety of social backgrounds. Most of Yogyakarta's youth population, after all, is university students who tend to move away after they graduate. Although they may form enduring friendships during their time in Yogya, along with useful social networks, the collectivities they form in and around distros are themselves ephemeral. People maintain ties with other individuals in the group but not the group itself. By the time I returned to Yogyakarta in 2010, the Reddoor community had long since dissipated and the distro had closed its doors. The space was rented out to a cellphone vendor.

However, there are several key differences between the Indonesian indie scene and the UK club scene that call into question the utility of the concept of "taste culture" for describing the Reddoor kids. For one, although a wide range of people spent time at Reddoor, and many of the practices of downplaying social and economic differences described by Thornton regularly occurred, not one of the Reddoor kids was even close to belonging to that category of the lower classes referred to in Indonesian as *kaum buruh,* or working class. Such people were utterly off of their radar. They were socially invisible. For another, taste—whether in music, fashion, or just about anything—was by no means consistent among them. As Fonso explained, he himself tended toward Britpop, while Ade was more into goth, Novan into metal, and Ito into post-rock and noise. As any self-professed metal, goth, or Britpop fan will tell you, these are by no means considered similar genres by their fans, and just about anywhere in the world that I have personally experienced the likelihood of a collectivity forming around such diverse musical tastes is small, to say the least. If distro communities are taste cultures, then what community isn't?

Instead, the elective community of Reddoor formed out of something less tangible: a common sensibility or disposition. Pipu described how she came to hang out at Reddoor as a sort of happy accident, something that just happened. She used to shop at Reddoor back at its original location on Jalan Gejayan, one of Northern Yogya's main streets, and gradually shifted into becoming a regular simply "because the kids there were fascinating" (*karena anak-anaknya asyik-asyik*). She recognized a kinship between herself and them. She had always been into drawing and thought of herself as creative, and the kids at Reddoor all seemed to be involved in something similar, like design, film, or music. For Fonso, hanging out at Reddoor was an outgrowth of spending time with his sister Agnes. She discovered Reddoor first and was already friends with a bunch of the kids there. Fonso began spending time there, too, discovering a common interest in playing music with a number of the regulars. Eventually, he got sucked up into a band himself. By the time I met him, he was more of a regular even than Agnes.

If the club kids described by Thornton constitute a "taste culture," then perhaps Reddoor and the numerous other communities congregating at distros and throughout the larger circuit of the indie scene can be described as *cultures of creative production,* elective communities formed around a desire—indeed, a sense of compulsion—to make stuff and make stuff happen. To be a part of the Reddoor kids was to be active in creative production in some way. It could have been as a musician, an artist, a writer, or even a band manager, but the important thing was *doing something,* even if that meant facilitating someone else's creative production. Hence, the sheer number of self-described "band managers" in the scene. Their common tie was active participation in cultural production, however small the scale.

This does not mean, however, that the Reddoor kids were always actively producing. That couldn't be further from the case.

A Typical Night at Reddoor

During the day, distros can get painfully slow. Reddoor usually opened at 11 a.m., but most of the customers, who were primarily university and high school students, would come by the shop in the early evenings. The real action at Reddoor, though, took place at night, after the final call to prayer of the evening. Two tires with cushions for seats were placed on the sidewalk alongside a couple of not-so-sturdy red chairs with missing backs, but most people would sit straight on the concrete. Ade, Pipu, and the gang would start gathering at around 7 or 8 p.m., when everyone was done with school or work, or sleeping, whatever kept them occupied during the day. Generally, someone would go on a beer run or, more commonly an *amer* run (*Anggur Merah,* literally, and jokingly referred to as Indonesian "red wine," is made from fermented papaya and tastes something like cough syrup). Whoever could, would *patungan* (contribute money to the pool). Usually 10,000 rupiah (a little over US$1) was more than enough.

There were a number of ways the evening could go from there. If there was some event happening, say, a concert for one of Reddoor's affiliated bands, we would pass around a few bottles of beer and *amer* then hop on motorbikes and head over to the show together. As I didn't have a motorbike of my own, I would usually hitch a ride on the back of Ade's, Ito's, or Aga's, and I would often find myself in the position of holding a bass or a guitar, pointed precariously upright and resting on my belt, so as not to collide with passing traffic. We would travel to the show in a motorcade and enter from backstage. Afterwards, depending on how late it was, we would head back to Reddoor for more drinks and talk.

If there were no event that night, then Reddoor would become an event in itself. Any number of people might stop by for short or longer periods, and the crowd would fluctuate in size from just a couple to some twenty or thirty people. This kind of diffuse socializing could go on until four or so in the morning. People would stay around and chat for a while, then go off to a nearby Internet café or *Warung PS2,* where one could rent Sony Playstation 2 game systems by the hour. Women in the scene, however, tended to leave at around eleven or midnight, generally giving as a reason an early morning appointment or class. Their boyfriend, or some other guy in the group, would give them a ride home (unless they had their own motorbike—but generally they deferred to their boyfriends, even so), then return to Reddoor for more drunken revelry. Although women held prominent positions in the community, often designers, musicians, and distro owners in their own right, there is no denying that late at night, it became a boy's scene.

Women in the Scene

No man I talked to ever denied a woman's right to be at Reddoor, and there were occasionally women there until late, always, as far I know, without incident, but as Wallach (2008b) and others have noted, *nongkrong* (hanging out) is still principally a male activity, and women out too late at night are liable to be accused of being *nakal* (naughty), or worse, *kupu-kupu malam* (night butterflies, that is, prostitutes). They exercised a strict self-censorship, going home earlier than their male counterparts so as not to arouse suspicion from their *ibu kost* (house "mother" of a boarding house) or the surrounding community.

Women, such as Diana Slackers or Dede Anonim, often occupy powerful and influential positions within the scene, but as Errington and other anthropologists working in the region have written, that does not necessarily imply equal status between men and women. Errington has argued that the status of women in Island Southeast Asia often appears to be quite high compared to other parts of the world, when in fact differences between men and women are simply marked in ways that are not "socially visible" to Western eyes (Errington 1990: 5). In Java, for instance, where much of this research was conducted, women tend to handle financial transactions, working as shopkeepers and bankers, positions that seem to imply economic power, when in actuality, such trifling with material matters is often thought of as beneath men. Men are supposed to be occupied with more spiritual and noble pursuits, pursuits requiring a higher degree of spiritual "potency" (Geertz 1960; Errington 1990; Keeler 1990). Whereas women tend to work behind the scenes, arranging events, handling money, and making things happen, men tend to occupy highly public roles that demonstrate their mastery over social forms, their charisma, and their power to influence others (Keeler 1990). One practical consequence is that occupying public space—such as hanging out at distros, playing in bands, and so on—tends to be a male activity, and by virtue of their public status, a number of behaviors strongly discouraged for women are quietly tolerated—even sometimes celebrated—for men. These include smoking, drinking, and engaging in extramarital (or premarital) sex.

My experience in the Indonesian indie scene gave me hope that cultural expectations around gender differences in Indonesia are beginning to change, but the emphasis here must be placed on *beginning*. Women in the indie scene often smoke, drink, hang out in mixed company, and play active, public, and highly valued roles in production. But they still constitute a relatively small percentage of scene members, and their roles in the scene are often gendered, as well. Women often play in bands, for instance, but are generally confined to the roles of singer, bassist, or keyboardist, unless the entire band is female. As Mahon notes about African American rock bands in the United States, there seems to be an almost "universally understood prohibition against women playing the guitar" (Mahon 2004: 206).

I would estimate that around seventy-five percent of participants in the Indonesian indie scene are men. Many women also told me that they became involved in the scene because their boyfriends were involved in it, and then changed their style and taste accordingly. Moreover, most prominent positions in the indie scene, for example, the entire "Senior Advisor Board" (*Dewan Penasehat*) of KICK (Kreative Independent Clothing Kommunity), the premier lobbying organization representing the political and economic interests of distros, is male.

A notable exception to this self-imposed curfew was Agnes, who made a point of flouting the late-night rule and other assorted conventions of female propriety, smoking, talking openly about taboo subjects like sex and politics, and otherwise consciously contributing to the construction of a new vision of female youth culture. Pipu, also a smoker and drinker, nonetheless routinely turned in before 11 p.m.

The Boys' Party

Late at night became a boys' party. At 1 or 2 a.m., the action would often move to one of two Circle K convenience stores, where we would swig more beer and eat taro chips on yet another sidewalk, or one of a number of low-grade nightclubs, Terrace and Tropis near the top of the list, where cheap, local brews—generally in suspicious shades of blue or green—were served in large pitchers with tiny, shot-like glasses.

Around two or three, in the morning someone would always get hungry, and we would meander to a roadside food stall (*angkringan*), where we'd chow down on *nasi gudeg* (a Yogya specialty made of steamed jackfruit and rice) or the perennial *indomie* (instant noodles served with greens and an egg, the Indonesian version of Top Ramen) and sip sugar-saturated jasmine tea.

Hanging out could last until sunrise, when a deathly calm would slowly descend on the group, and no one could stomach another round of beer. The early morning call to prayer, broadcast from the scratchy loudspeakers of neighborhood mosques, started at around 4:30 a.m., and it would rouse the few stragglers left to dust themselves off and head home.

It was always unclear to me why we had hung out until this point. Everyone was clearly exhausted by 3 a.m. As I hitched rides home with Ade on the back of his motorbike, he would often confess to me that he would rather not have hung out so late, but since other people wanted to, and he felt responsible for their well-being, he did, too. Ito told me something similar once on a ride home, as did several other male Reddoor regulars, and I got the distinct impression that, in fact, no one actually wanted to hang out that late. I certainly did not. But no one wanted to be the first one to go home, either. Life at distros, as with all aspects of life in Indonesia, involves continually negotiating one's own desires with those of the group.

Even more to the point, life in the distros involves a kind of continual sociality, an emphasis on being part of the group that goes well beyond what an American observer like myself can readily relate to. The Reddoor kids spent hours a day together, and long alcohol-lubricated nights together. They had little sense of a personal or private life apart from the group, nor did they want one. They minimized time alone, often complaining about having to go home. The group was their life, and even in the wee hours of morning, breaking from the group took overcoming some serious inertia.

The Distro as Educational Center

A few weeks before I went home, I sat down with five of the kids from Reddoor, now hanging out at Ade and Pipu's new shop, Pipuangpu, for a more formal, recorded discussion of many of the issues we had been discussing informally late at night for months. It was an awkward moment. Everyone had been fully aware that I was doing research from the beginning, but I had become a scene regular, a friend, and the procedural formality of consent forms and digital recording created a palpable nervous tension I had hoped to avoid. Ade sent one of his staff members on a beer run, so that the mood would be more relaxed and similar in character to a typical Reddoor night. We sat behind a wall in front of the new shop, where in the morning a food stall sells *bubur ayam* (a porridge of rice and chicken) and in the late afternoons, employees and friends play cards.

I asked Ade, Pipu, Novan, Fonso, and Ito about the *konsep* (concept) behind their new shop. Ade started the conversation, explaining that Pipuangpu was a distro—a distribution outlet for self-produced clothing, music, and magazines—but also a place that "anyone could be a part of," whether selling their clothing label there, showing their art there, or playing their music there. It is a shop, an exhibition space, and a concert venue, he told me. It is also, he went on to say, something of an educational center, where young people are made aware of various creative movements happening in Indonesia and elsewhere, and given guidance by other members of the scene about which of these are good, interesting, or sophisticated, and which are not worth their time.

"Actually," Ito added, "Pipuangpu is media" (*Pipuangpua itu media*), adding, "media movement" in English to drive home the point. It is a place, he explained, where kids who want to do something creative, but don't know what, can come for direction and guidance from other people who may have more experience than them. For bands, he went on to say, it is a place where they can be mentored by other bands, and for a lot of kids, it is also a space where they can explore musical styles. The computer at Reddoor, and then later at Pipuangpu, was a massive archive of MP3s, featuring indie, electronica, punk, metal, and any number of other self-consciously alternative musical genres from all over Indonesia and around the world. Kids came in with memory disks and thumbdrives to update it or download content, and the end result was a vast collection of music and musical styles passed back and forth among community members. It had become a musical library and shared reference bank for bands to use to find their own sound.

Pipu then jumped in to say that Pipuangpu is a place to learn about design. Hopefully, she went on, the kids who come here are able to get a sense from the brands they sell and the designs they showcase of what constitutes good design. She sees Pipuangpu as a center for amateur designers. "Not all designs have to be done by professionals," she said (*Semua design ngak harus orang professional aja yang bisa lakukannya*). "We can also learn from each other."

Ade built on Pipu's comments. "I guess for me it's a kind of common space for playing (*main*). Playing with imagination and heart." From the beginning, he went on to say, the idea behind Pipuangpu was collaboration (*kolaborasi*), between artists, designers, musicians, and other creative people. Through spending time at a distro like Reddoor or Pipuangpu, young Indonesians are activated as creative producers, incorporated into a community of people involved in similar activities, and ultimately pushed toward producing themselves. In the space of a distro, peer pressure makes peers into producers.

I often heard this kind of educational description of distro life from participants in the indie scene more broadly. Hamid Ariwinata of Triggers Syndicate distro, also in Yogya, describes his designs as informing shoppers about the "roots" behind the music they like. Diana Slackers sees working at her shop as a kind of residency in production. Dendy Darman of Unkl347 sees his distro as a mentor to other distros, showing kids how to design and distribute with integrity.

As communities ranging in age from late teens to early thirties, distros create a space where people of differing experience in types of DIY production can meet and discuss how to take on a certain task. Ade and Pipu told me that they learned how to set up a distro from other friends they knew through Reddoor. Ito learned to make films through his friends at Reddoor. Rezka, Hamid, and many other aspiring designers learned to use design software from hanging out at Reddoor and similar distros.

Reddoor was as much an educational center as a community meeting place, not in any formal capacity—there are no design and software workshops there (although there are distros that do have them)—but in the sense of providing a space for cooperation, collaboration, and, above all, information-sharing to take place. Each Reddoor regular brought a small piece of expertise to the table, and together, these composed a collective knowledge pool (see Levy 1997; Jenkins 2006) each participant could tap into in pursuing a given project. It is this knowledge pool that makes DIY a tenable possibility.

Collective Processing

I do not want to overestimate the educational aspect of distros, however. Although informants repeatedly cited this purpose for distros in interviews and casual conversations, in my own observations, it always took a back seat to the much more important dimension of *nongkrong aja* (just hanging out). People hang out at distros not so much for purposes of self-edification as for social inebriation. They hang out, drink, and *ngobrol* (talk casually) until late at night, mainly because it is fun. During these long hangout sessions, however, they do real cultural work, figuring out common positions on everything from music to fashion to politics. They hash out ideas, argue points, and generally place themselves within larger debates occurring in Yogyakarta and Indonesia at large.

In the simplest sense, this could be a song coming on the sound system and the Reddoor kids discussing whether it was cool or not. At a more complex level, this could be multiple parties discussing multiple positions in regard to fundamentalist Islamic movements in Indonesia and each party consenting some points in order to reach a larger group consensus. Opinions are nebulous things. Reddoor kids don't just discuss their opinions in these conversations; they form them.

Some of the more memorable discussions to occur during my time at Reddoor involved a subject that was quite taboo my first time in Indonesia, back in 1996: politics, and particularly such issues as the corruption of politicians, the role of Islam in the government, and the push toward democratization. Robison has noted that the Indonesian middle class has yet to establish for itself a clear political agenda (Robison 1996), and my experience among Indonesian indie scenesters would suggest that this is true. It is not so much that young people don't agree on political issues because, as with youth in the United States and elsewhere, they are not sure where they stand on them, or whether, in fact, they even care to have a position.

One case in point is the issue of censorship of the media. The majority of Indonesians I have discussed the issue with think government monitoring of television and film is critical to protect viewers from morally "dangerous" (*bahaya*) content, particularly crude language and sexuality. This is, after all, the view they were brought up with, taught in schools, and told is necessary in countless newspaper editorials since they were young. In the indie scene, there is no single opinion on this issue. Many of the young scenesters I have met reiterate the standard sentiment, but others are not so sure, seeing their own activities in media production as themselves potentially suffering from government oversight.

One of the few places I encountered a universally hostile attitude toward censorship was at Reddoor. Late night, semi-drunken discussions had constructed a shared understanding of censorship as anathema to self-expression. In fact, the Reddoor kids had developed something of a rebellious bravado in regards to censorship, egged on by one another in heated debate. One of the guys I knew from there, a keyboardist in a relatively well-known indie rock band called De Sisters, told me that shock and discomfort is simply a prerequisite of rock 'n' roll. Reddoor had forged the collective interpretation, deeply at odds with that of most middle-class Indonesians I have talked to, of censorship as fundamentally bad, even when it is carried out with positive intentions. This attitude is undoubtedly one of the reasons I got along so well with the Reddoor kids.

Production as a Term of Participation

Hanging out at distros is also where the productive activities each scene member participates in are brought under social surveillance, publicly discussed and assigned meaning. The quality of each other's designs was a topic of interest, as was the success of a band's melody, use of English, or stage antics. The concerts of other members of the scene were talked about with particular zeal, and I was sometimes shocked by how blunt and unflattering peoples' descriptions of their friends' shows could be. These discussions did not just debate the success of a given performance, however, but called attention to, and brought under peer surveillance, the individual contributions of a scene member to larger community achievements.

Participation in the Indonesian indie scene, in other words, is largely a function of one's assuming a particular subject position within the scene. And this means having a distinctive mode of involvement in some form of scene production. This can mean being a clothing designer, a musician, a store employee, a magazine writer, or even an anthropologist chronicling the scene for an academic audience, but it requires participating in cultural production in some way. This social fact was perhaps most evident in the larger scene practice of referring to someone as their first name followed by their productive affiliation. Ade, for instance, was "Ade Reddoor." Fonso was "Fonso Nervous." Hamid of Triggers Syndicate was "Hamid Triggers." Diana of Slackers was "Diana Slackers." And Dede of Anonim in Bandung goes by "Dede Anonim." Sometimes people call her "Denim" as an affectionate shorthand.

Of course, this is in part a function of Indonesian grammar. Placing two nouns together in Indonesian implies a prepositional relationship. Dede Anonim can also mean "Dede *of* Anonim." Nonetheless, scene members often use this construction as if it were their formal name, preferring to be referred to in media reports as "Dede Anonim," "Diana Slackers," or "Ariel PeterPan," even using such a name on their Facebook accounts. Many of the names used in this book, thus, are based on such a preference.

The point is, in the Indonesian indie scene, you are what you do. It is how people think of you. It is even how they refer to you. Social identity is a function of participation in cultural production. And if you are not involved in cultural production in some way, you have no place in the scene.

I should point out, though, that being affiliated with a particular productive grouping, say the band Nervous or the distro Reddoor, does not preclude membership in some other productive grouping, and there is a high degree of flexibility in terms of what someone is called and how they are placed. Novan, for instance, was both "Novan Nervous" and "Novan Captain Jack." I have even heard him referred to as "Novan Pipuangpu," as by the time I left he had officially become an employee of the shop. Scene positions are always tentative and partial. They are continually made and re-made through everyday practice.

The Distro as Practical Resource

Hanging out at distros, then, provides an important site for any number of social, cultural, and identity production to take place. It also, however, provides scene members with more tangible resources for getting things done. People make extensive use of their social networks to put on events, promote products, and otherwise make things happen. When Ade and the Reddoor kids had the idea for "Monster Therapy," a music, dance, and installation art event designed to promote Reddoor, they employed an expansive network of friends and collaborators. Ade went from distro to distro asking friends and colleagues in management positions to "sponsor" the event with contributions of around 200,000 rupiah each (roughly US$22). In exchange, their logo would be featured on the banners, posters, and fliers advertising the event.

Ito, Novan, and other Reddoor regulars text-messaged, e-mailed, and otherwise contacted a variety of friends involved with music production to secure local bands for the event. Music equipment, meanwhile, was secured through collective pitching in—an amplifier from here, a drum kit from there. The event, in other words, was a collaborative effort put together by a number of unpaid parties operating through a system of friend reciprocity. Communal assistance, like the *gotong royong* of a small Javanese village, is an integral component of scene practice. Networks are forged through chipping in, helping each other out, and participating in communal projects. Events like Monster Therapy, in this sense, are a critical component of establishing the networks of friends and collaborators referred to as "the scene." They require social collaboration across smaller distro communities and create intricate alliances based on productive activities.

Moreover, because cross-distro networks are so critical to establishing an individual's place in the scene and one's ability to get things done, individual participants in the distro scene spend a good deal of time checking in with distros other than the one where they spend most of their time. The practice of *main* (literally "playing," but used like dropping in or stopping by casually) is deeply ingrained, and when someone hasn't done so in a while, they could very well fall off the distro map.

I, too, got caught up in the politics of *main,* making sure I had stopped by all the primary distros in my study at least every week. When it had been a while or if I had been out of town, I would get comments like the friendly, "Wow, it's been a long time since we've seen you. Where have you been?" (*Wah, udah lama banget ngak ketemu! Ke mana kamu?*) or the somewhat harsher rebuke "How come it's been so long since you've been here? Don't you like us anymore?" (*Kok lama gak ke sini? Gak suka kami lagi?*). There are, of course, no firm rules about how often one needs to *main,* but the point is, maintaining social networks, and hence pools of collective labor and support, requires continual work. Hanging out secures social ties necessary for cultural production to take place.

DIY Is a Misnomer

Nongkrong, or hanging out, is by no means an ancillary aspect of scene social life. It is, rather, the critical social medium through which cultural production is made possible and put into practice. It is where the work of maintaining the scene takes place, and it provides the critical pool of labor and knowledge scene members make use of in personal DIY projects. Moreover, it is through hanging out that the DIY ethos is most actively maintained and developed.

In this sense, DIY is a misnomer. There is no "doing it" oneself, no strictly autonomous production. All production is in some way social, whether the moment of production involves other people or not. "Making is connecting" as Gauntlett (2011) has argued. Producers in the indie scene look to others for inspiration and guidance, distinction and differentiation, and are actively involved in broad social networks that make their own productive activities possible. To create, then, is as a much a force of connection as it is an expression of individual selfhood. It unites divergent communities and organizes experience into a tenuous, meaningful whole.

–4–

DIY Chic: Notes on Indie Style

Be an original in a land full of fakes and duplicates.

—Ad for The Emperor's Avenue Distro in Bandung

As for originality, only God has that.

—Adegreden Adhari Donora, designer for Reddoor and FireFighter Fight!

On the Road at Home

Venus had only been in Yogyakarta for a couple years when I started this project, but she already referred to it as home. She likes the laidback (*santai*) feel of the city, and the fact that social life there still seems to take precedence over commerce. She likes its cosmopolitan outlook and its low-key tropical vibe: how students, musicians, and artists linger at street-side *warung* until all hours of the night. "*Begadang*," they call it. It's one of Yogya's most popular pastimes.

Born in Semarang, an industrial port town on the northern coast of Java and raised primarily in Jakarta, the capital city, she is no big fan of either place. "Too money-oriented," she told me. So when she finished high school, she thought she would try out something new, and island-hopped over to Bali to study in Denpasar. It was a good place for her—for a while, anyway—and plenty different from Jakarta, in any case. She made friends in the local metal scene and the expatriate community, spent lots of time in the notorious tourist district of Kuta Beach, where Jerinx and the boys of pop-punk group Superman Is Dead had built their own little rock 'n' roll empire on Poppies Gang II (see Baulch 2007). She took to wearing black, got herself tattooed, and went to lots of smoky, late-night gigs. Music was rapidly becoming a much bigger part of her life than school. She lost interest in her studies and eventually went on leave. She isn't planning on returning.

Venus describes herself as a "backpacker," a traveler who would rather meander from place to place than set down deep roots. She espouses a familiar philosophy of the open road, an idealization of homelessness and displacement reminiscent of Jack Kerouac or Henry Miller, and claims not to care much about the creature comforts of the settled life.

Eventually, she said, she grew restless in Bali, too, and thought she would see what else is out there. She moved to Bandung for a few months, drawn in by its reputation as the center of Indonesia's indie scene, but it didn't stick, either. She just didn't feel at home there, she said, for reasons she can't quite articulate. So she caught a train and made the seven-hour journey east to Yogyakarta, city of students. She took to it right away.

Venus wasted no time making friends in Yogya. She was taken in by a couple of "skinheads" she met at a concert and introduced around. After a few months, she was pretty hooked in to the local scene. She formed a "Swedish-style black metal" band called Salient Insanity with some of her new buddies, and became the vocalist and primary lyricist. The motley crew of indie kids, each with their own dramatically different taste in music, became part of a small cohort of groups with a female singer in a male-dominated genre. With their short, pageboy hair-cuts, too-tight T-shirts, and perpetual black denim skinny jeans, they looked a little out of place in a style of music dominated by long-haired metalheads in theatrical make-up, but Venus didn't let it get to her. She likes being a little off kilter, a little out of place. She learned how to scream in a raspy, menacing style that conjures up images of vengeful Norse deities and Balinese witches. She got a job, too, as the stock manager for an up-and-coming hard rock and metal-themed distro, Triggers Syndicate. That's where I first met her.

Triggers Syndicate was on a dusty stretch of Jalan Seturan in the student ghetto of northern Yogyakarta. It was one of several distros to pop up on the street between 2004 and 2007, targeting the students of nearby universities like Sanata Dharma, UPN, and Atma Jaya. I stumbled upon it one hot afternoon in the middle of the fasting month of Ramadan. I had been wandering the alleyways, fighting off dehydration, and looking for a number of distros I had spotted on a map included with the first (and only) issue of *ELV* youth lifestyle magazine, when I noticed the bold red sign perched above the rusted-metal security spikes of a concrete wall. I was the only customer in the store.

Venus was behind the counter and paid scant attention to me when I came in. She was watching the second season of the fashion designer competition reality show *Project Runway* on Discovery's Travel and Living channel and was clearly wrapped up in what she was watching, despite the lack of Indonesian subtitles. I used this fact as an excuse to break the ice, and I asked Venus if she could understand what the designers were saying. "Of course," she told me, nonchalantly. She had learned textbook English throughout school, then American slang from her ex-pat friends in Bali, along with Tim Burton and Robert Rodriguez films, heavy metal lyrics, and social networking websites like Friendster and MySpace. English is easy for her, she said. "It's more expressive than Indonesian."

The comment turned into a conversation, and we talked a little about her life history, discussed music and design, clothing and tattoos, argued who was a better designer on *Project Runway,* Chloe or Santino—I was on Santino's side (of course), she (unbelievably) on Chloe's. We hit it off pretty well—even if we couldn't agree on who should have won *Project Runway,* Season 2. We shared, as it turned out, a campy affection for popular culture that gave us plenty to talk enthusiastically about, even as we peppered our conversation with subtle markers of ironic distance, a few pieces of exaggerated praise here, some comically enlarged eyes and elongated consonants there. I wrote in my fieldnotes that evening that I felt like I had finally met someone in town I could relate to, with whom I could easily imagine being friends.

I was impressed with Venus. She had an unstudied yet sophisticated air about her, a cool demeanor, belied by her outgoing personality. I had never seen an Indonesian woman with tattoos before—but then I had only been back in the country for a month—and at twenty-two, she already had plenty of ink on her torso, stars going up one arm, a Japanese-style anime girl on the other. It gave her an edge, set her apart, and sometimes, she said, got her into trouble with the older generation. She had gotten used to being labeled a *cewek nakal* (naughty girl, or slut), or even a *preman* (thug) by those people who didn't know her, and she'd had to develop a fairly thick skin about the whole thing. But Indonesia is changing rapidly, she told me, and that sort of judgment seems to be on the decline. Tattoos are on the verge of becoming mainstream, she said, and she tries to make a habit of being before the tide.

Venus wore a perpetual pair of black-framed Buddy Holly glasses and did her hair in a messy ponytail with blunt-cut bangs that managed at once to convey style and a complete lack of interest in it. She wore heavy-metal T-shirts, some faded like a favorite pair of old pajamas, some crisp and shiny new, but always form-fitting with the sleeves cut and hemmed above the bicep in standard scenester protocol, and faded denim jeans, pre-washed for maximum effect and tapered at the ankle, often ripped—whether deliberately or through wear is hard to say—at the knees. Sometimes they were made into cutoffs, loose threads of denim hanging down like a hula skirt. Other times, they were left more or less intact, with perhaps a few patches of local bands sewn onto the thighs. Her shoes alternated between beat-up Converse All-Stars and a pair of Vans, customized tagger-style with a permanent marker. She wore a variety of friendship bracelets and new age jewelry, sometimes paired with gaudy silver rings of skulls, demons, and other items of performative moroseness associated with metal and punk. Sometimes she topped it all off with a distro-produced plaid, Western-style shirt or a hip hop hoodie, decorated, perhaps, in repeated, multicolored logos from a local brand, a sweatjacket resembling nothing so much as moving wallpaper.

Venus had a quality about her, which, though hard to describe, was immediately familiar to me from years of living in Los Angeles and the San Francisco Bay Area. She seemed "cool" and disdainful of "cool" at the same time, sharply aware of the currents of popular culture at home and abroad, but somehow removed from them. She valued creativity, wrote poetry, but also knew how to appreciate shallow pop culture excess like *Project Runway*. She was into metal, but was, in her words, "not really a heavy metal kind of person," listened to a variety of other kinds of music, and hung out with a variety of "open-minded" people. She seemed to thwart any easy self-definition. She was, in a word, "hip."

In this chapter, I examine the stylistic preoccupations of Indonesian indie kids such as Venus, the way they present themselves to each other and the outside world, and tie these tendencies in with emergent class politics and increasingly globalized cultural dynamics. In particular, I focus on the emergence of "hip" in Indonesian indie style—that slippery, intentionally elusive aesthetic attitude that holds up critical "consciousness" and semiotic ambiguity as essential criteria for determining value. Hip, I conclude, is not the opposite of DIY, as the hipster backlash in the United States and Europe might have it, the cheapening of subcultural aesthetics for mass consumption. It is, on the contrary, an application of the DIY ethos to one's own individual style, a kind of cut-and-paste approach to personal adornment adopted by the ambivalent, by people enmeshed in multiple discourses at once, who choose, in fact, not to choose between opposed positions. In the case of Indonesia more specifically, it is the aesthetic attitude of those who value their rising socio-economic status, the doors it opens for them, and the connections it grants them, and yet resent the intrusion of economic logic into all aspects of their daily lives. More to the point, it is a mode of distinction for the digital age, where access to cultural resources is greater and more varied than ever before—an age, I argue, where distinction itself already seems dated.

Meanings and Translations

John Leland, in his comprehensive genealogy of American hipsters, *Hip: The History*, traces the word "hip" back to the West African language of Wolof and the cognate *hepi* or *hipi,* meaning "to see" or "to open one's eyes" (Leland 2004). It traveled to the United States, he argues, with the imprisoned passengers of slave ships, and it is through the prism of slavery and its legacy that hip became a distinctive American mode of practice. The first incipient expressions of modern hip, Leland explains, developed on the antebellum plantation as a secret language, a subtle "signification" slaves used to slip critique beneath the understanding of their masters. It was further articulated through blues and jazz, before eventually being taken on by middle-class white kids as a stylistic "antithesis to the man in the gray flannel suit" (Frank 1997: 12). Hip has assumed any number of forms over the years, from the slim-cut suits and tilted fedoras of the noir detective to the puffy coats and asymmetrical haircuts of the contemporary New York indie band; and yet, throughout all of its changes, it "maintains some constants: a dance between black and white; a love of the outsider; a straddle of high and low culture; a grimy sense of nobility; language that means more than it says" (Leland 2004: 10).

But hip is never one to be pinned down. As Leland writes, hip grounds its practitioners in the "isolated present tense," the vagaries of fashion and style (Leland 2004: 8). It is between states, "forever on the road" (Leland 2004: 356). Hip, in fact, depends upon this marginal, nomadic status to have any meaning at all. If everyone's hip, no one is. And so hipsters strive to be perpetually ahead of the game, or at least, way off on the sidelines where the great hordes of players can't get a good look at what they're up to. When everyone catches up, it is time to move on to something else, a feat, Leland notes, which is increasingly difficult in an era of such easy access to information. In the digital age, claims Greif (2010), the only recourse left to the distinction-conscious hipster is to practice the micro-politics of hip, to latch on to the small nuances of trends and exploit them for all they are worth, perform them in ways that elude the public at large, even undermine their apparent meaning. The hipster has learned to cover her tracks.

Venus's version of hipness is not exactly the same as the one I know from back home. Although she dabbles in irony, employs plenty of sarcasm in her speech, adorns herself in contradictory symbols, and knows how to appreciate her pop culture kitsch, she doesn't construct an impenetrable ironic shield around herself (Lanham 2003), claim to like metal for its schlock value, or flaunt her taste in music as if it were demonstrable proof of her superior social worth. She, like the other Indonesian indie scenesters I know, expresses a kind of humility and sincerity that indie hipsters in the United States often steadfastly avoid. She has no knee-jerk reaction against melodrama, or pouring out one's heart (*curhat*). And she's unlikely to use the word "hip" to describe herself. "Cool" is in far more common circulation in Indonesia, as is the rough Indonesian equivalent *keren*. There is not, however, any English word that better expresses what Venus is than "hip." The term captures the fluidity of her personal fashion, its grounding in knowledge and intentionality, its unmoored international orientation, and it differentiates this contemporary pose from earlier manifestations of Indonesian youth style.

In the 1990s, Indonesia seemed to have imported the iconography of hip without its underlying attitude. This was a time, as a number of scene participants intimated to me, when people felt unequipped to selectively adopt foreign trends, when they mimicked imported styles as accurately as they could, without evaluating their appropriateness to local context or adapting them to local conditions. Borrowed styles, like punk and metal, often became calcified in purist forms of youth practice, conservative subcultural traditions (Wallach 2008a), more concerned with demonstrating their genuine allegiance to the imported style than the style's own dynamism, adaptivity, or even relevance.

My first Indonesian underground music gig, for example, was a micro-festival of punk, hardcore, and metal bands from around Bali and Java put on by the Indonesian Art Institute (ISI) at the Kridosono Stadium in downtown Yogyakarta in early 1997. It was called Twenty-Something, Twenty-Nothing, and, as the name implies, featured twenty bands, with members aged in their early twenties. The groups were garbed in chains, spikes, and torn up T-shirts, had gravity-defying hairstyles, and looked like they could have just as easily been panhandling in Piccadilly Circus as playing a gig in this predominantly Muslim Southeast Asian nation. It was a familiar enough style to me, but here it seemed exaggerated, almost cartoonish, like a pageant version of a rock opera. This was youth style as both drama and farce, an enactment of extreme fashion that created an almost accidental parody of what it mimicked (Bhabha 1994).

But Venus, and dozens of other young Indonesians I met in 2006–2007, and then again, to an even greater degree in the summer of 2010, had a much more discerning, headier approach to the consumption of imported styles. They no longer adopted foreign styles wholesale; they played with them, manipulated them, and made them their own. They valued knowledge of the styles they emulated, *tahu rootsnya* (knowing the roots), as Indonesian scenesters so often put it, and critiqued others for simply *ikut-ikutan* (blindly joining in). Venus, for instance, has spent weeks of her life researching styles of black metal from Sweden and Norway, establishing online links with bands from all over Europe and the Western world on MySpace, Friendster, and, more recently, Facebook. But the music she produced drew from these styles without copying them. She combined the stark musicality of Scandinavian black metal with the lyricism of Icelandic songstress Björk, and wrote songs in English about little girls coming of age in Indonesia.

Plus, young Indonesians like her had a sense of humor about their own styles. They tried not to take themselves too seriously as punk, metal, or even as indie kids, no longer divided into strictly antagonistic factions that upheld their genre preferences as if they were statements about the condition of their souls. Indie kids continually

Figure 6 Hip, Indonesian style. A distro employee in Yogyakarta.

made fun of each other's styles, came up with new monikers for them, compared them to those of well-known musicians and other celebrities. Style was something they identified with, but not too closely. It was always held at a safe distance.

No doubt, most participants in the indie scene tended toward one genre of music and fashion or another, but they expressed this affiliation in just those terms. "*Aku cenderung ke hardcore*," I might have heard them say, "I tend toward hardcore," rather than the far less self-conscious, and decidedly less hip, "*aku hardcore*," or, "I am hardcore." Most did not listen exclusively to one style of music. Most mixed up aesthetics in their personal look. Genre was just a tendency, something one gravitates toward at certain moments, but at other moments may very well move away from. Contemporary Indonesian indie style, then, exhibits a playful self-scrutiny, a valuing of critical consciousness and distanced awareness, that, if not strictly "hip" in the terms Leland lays out, at least feels something very much like it.

The Indie Look

It stands to reason, then, that the indie look in Indonesia would have certain key differences from its counterparts in the United States or the UK. Adopted with critical precision and customized for the individual, it has been edited and remixed, filtered through a local lens, and invested with its own character and feel. There are certain commonalities, of course. Indonesian indie hipsters, like the ones I know from back home, often wear the carefully disheveled hair of an American Apparel model; the perpetual skinny jeans of a suburban emo scream-core band; the too-tight T-shirts with bold, often ironic statements printed across them that line the aisles of Melrose Avenue vintage clothing boutiques; the thick-framed plastic glasses of Weezer front man Rivers Cuomo; the pseudo working-class "trucker hats" that Ashton Kutcher popularized at the end of the 1990s; and the Chuck Taylor Converse All-Stars that seem everywhere to signify a vague allegiance to an unspecified alternative culture. They want, after all, to be recognizable to indie kids the world over. But indie's fundamental preoccupation, what Fonarow describes as its peculiar reverence for its own childhood (2006: 44), is conspicuously missing.

Seeking an aesthetic untainted by commercial interests and the corruption of consumer culture, the English indie scenesters that Fonarow described in her 2006 book scoured the racks of charity shops and clothing swaps in search of items that conjured up a simpler time: grandpa sweaters and granny glasses, anoraks and baby doll dresses, T-shirts for brands from their childhood, and classic sneakers that went out of style in the 1980s. They favored the oversized (for its resemblance to hand-me-downs from older siblings) and the too tight (as in clothing they have already grown out of) (Fonarow 2006: 44–45). Some of indie's look, she explained, was carried over from earlier subcultural traditions, including punk and mod, particularly its emphasis on androgyny, slenderness, and "childlike sexuality" (Fonarow

2006: 45), and its penchant for Beatles-esque moptop haircuts, but in all of its manifestations, indie maintained associations with an imagined, simpler past. As Fonarow wrote, "Indie's clothes typically do not fit—either the person or the time" (Fonarow 2006: 45).

Indonesian indie clothing, in stark contrast, is painstakingly current, borrowing elements from contemporary youth cultures in the United States, Europe, and East Asia, with a kind of omnivorous hunger that would no doubt feel foreign to the indie kids of Fonarow's study. I have, to be sure, seen plenty of Indonesian indie kids that conform pretty precisely to Fonarow's description. Cardigans, parkas, and ironic T-shirts are well represented in the scene, and thick-framed glasses are so popular as to be nearly ubiquitous. In ads for indie clothing lines like Monik and Cosmic, for instance, moptopped hipsters in scarves, Burberry-inspired raincoats, and granny glasses picnic in the park and smile adoringly from café benches. But this is simply one of indie's manifestations, one style option among many. There are also visible elements of metal, as is so clear in Venus's case, along with punk, emo, skate, and even mid-twentieth-century jazz, as filtered through contemporary French and Scandinavian crooners. There are splashes of hip hop, tinges of mod, oligopolies of style, with no one genre ever gaining the upper hand. The Yogyakarta indie fashion catalog *Zek!* paid tribute to the diversity of styles evident in the scene through devoting each issue in 2006–2007 to a different subcultural theme.

One was on indie pop, another on disco punk, one on grunge, and even one on oi! Each style was depicted on the front cover as a selection of identifiable wardrobe items: a wool raincoat, a knitted scarf, and a pixie-ish bob, for instance, for indie pop. And these items were then listed later on in the issue as "must haves" to complete the look. Indie in Indonesia, and certainly as displayed in *Zek!*, is a range of possible associations, rather than a clearly prescribed look.

Indonesian scenesters also have a much crisper and sharper take on indie fashion than do their American or British counterparts, preferring new to second-hand, well-pressed and freshly ironed to just out of the drawer. I was continually amazed by how precise peoples' hairstyles were: bangs perfectly positioned, no lock out of place, as if they had come directly from the salon. Many times, they had. Even the bed-head look common to indie the world over had a calculated quality to it, blow-dried from the back to maximize the cowlick. And alteration, either done oneself or by one of the many affordable tailors that line the city streets of Indonesia, was simply expected. Clothes should conform to the body perfectly, in the form-fitting, tattoos-exposed style of a Calvin Klein ad.

Like British indie scenesters, Indonesian indie kids compose their look out of a kind of existential longing. It is chock full of references to fashion trends happening on the other side of the world. But it is not a simpler, less-corporate past that the Indonesian indie style evokes. Indie traveled to Indonesia through the circuits of corporate capitalism to begin with, through MTV and the Rupert Murdoch-owned MySpace, smuggled-in music mags, and copied cassettes. Its stylistic inspirations

Figure 7 *Zek!* #4, the Indie Pop issue.

come from feverish Internet searches, not glances through old photo albums. Theirs is a spatial rather than a temporal nostalgia (see chapter 6), a longing for what lies beyond Indonesia's borders. The Indonesian indie look links them with other places and other people, forges a global "imagined community" (Anderson 1983) out of dissociated styles. It employs a hipster's continual demonstrated awareness of global currents in music and fashion, and yet, as the next few sections demonstrate, refuses to identify too closely with any one of them.

After Distinction

So what had changed between 1996 and 2006? What led to this efflorescence of subcultural styles and this new mode of picking and choosing so restlessly between them? Why did the Indonesian underground of the 1990s repackage itself as the hipper, and more stylistically evasive indie scene?

It warrants pointing out at this juncture that hip is not entirely without precedent in Indonesia. Mràzek (2002), for example, has described the "Indonesian dandy" of the late colonial period as a kind of theatrical imposter, a local posing in colonial garb. The dandy appeared to emulate, down to his carefully starched collar, the symbolic attributes of colonial power, and yet there was a certain exaggerated neatness about his look, a certain over-extension of the limits of propriety that simultaneously paid tribute to and denaturalized the object of its emulation. Was this not, in some sense, hip?

Bhabha (1994) famously has argued that colonial mimicry always involves such subtle alterations, such slippages in meaning and intent that distort as they replicate. It may, in fact, be characteristic of the enslaved and the colonized in general to assume modes of resistance that appear to give in to the colonizers' demands, "weapons of the weak," as Scott (1985) calls them. And in Indonesia, such practices certainly didn't end with colonialism. Heryanto (2008) identifies a strategy, following Mbembe (2001), of "hyper-obedience" common to the New Order era, in which would-be activists presented themselves as staunch supporters of a grossly flawed electoral system as a means of both reveling in the pageantry of the event and calling attention to its profound absurdity. Baulch, similarly, describes 1990s Balinese "alternapunk" as "deceptive and slippery, refusing to be pinned to conventional notions of opposition and hybridization" (2007: 110).

Double-meanings and *entendres*, complex positionalities and slippery subjectivities, then, are nothing new in Indonesia. Indonesians have never needed training to achieve such an effect. Nor is the cool detachment or contrived inscrutability of hip anything fundamentally novel. One need only see one of the famous black and white photographs of revolutionary poet Chairil Anwar back in the 1940s to find a local inflection of the jaded bohemian type, disconnected from "society," but tethered to it, at least by a dangling thread.

Nonetheless, hip is not, and has never been, the signature Indonesian style, a dominant attitude or mode of self-presentation, the way Leland and Frank argue it has become in the United States. The saccharine sentimentality of so much Indonesian pop music (see Yampolsky 1989; Lockard 1998), the intense melodrama of so many Indonesian films (see Heider 1991; Sen and Hill 2000), and the staunch literalism of events like Twenty-Something, Twenty-Nothing makes that evident enough. The fact that hip has become so widespread in Indonesia in recent years still requires explanation.

My explanation is rather simple. Hip, as a stylistic sensibility, just makes sense in Indonesia today. As Indonesia has moved over the course of the last couple of decades from an agricultural to an industrial, and now partially postindustrial, economy, it has developed an urban intellectual labor pool, widely referred to as "the new middle class" (Dick 1985; Robison 1996; Heryanto 1999; Werner 1999; Gerke 2000). These are the highly-trained white collar workers of the increasingly export-based Indonesian economy, the managers and marketers, the graphic designers and software developers, all of whom have some stake in presenting themselves as innovative thinkers with a creative bent, in short, what Florida (2002) would label the "creative class." Showing a quirky, "artsy" side, thus, has an economic incentive in Indonesia's current economy—just so long as it's not too artsy. We wouldn't want to alienate our employers, after all. And who better to pull off the hat trick of working within the box while thinking outside of it than the hipster, the stylistic trickster refusing to fully identify with one thing or another? Hip, in this context, has a distinct competitive advantage (Florida 2002; Lloyd 2006). The hipster, then, is a contemporary articulation of Indonesian middle-classness, one configured for its strategic utility in current circumstances, an information-based, neoliberal economy, where awareness is of critical importance, risk and flexibility valorized, and creative "quirkiness" a highly marketable asset.

It is also, however, possible to see the hipster as a concerted reaction of the middle class to the increasing tenuousness of its own position. "These days," Elang Eby, designer, blogger, and vocalist for the popular indie rock band Polyester Embassy, told me as we chatted in the upstairs office at Common Room Networks Foundation, an arts and media collective in Bandung where I lived for three months in 2007, "even the poorest kids in the *kampung* (ghetto or village) can afford to be stylish." Cheap access to the Internet, a plethora of free-style publications, magazines, and zines, hordes of low-price distros, and an onslaught of pirated fashion and media have brought "cool" to the masses. Being *bergaya* (stylish), Elang explains, used to be strictly an elite urban phenomenon. Throughout the 1980s and 1990s, a growing urban middle class used whatever means they could to establish their difference from the Indonesian majority. Heryanto (1999) describes a set of ostentatious class practices this new bourgeoisie acted out in public, much to the dismay of everyone else. A number of other theorists have depicted a new consumer class caught up in its own opulent display, drivers of Hummers, BMWs, and Benzes, eaters of sushi and swiggers of martinis, yuppie fitness buffs who work out in mall athletic clubs in front of large untinted windows so that everyone else can witness their routine. For Indonesia's elite, these writers concur, "visibility is everything" (Ong 1999: 173).

Things, however, are beginning to change. And rather quickly at that. As the Asian financial crisis began to level the playing field, cutting the newly rich back down to size and substantially reducing the class mobility of a generation, many young people began to reevaluate their own habits of consumption and display. Conspicuousness became gauche, and luxury something you seal behind closed doors. At the same time, new media opened new corridors to fashion and trends happening elsewhere. Distros and pirates alike expanded their businesses to a larger and larger sector of the population, and innumerable avenues for gaining access to the cultural capital once possessed by the elite began to open up.

The fact is that style and taste are no longer accurate barometers of socio-economic status in Indonesia, and, I would suspect, in large portions of the rest of the world. Bourdieu's famous hierarchy of tastes (Bourdieu 1984) is becoming less and less easy to map. Figuring out what is "cool" and finding out how to get it is simply easier to accomplish than it has ever been, and hence, by definition can no longer be the defining attribute of cool.

No doubt Elang's statement about the poorest kids in the *kampung* is an exaggeration. In a country where the majority of citizens make less than 20,000 rupiah a day (around US$2), 70,000 is still a lot to spend on a distro label T-shirt. As mentioned in chapter 1, seventy percent of the population lives in rural areas, often without access to running water, let alone the Internet, and even in big cities, many people lack the basic computer and literacy skills necessary to navigate the virtual world (Hill and Sen 2005).

But walking around Bandung, or any other major city in Indonesia these days, it feels true. Fitted, distro-label T-shirts and dirty skinny jeans have become a fashion staple of everyone from street musicians (*pengamen*), to well-to-do university students and urban professionals. And "subcultural" styles, which romanticize the visual attributes of poverty (Fonarow 2006; Lloyd 2006) have blurred the parameters of class distinctions even further (Lipovetsky 2002).

Plus, young Indonesians have proven extremely resourceful in overcoming obstacles to participating in youth culture. In cities such as Bandung and Yogyakarta, kids from a variety of backgrounds are making do with what they've got. They pool their resources to maximize their access to global trends (Gerke 2000), share luxury items, and improvise when they can. Friends pass around burned CDs of music they have acquired online, carry around memory disks to pull out and fill up at a moment's notice. They share computers to keep costs down, and share Internet access rates. And they get most of their information mouth-to-mouth, anyway. Friends assist each other in bridging social differences, filling in gaps in one another's cultural capital. Consequently, Indonesia's cool kids hold a slipping grip on those informational resources that used to maintain their status as uniquely connected with global culture. Faced with a dramatically different set of circumstances surrounding consumption than did a previous generation of Indonesia's elite, today's young and middle-class are faced with two options: either find new ways to distinguish themselves or simply focus their attention on something else. No doubt, they do a little of both.

For the Indonesian middle-class today, or at least that segment of the middle class that identifies as "indie," *what* one consumes is simply no longer as important as *how* one consumes it. Whereas Indonesian indie kids imagine a faceless majority with only some cursory understanding of youth trends happening elsewhere, they cultivate a deep and abiding knowledge of those trends. They read the latest imported magazines and spend hours a day on the Internet researching their favorite bands and brands. They develop an intimate relationship with what they consume, even become producers of similar products themselves. DIY, in this sense, is the logical end result of a sequence of ever more active forms of consumption, carried out in an increasingly difficult game of middle-class distinction.

At the same time, indie kids cultivate a seemingly contradictory disdain for what they consume. They glance at friends' *Rolling Stone* magazines rather than condescend to buy them themselves, or download the latest performance by Arcade Fire from YouTube, rather than watch it on network TV. They buy name-brand laptops and motorbikes, then cover them over with stickers of local bands, or name-brand shoes like Converse and Vans, then scrawl over them with permanent markers. Whereas the cool, middle-class Indonesians of the early 1990s took dates to McDonald's, yammered conspicuously on cell phones, and bought all the latest Bon Jovi CDs, the indie kids of the 2000s sit on the wall outside McDonald's while they sip their milkshakes, discretely text their friends, and exchange illegally downloaded MP3s of obscure bands from Omaha, Nebraska. They cultivate a too-cool-to-consume attitude, even as they consume avidly. In other words, they have adopted a third position, outside consumer and anti-consumer, the position of the critical and ambivalent hipster.

Hip, however, is not just a matter of delving deeply into popular culture, then putting on the veneer of indifference. It is also critical to exert some greater degree of control over what one consumes. Hipsters are not defined by their consumption; they define themselves *through* consumption. This means personalizing popular culture instead of just emulating it, painstakingly separating out worthwhile trends from the merely trendy, and for an increasingly large portion of youth, it means going into cultural production for oneself.

And hip, unlike earlier manifestations of Indonesian cool, never revels openly in its class elitism. The hip outright deny that the material is a significant component of identity. They take their cues from those neo-bohemian (Lloyd 2006) artsy types living in pre-gentrified urban squalor. As Venus claims, "class just isn't very important in the scene." Sure, if someone's got his own car, it's a significant asset. He can use it to drive around his band member friends. If someone's got an amplifier, he can donate it to the common pool. But hording wealth and showing it off, a la Thorston Veblen's depiction of the moneyed elite, just isn't done.

The New Rules of the Fashion Game

The new rules of the fashion game are something Elang knows a little about. As the vocalist for the post-rock band Polyester Embassy as well as one half of the experimental electronic duo Alphawaves, he has become something of a style icon himself in recent years, "endorsed" by such indie clothing labels as Unkl347 and featured in a variety of indie publications as one of the "it" boys of the moment. His formal training in fashion happened under the Bandung clothing label Airplane Systm, where he served as "traffic controller," responsible for overseeing distribution for a number of years prior to breaking away and starting two of his own labels, the sustainable headwear company Cool Caps, and the up-market denim line Easton. The former is sold in a variety of indie boutiques and distros, the latter traded exclusively on the Internet.

Elang's personal style is textbook hipster, but only in the sense that it conforms to no one style in particular. It is a scavenger's aesthetic, a merging of hip hop and golf punk, DJ and mathrocker, a mish-mash of print T-shirts, plaid slacks, and schoolboy caps that has yet to be assigned any definitive classification. He prefers it that way. Elang tries to keep himself on the cutting edge. His style is very much a work in progress, an ongoing project of reinvention that works according to the logic of mix 'n' match—style's own version of cut and paste. Pick up any Indonesian teen style or fashion magazine, consult any one of a number of Indonesian fashion blogs, and it is immediately obvious that "c'mon, everyone's wearing it!" has long since been replaced by "don't be afraid to look different!" as the dominant fashion ideology in today's Indonesia. No one wants to blend in anymore, at least according to this rhetoric, not if they want to stake some claim to coolness. This is not to say that any old style will do. The appropriate raw materials for constructing one's own style are subject to trends, just as the old prefabricated types were.

Figure 8 An employee at a distro in Yogyakarta, whose style has elements of punk, emo, indie, and *harajuku*.

To be different means to assemble a set of pre-approved styles in a unique config-uration, not to invent your own. Singer Melly Goeslaw was pegged by the September 2004 issue of *MTV Indonesia's Trax* magazine as a "fashion innovator" because she knows how to piece fashions together in a way that is distinctive and recognizable: a traditional "Asian" base, with a touch of punk, a splash of pop, and an undercur-rent of hip hop. Jakarta garage rock group The Brandals were described as "stylish renegades" (*berandalan*) for their recycling of "products from the styles of mod and punk rock." In other words, the ideal fashionista is something of a fashion *bricoleur* (Lévi-Strauss 1966; Hebdige 1979), picking and choosing from a smorgasbord of available styles. Elang is a skilled practitioner of this craft.

For me, though, no one I met in Indonesia personified the pieced-together aesthetic of contemporary indie better than Nadya Asteria, "Pipu" of Reddoor and Pipuangpu. As with Venus, I first met Pipu at Triggers Syndicate, when I was lounging on the black pleather ottoman in the middle of the showroom floor, watching some program or other on cable television and chatting with Venus and Ekil about something or other related to that. She immediately caught my attention when she walked in. A petite, light-skinned nineteen-year-old in a fitted black T-shirt; a plaid ultra mini-skirt; thigh-high, black leather lace-up boots, with white cotton stockings held up by garters; and a Weimar-era bob hairstyle with asymmetrical, multi-level bangs, she looked like the ideal of urban sophistication I had as a disaffected indie teenager in Northern California. I was surprised, frankly, to see a young woman dressed in such severe—and potentially scandalous—attire in this often conservative, majority Muslim country. She didn't say much to me, just stopped in, chatted with Venus for a minute, and took off, but I would run into her again and again at Reddoor, where she was a regular. Through her boyfriend Ade, she and I eventually became friends. But it always seemed to me that she maintained a conscious distance from the group, a carefully constructed cool persona that both established her place as a member of the scene and erected a protective barrier around her.

Pipu has become adept at life posing, the art of looking like she's being photo-graphed no matter what she's doing. She adopts a modelesque poise in the most prosaic of situations—leaning against a graffitied wall, cigarette in open fist, or re-clining listlessly on a motorbike—that has, in fact, led her to be one of the most pho-tographed figures in the Yogyakarta indie scene. She has been featured in a range of ads for friends' distros and clothing labels, including Rebel Stars and Triggers Syn-dicate. On the cover of *Trash*, the inaugural issue of Triggers Syndicate's "monthly free fashion magazine" (which, to my knowledge, only produced one issue ever), she stands dispassionately, arms at her side, staring straight at the camera as if she were challenging it, with lips slightly parted in a haute couture pout and streaks of red in her choppy black hair. She wears a white T-shirt that reads "Love Kill [*sic*] Slowly" in minimal black letters that convey a kind of bare-bones elegance. In this shot, and throughout the loosely disguised catalog of Triggers Syndicate's clothes, she personifies the look of apocalyptic teenage nihilism that characterizes the signature Triggers Syndicate aesthetic.

Pipu's look is put-together and deliberate. She "mixes 'n' matches" to create a style that is "uniquely her," takes (*ambil*) from pop cultural resources around her to piece together a distinctive *ensemble.* "My style," she told me, "is my style alone. I've invented it myself." That doesn't mean, however, that it is original or idiosyncratic. Her lace-up, twenty-eye Converse boots align her with a traditionally indie and punk aesthetic. Her caked-on white foundation and heavy black eyeliner are recognizably gothic. Her plaid miniskirt conjures up Twiggy and the "Swinging 60s" rendition of British mod, by way of early 1970s punk rock. Rather, her style is a constructed assemblage of recognizable types.

If older, British and American models of indie emphasized one's membership in a distinctive subcultural community with its own brand of quirky cool, the newer, hipper, Indonesian model, as represented by Pipu or Elang, promotes a chameleonesque approach to style, where one could potentially fit in anywhere, and yet can be pinned down to exactly nowhere (see Polhemus 1996). It strives to be elusive and indexical at once. It points to any number of styles without ever fully, or finally, settling into a single one.

The "Self" in "Do-It-Yourself"

For Pipu or Elang, maintaining a hip persona means being at the center of multiple trends, forging one's own constellation of cool. To be hip is to tinker with style, play with its elements, and rearrange them into customized forms. It makes the simplest act of picking and choosing one's clothes into a DIY project. And what emerges from this project of stylistic bricolage is a fluid, unstable conception of selfhood, a construction of subjectivity expressed through the logic of appropriation and assemblage. This is the nomadic (Deleuze and Guattari 1987) self of an interconnected Indonesia, of a nation saturated with multiple streams of style, a self firmly planted on the un-firm grounds of the digital age. It is hardly the rational individual described by theorists of neoliberalism, that alienated, atomized subject of self-governance. The "self" in "do-it-yourself," rather, is a nodal self. It is the self as nexus, a point of friction and connection between divergent flows and intensities (Massumi 2002). The self in do-it-yourself is a stylized collage, a frail, syncretic whole, cut-and-pasted and mix 'n' matched into existence.

In the late modern age, sociologist Anthony Giddens has famously argued, the self is no longer an ontological given, inherited or predetermined by one's social position, but a project (Sartre 1963; Ortner 2006: 40) reflexively and continually made (Giddens 1991). An individual actively constructs the self in dialogue with larger "abstract systems," both local and global, through multiple choices—what clothes to wear, what food to eat, what kind of car to drive (Giddens 1991: 5). In "traditional" social contexts, he claims, the self is a status one achieves upon adulthood, a position acquired through undergoing rites of passage nearly uniform in character from individual to individual. It is a fairly predictable process of social reproduction. But in the late modern, "post-traditional" age, which, according to Giddens, is characterized by "profound processes of reorganization of time and space, coupled to the expansion of disembedding mechanisms that prize social relations free from the hold of specific locales" (Giddens 1991: 2), the self is anything but predetermined; it must be achieved.

No doubt Giddens overstates his case a bit here. Social reproduction was never quite as smooth and predictable as he suggests, and well before the modern era, especially in a multicultural society like Indonesia, where cultures themselves have long maintained a similarly piecemeal quality, situated social actors in all sorts of settings had learned to manipulate pre-established types for their own ends (see Bourdieu 1977), to employ some degree of agency over who they are within a given group of people. But I think Giddens's essential point, that the self has become a project of continual attention, carefully monitored (Foucault 1986) and consciously constructed through active social practice, is a good one; that is, so long as we see this process as always tentative, partial, and above all, social. There is a sense of indeterminacy that characterizes contemporary identity formation, which if not wholly new, is at least more pronounced than it was previously, an indeterminacy that is at once potentially liberating and unquestionably anxiety-producing (Evans 2007).

Indonesia in the last few decades, as should already be obvious from the previous chapters, has undergone profound social transformation. Its government is reforming toward democracy. Its economy has been deregulated. Ties with international investors have multiplied. Increased mobility within and across national borders, along with the "disembedding mechanisms" of mass mediation and (relatively) free trade, have reorganized Indonesian experiences of time and space, expanded the repertoire of possible lifestyle choices, and created a vast set of imaginative resources (see Appaduarai 1996) from which young Indonesians can choose in the construction of self.

But the use of the term "disembedding" implies for me a free-floating, unencumbered quality at odds with the realities of contemporary middle-class Indonesian life. Young people like Pipu, Venus, and Elang are hardly free of locality. They are, in fact, deeply conscious of it. All too conscious. Although both Venus and Pipu have lived in multiple locations—Pipu in Kalimantan and Yogyakarta, and Venus in Semarang, Jakarta, Bali, Bandung, and Yogyakarta—neither have ever left the country, lacking the monetary resources to do so. Rather, their mobility, limited as it is, has made them even more conscious of the boundaries of space and place. They are keenly aware of all sorts of "youth movements" happening elsewhere that they can only minimally take part in. They bemoan the feeling of stuckness that keeps them rooted in Indonesian soil, often discuss their fantasies of roaming abroad— Pipu dreams of studying architecture in Germany, and Venus of backpacking through England and Scandinavia.

Sure, their mobility is greater than most Indonesians. The majority of the population, after all, lives its entire life in rural areas, never even leaving the confines of the province in which they were born. But these middle-class indie kids are just mobile enough to recognize how limited their mobility still is. My own ability to cross borders with relative freedom and ease created an uncomfortable hierarchy between informants and me, of which I was always keenly aware. Before my one brief trip home in April 2007, my friends in Indonesia compiled a list of media products they hoped I could bring back for them from abroad. This is not, after all, the moneyed elite, but it isn't the rural peasantry, either. They all have motorbikes and cell phones, access to computers and the Internet. What characterizes the middle-class experience of young people like Pipu, Elang, and Venus, is a kind of mid-level mobility, between localities but still only within national boundaries, within the circuits of cyberspace but never the roads and highways of actual, international space.

Iyo, singer for the indie pop band Pure Saturday and long-time Chief Executive of *Ripple* magazine, sums up this middle-class positionality through the expression *di tengah-tengah* (being in the middle). In Iyo's words:

We're a third world country still. The thing is, back in the '90s, when I was growing up, what was cool wasn't the traditional. Because people here were still thirsty [for something else]. Back then it was the culture of the Suharto era. Information was difficult to come by. And expensive, too. The cool people, then, were people who went outside the country. People with big inheritances who could travel. Rich people. In the Suharto era, I think it was like that. Everything was totally controlled (by the government). So it was difficult for kids [*anak muda*] to be cool. And to be cool you needed information, you needed new stuff, right? So everything came from outside the country … The cultural movers, the pioneers, were from the skateboarding and surfing communities. And that culture was really strong, you know. That culture [that came from] outside the country was really strong. In terms of its music, its attitude, it was rooted in the foreign too. And these days that's more what I'm familiar with. But actually I'm still in the middle, because my influences are from America, [and] from England. I'm more comfortable with that stuff. But in truth, I'm still in the middle. [We] haven't yet reached our goal. We still aren't on the same level as Europeans. We remain in the middle.

Iyo describes an earlier era, where cool was defined solely by one's degree of access to foreign cultural goods. Although that era is fading away, in part because of his own magazine's contribution to making information about such trends available to any literate urban kid (for free no less), he remains conscious of his own relative lack.

Indonesia's indie kids still work to actively position themselves in terms of elsewhere, but they do so with a kind of knowledge and discernment impossible for all but the richest of the rich just ten years previous. They extend their pop culture feelers in a thousand directions but find that they never quite reach far enough.

Rather than being disembedded from time and space, then, the predicament of being "in the middle" is one of being embedded into discourses and informational flows of multiple times and spaces, while remaining all too firmly grounded in material locality.

Sociality, Connectivity, and the Lurking Specter of the Mainstream

I want to end this chapter with something of a disclaimer. I have argued that as Indonesia becomes more deeply implicated in a global media system and an informational economy, access to information, distro fashion, and pirated goods have conspired to make what one consumes less important than how one consumes it. The style game, these days, is more about degree and scale than about form and type, more about customization and cutting and pasting than about copying and conforming. The implication, of course, is that consumption itself still matters, and what's more, that it matters in large part because it is a way of distinguishing oneself from others.

I do not, however, mean to overemphasize the elitism and exclusivity of the Indonesian indie scene. In fact, I would argue that an emphasis on consciousness and participation is gradually replacing middle-class identity practices based on invidious distinction. For indie kids today, it is more important to contribute positively to cultural production and establish connections across borders than to actively prove that they are better than those lower down on the totem pole.

No doubt there is still elitism in the indie scene, as there is in the American indie scene of which I have long been a part, but it is an elitism based on subcultural participation, rather than class status per se, an elitism premised on self-imposed marginality rather than class-based superiority, and an elitism that distinguishes itself not from any particular class formation, but from an abstract social specter (see Siegel 1998), " the mainstream" (Thornton 1996), whose very conceptual utility lies precisely in its vague articulation. The mainstream toward which indie scenesters continuously pose themselves in opposition has the conceptual advantage of having no direct real-world equivalent. It is everyone and no one; most Indonesians, but not anyone we know. It is, in other words, a kind of faceless boogeyman, a "specter" (Siegel 1998) lurking somewhere out there in the dark, dank streets of the social imaginary.

Indie kids may be snobs with superior knowledge of un-signed bands from Middle America, obscure fashion magazines from Tokyo, and the latest developments in South Korean comic books, but they are not snobs toward anyone in particular. They demonize, instead, a kind of formless mass, an imagined mainstream (Thornton 1996) that represents not one particular group of consumers, but the very idea of the passive consuming subject. They want to be something other than that subject, someone more deeply committed, critical, and engaged.

"Fashion," writes philosopher Gilles Lipovetsky of twentieth-century trends in Western pop culture, "is less a sign of class ambition than a way out of the world of tradition" (Lipovetsky 2002: 4). This is no less true in Indonesia. The indie style, in this case, is an aesthetic of dis-articulation as much as it is a means of articulating identity. It is a breaking free from. For Indonesian middle-class youth, those who most conspicuously display a hip indie sensibility, fashion is more a force of connectivity than it is a method of differentiation. It links Indonesian youth with other youth in other places, even if only symbolically, assuaging the sense of marginality often experienced by the new middle class. Today's indie style is testimony, thus, not to the atomization of the individual under a late capitalist regime, but to "the multiplicity of the self" (Maffesoli 1996) in the global sensorium, the contradictions and compromises that one willfully, and stylistically, embodies. And it is testimony to the importance of creative production to new articulations of selfhood. To be hip is not to follow trends; it is to help forge them, to piece them together as a fashion bricoleur.

—5—

On Cutting and Pasting: The Art and Politics of DIY Streetwear

Now is the era of cut and paste.

—Dendy Darman, co-founder and owner of Unkl347

Graphic Manipulation

Adhari Adegreden Donora (Ade) and I sat in the cramped backroom of Reddoor distro in Yogyakarta amid toppling-over stacks of plastic-sheathed T-shirts, some American indie rock band blaring over the loudspeakers, while he hunched over the computer and tinkered with a new design. So far he had etched out a bright yellow telephone with the "paintbrush" tool of Corel Draw. It was an old-fashioned phone, clunky and cumbersome, and Ade had most likely never used one like it. It had that picturesque, nostalgic quality common to phones in movies or high school drama productions, a phone archetype. Beneath it, he had spelled out in a bold black font the name of the clothing label he sold through the shop: "FireFighter Fight!"—as much an exclamation as a name. He was now using the "shape" tool to construct a black, spiral telephone chord out of small, overlapping circles. "Naïve," he told me, laughing, pointing out the commonality between his own mouse drawn-efforts and the kind of anti-skill conceptual art emerging out of New York in the 1980s.

The final motif might become the graphic on a T-shirt. It might become the print pattern of a blazer or a hooded sweatjacket. It might be the singular logo placed strategically over the right breast of a sweater. More likely it will become nothing at all, one of many discarded visual ideas, left in the archives of the "Document" folder of Ade's PC.

Ade spun back around in his chair and closed out his composition, opening up another file he had been working on over the last couple of weeks, a poster for Reddoor's upcoming show "Monster Therapy." Most of the work for the event had already been done. The talent had been booked, sponsorships had been secured—a list of distros mounted on the wall had checks marked next to them in black, perma-nent ink. But one of the most important tasks had yet to be finished, constructing a consistent image for the event. Ade had an assortment of graphics he was using for that purpose, all with a Japanese monster movie feel. The poster he had completed so far featured a Godzilla-like lizard stomping through an urban landscape under construction. A sign for Reddoor stood in the forefront of the image, straight in the monster's path. Portions of the piece had been lifted from online photo galleries. Others had been "drawn" in Corel Draw, still others imported through Adobe Photoshop. It was a hybrid of the cartoon and the real.

"How long does it usually take you to finish one of these things?" I asked as I pointed at the screen.

It varies, Ade told me. It could be a few days. It could be a week. It's hard to get things done at Reddoor, after all. There are always other people around, chatting, playing music, or drinking beer on the sidewalk out front. The small stockroom where we sat was often crowded with friends and employees. An assortment of seat pads and improvised chairs littered the floor. There is always someone watching at Reddoor, peering over Ade's shoulder and offering suggestions on whatever he's doing. Sometimes these are helpful, Ade told me. Other times, they just keep him from concentrating.

So Ade does a lot of his work in his off-hours—a nebulous distinction to be sure in a setting where work and play are so inextricably intermingled—at his boarding house (*kos-kosan*) in the southern part of Yogyakarta. It's not much of a space, just a single room in a run-down complex full of students and the recently graduated, but his room is his alone. When he needs to get things done without distraction, that's where he goes.

Ade and I had become good friends. This, however, was the first time I had watched him work. I wanted to know more about his process of constructing images, and I asked him a number of technical points, about what software he uses (Corel Draw, sometimes Adobe Photoshop or Illustrator), where he gets his images (websites, Japanese fashion magazines, French design books). It was important stuff, and I wanted to record it in a more formal way.

"When do I get to interview you?"

Ade hesitated. "As what?"

I was a bit confused by Ade's response, thinking the answer was obvious. So I asked him in return, "What do *you* mean?"

"Well, as the manager of Reddoor?" he explained. "Or as a student?"

"No, as a designer."

Ade grimaced and reflected for a moment before responding. "If you want to interview a designer, you should interview someone else. I'm not a designer at all. I don't really design anything. I'm more of a graphic manipulator." He used the English term, then added the Indonesian translation "*manipulator grafis.*"

It is a term Ade is particularly fond of. It shows up in his designs, peppers his speech, steps in as a descriptive term for the pieced together look of his compositions. But it's not as if Ade doesn't know how to design. In fact, at the time of this research he was enrolled in one of the top design programs in the country. He knows the foundations of design inside and out. He's just not all that interested in design as it's most commonly conceptualized, making pretty little pictures that help sell products.

Ade was raised by a conservative Muslim family in Riau, a relatively wealthy region in Sumatra. He grew up comfortably middle-class and could have gone on to any number of professional positions in Riau's booming oil industry, but that was never really Ade's thing. He had always liked to draw, to paint, to create things with his mind and his hands. His parents discouraged him from thinking of art as a career option, though, and Ade never really gave it serious consideration. They would have preferred something more practical for him, economics, perhaps, or engineering. Those are the two fields, Ade told me, that Indonesian parents tend to want their children to go into, sort of what law and medicine are to American parents.

Ade said it never really occurred to him that he could even make a career out of art until his sister moved to Yogyakarta and recommended to their parents that they send him to ISI to study design. She convinced them that he could live a comfortable, respectable life as a designer. There are plenty of opportunities in that field these days, as the Indonesian economy adapts to the global marketplace and expands its cultural sector, and besides, Ade would have his sister to look after him in Yogya and keep him from getting into too much trouble. His parents eventually gave their consent.

ISI, it turns out, was a good place for Ade, but not for the reasons his parents or sister had in mind. He discovered punk at ISI, gothic fashion, and indie rock. He learned about radical European art movements like Surrealism, Dadaism, and Situationism; got involved with the House of Natural Fiber, "an informal creative community of collaborative expression" (www.natural-fiber.com/about.html); and began taking part in large media installations that involved lots of flashing lights, disorienting imagery, and music made from scraping metal and amplifying cell-phone frequencies.

Ade quickly lost any interest he once might have had in the textbook variety of design work. Instead, he pursued design as experimentation and critique. It became for him part of a larger project of visual "education," of "waking up" the Indonesian populace, as he liked to put it, challenging their thinking about the aesthetic universe they occupy. It is hardly a revolutionary concept for an art academy design program, but it felt new to Ade, an approach to design based more on the desire to communicate than to sell.

In his design work, Ade attempts to lure in his viewers with familiar imagery, then present to them something different from what they expected, something incongruous, even disconcerting. He borrows from a repertoire of dislocated imagery: innocuous woodland creatures, fire-breathing dinosaurs, cartoon aliens, and in keeping with the name of his clothing label, anything having to do with firefighting (Dalmatians and fire hydrants, flames and hoses).

But there is always something slightly off about this work, some uncomfortable juxtaposition (see Hebdige 1979) that challenges the innocuousness of what he is depicting. One of his favorite motifs involves a simple image of a deer with its antlers missing from its head. A single antler protrudes from the creature's nose like a unicorn's horn. It looks clumsy, its weight unevenly distributed, as if it is about to fall over. A number of his pieces also involve firefighters, those public servants who (presumably) protect us from harm. Ade's firefighters, however, tend to be monstrous, anonymous figures hidden behind gas masks and helmets. In Ade's work, the dangerous is rendered harmless. The harmless, in turn, becomes grotesque.

The term "graphic manipulation," then, has more than one meaning here. It refers to the manipulation of existing graphics, the collaging, that is, of sampled materials, and to the "graphic" nature of such manipulation, its underlying violence, its subversion of visual forms. And it also refers to the more practical aspects of Ade's fashion production. For him, the design of garments themselves happens elsewhere, with limited direction from him. His design work is almost purely graphic in orientation, composed on a computer and delivered to production houses in digital format. It challenges the very notion of what fashion design means, makes it far simpler, far more accessible, a practice available to anyone with a computer and access to pirated software, in other words, to pretty much everyone Ade knows. It should come as no surprise, then, that so many people Ade knows are themselves designers.

In this chapter, I discuss the art and politics of Indonesian DIY streetwear design such as Ade's, the way indie designers construct compositions out of existing graphics and forge new relationships with both fashion production and global commerce in the process. Cut and paste, I argue, is not just a quick and easy method of producing images, though it is certainly that; it is also a tactic of global re-positioning, a rewriting of the power relationships embedded in neoliberal capitalism. Designers such as Ade, I suggest, sample materials from those more powerful others—corporations, political bodies, designers with established cachet—who exert such a fundamental influence over the ways they imagine and relate to everyday life. And in so doing, they take possession over those institutions, put their own stamp on them, and make them their own. They infuse the branded imagery of global commerce with a new democratic potency, a new dynamic sociality.

The Global Ascendance of Streetwear

The reduction of fashion to graphics is, of course, no Indonesian innovation. Designers like Ade proudly trace their aesthetic lineage back through a canon of streetwear labels out of California, New York, and, more recently, London, Vancouver, and Tokyo, for whom the graphic T-shirt remains the most significant, and frequently employed, medium. As Carbone and Johnson (2011) point out in their recent "Oral History of the Graphic T-shirt," the history of streetwear itself is largely the history of graphic manipulation, repurposing existing imagery for the design of boards, T-shirts, and sneakers. Born out of the subcultural intersections of surfing, skateboarding, punk, and hip hop, streetwear's roots lie in the ethnically diverse and stylistically eclectic Southern Californian surf scene of the late 1970s and early 1980s. It soon expanded to New York, where the budding hip hop scene helped launch it into public visibility. Early brands like Powell Peralta, Santa Cruz, and perhaps most influential of all, Stüssy, converted board art to T-shirt art, transposing one graphic medium onto another (Vogel 2007; Sims 2010; Carbone and Johnson 2011). As they did so, they emphasized the graphic element as the central visual focus of a garment, erasing the authorial contributions of the garment's designers, and consigning non-graphic creative production to the unglamorous position of manual labor. The graphic *was* the fashion, an innovation that not only played to the strengths of a board designer, but also appealed to the punk-influenced DIY ethos of the surf and skate community. Not everyone could design clothing, but most people can put some sort of image together, either by drawing or spraypainting, or at least through collaging some moderately novel composition. Streetwear designers did all of the above, and as they became more and more influential figures in the world of international fashion, they became a greater and greater challenge to the fashion industry as usual.

According to Paul Mittleman of the long-lived Southern California streetwear company Stüssy, streetwear borrowed the DIY tactics of both punk and hip hop (in Carbone and Johnson 2011). Designers cut and pasted from popular culture, remixed the logos of well-known brands, "mixed and matched" from innumerable subcultural sources (Fujiwara, as cited in Sims 2010: 117), and took to regularly satirizing those staples of couture that had come to represent the state of fashion worldwide. Says Bobby Hundreds of the respected Los Angeles streetwear line The Hundreds, "Stüssy was founded upon parody. The line was a direct rip-off of high-end fashion lines, but [Shawn Stüssy] brought it to the street level" (Fujiwara, as cited in Sims 2010). The original Stüssy logo was based on Chanel's. Later renditions referenced Louis Vuitton, Commes des Garçons, and Avenue B.

And it wasn't just fashion that the early streetwear scene took on. Los Angeles label Freshjive created brand parodies of Tide, the laundry detergent giant, along with Special K cereal and 7–11 convenience stores. Fellow Los Angeles label X-Large borrowed from video game companies, pulpy old Hollywood films, and major fast food franchises. Fuct took from science fiction films and sports paraphernalia, Obey from professional wrestling and mainstream newspapers. When surf and skate brands Quicksilver, Volcom, Stüssy, and Obey became international names, their fellow streetwear designers took from them, too, lumping together the former scene mainstays with the rest of corporate capitalism that they saw as so fundamentally opposed to their scene's own way of doing business. Parody became a strategy of brand distinction, a way of distancing themselves from capitalism as usual. This was street level anti-fashion, a declaration of sartorial independence.

Of course, that sense of independence from mainstream capitalism was perhaps always a bit more gestural than actual, as much a part of streetwear's brand appeal as its politics. Streetwear labels are in the apparel industry, too, after all, selling garments—albeit in smaller batches than major fashion labels—and tailoring their goods to changing markets. Style journalist Josh Sims estimates that streetwear is now one of the world's biggest clothing sectors, with sales in the billions of U.S. dollars per year. Sims is no doubt lumping together athletic clothing goliaths such as Nike, Adidas, and Puma with smaller brands such as Mooks and Mecca, but it nonetheless begs the question of just how "outside" streetwear labels can claim to be. Plus, for decades now, respected streetwear labels such as AKA, Undefeated, and Alife have partnered with athletic giants such as Nike, Adidas, and Puma to produce limited-edition shoes of their own. The conceptual distinction between streetwear and ready-to-wear is getting more and more difficult to maintain.

This is especially true as couture brands, from Paul Smith to Commes des Garçons, borrow continually from streetwear in their designs. Early streetwear labels may have appropriated imagery from couture brands, but clearly the influence goes both ways. This is largely because of the street credibility brands such as Obey, Undefeated, and A Bathing Ape are perceived to have by couture labels, and it also speaks to the decline in the brash confidence of couture to manufacture global trends. Where once the fashion world presumed to hold a monopoly on popular taste, to forge the new looks of the moment by tailoring the wardrobes of the elite and letting them "trickle down" (Aspelund 2009) to the masses, today, fashion much more often goes in the opposite direction, "bubbling up" (Polhemus 1994; Sims 2010) from "the streets." Beginning, arguably, with Yves Saint-Laurent, the top houses of fashion have looked to urban streetwear for inspiration for their designs (Polhemus 1994; Aspelund 2009), co-opting elements of subcultural style (the "Beat" style, famously, for Saint-Laurent; punk for Jean-Paul Gautier and Betsey Johnson; mod for John Galliano and Mary Quaint; goth, industrial, and steam punk for Alexander McQueen) and re-interpreting them as couture. While the grand couturiers of yesteryear prided themselves on setting the standards for elite fashion, conjuring, as if from nothing, the hot new looks for tomorrow, today's designers attempt to predict what fashions will sell tomorrow by carefully scrutinizing what the cool kids already have on. These days, many brands prefer the street-tested product to the unproven experiment. They employ "coolhunters" (Gladwell 2000) to track down the latest trends, borrow from youth styles, and check out what the small streetwear labels are selling in New York, London, and Tokyo. "High fashion and street fashion are now blended," claims Jake Burton, creative director of the extreme sports clothing label of the same name. "The irreverence of street is now demanded at the highest levels of fashion" (cited in Vogel 2007: 49–50).

The Indonesian indie scene, for its part, first encountered streetwear brands like Stüssy, Juice, and Volcom through surf shops that popped up in Bali and other major surf destinations in Indonesia in the mid-1980s, and then again through the Australian clothing chain Planet Surf, who, by the mid-1990s had established outlets at malls throughout urban Indonesia. By the time it reached them, streetwear was already inextricably caught up in international couture, part of the same markets, the same systems of status production and distinction. And yet it retained something of its countercultural cachet. Streetwear both linked its customers with a larger world of transnational commerce and differentiated them from it. It captured something of the hipster's ambivalence and ambiguity. Streetwear was both *fashionable* and yet not *fashion*, per se. That was no doubt its appeal to middle-class self-professed rebels like Dendy, Adjie, and Marin, and when they, in the mid-to-late 1990s started producing clothing of their own, it should come as no surprise to learn that they borrowed these streetwear brands' cut-and-paste approach to design. Ade, inspired to go into streetwear design himself from the earlier examples of Unkl347, No Label Stuff, and Monik/Celtic, followed their lead.

Bricolage Redux

Lévi-Strauss first coined the term *bricolage* to describe the "science of the concrete" (Lévi-Strauss 1966), whereby an individual "makes do with 'whatever is at hand'" to conduct a number of diverse tasks (Lévi-Strauss 1966: 17). The bricoleur, he explains, constructs works out of available materials, whether they were intended for this purpose or not. Unlike "the engineer," who constructs from raw materials "conceived and procured for the purpose of a project," (Lévi-Strauss 1966) the bricoleur puts existing things to new purposes. The engineer creates; the bricoleur tinkers. And this is not just tinkering for the sake of tinkering. The bricoleur "speaks through the medium of things" (Lévi-Strauss 1966: 21), makes meaning out of assemblage.

Since Lévi-Strauss developed the concept, bricolage has been packaged and repackaged for use by a variety of social theorists. Anthropologists, in particular, have made heavy use of the concept, employing it for a diverse range of theoretical tasks, from describing how educators design instructional curricula (Hatton 1989; Wagner 1990) to accounting for the hodgepodge religious rituals of colonial subjects (Chao 1999). At its most banal, bricolage in these texts simply refers to how people put pieces of things together to form a complex whole. At its most extravagant, bricolage is no less than the dynamic subversion of dominant forms.

The way cultural theorists have used bricolage has tended to lie somewhere between these two extreme poles. On the one end, is the position most closely associated with Hebdige (1979), Clarke (1976), and the Centre for Contemporary Cultural Studies (CCCS) in Birmingham, England. These cultural studies theorists used the concept of bricolage to describe the aesthetic practices of working-class subcultures of the 1960s and 1970s. Such theorists argued that subcultural practitioners challenge the hegemony of the dominant (read, bourgeois) culture not through explicit acts of resistance, but "obliquely" through style (Hebdige 1979: 17). They take everyday items associated with respectability and upward-mobility, a business suit or a school girl uniform, for instance, and deconstruct them through their personal attire, juxtapose them with incongruous elements, or sometimes even literally rip them apart and reassemble them with precarious materials like safety pins or duct tape. In the process, the appropriated materials take on new resonance and significance. They become dissociated from their original context and come to signify group solidarity, rebellion against the "mainstream," and self-imposed marginality. Hebdige thus read punk and mod fashions as forms of "semiotic guerilla warfare" (Eco 1972), attempts to "disrupt and reorganize meaning" (Hedbige 1979: 106). For him and others within the CCCS, bricolage was a method of aesthetic subversion, an act of visual resistance in line with the tradition of surrealist collage.

At the other end of the pole is the more pessimistic position assumed by a certain brand of poststructuralist thinker, most notably Derrida (1980), who sees nothing particularly resistant or subversive in the practice. For Derrida, bricolage is not only quite prosaic and ordinary, but in fact, the only kind of aesthetic practice possible. He takes issue with Lévi-Strauss's juxtaposition between the bricoleur and the engineer, claiming that since every act of linguistic communication entails the structuring elements of syntax and lexicon, all discourse is already bricolage. For Derrida, then, bricolage is little more than business as usual.

My own understanding of bricolage as a cultural practice lies somewhere in between Hebdige and Derrida. I am sympathetic with claims by Derrida that the logic of bricolage is intrinsic to human linguistic practice, but I would argue that his use of the term fails to recognize a significant qualitative difference between compositions that base their value on their perceived originality, and compositions whose assembled nature is a deliberate, and meaning-laden aspect of their value. Bricolage of the latter sort, I would argue, can be, and often is, fundamentally transformative, rendering explicit what would otherwise be unacknowledged, hidden, or even outright denied in one's work. Similarly, I share Hebdige's belief that bricolage can serve as a potent mechanism for reworking dominant meanings, but I would argue that the emphasis on bricolage as resistance misses the more complex positionalities it often enacts, namely, the ambivalence and "in-betweenness" of contemporary consuming subjects.

The rest of this chapter will consider examples of bricolage put into practice by Indonesian indie streetwear designers and attempt to develop a more useful conception of the term for our times, one that maintains critical aspects of both of these two bodies of argument without being reducible to either one. Ade and other Indonesian indie designers' graphic manipulation, I demonstrate, is a variety of bricolage that speaks volumes about the state of contemporary cultural production, the social meaning and value of fashion, and the position of Indonesian youth in the larger global economy.

Pastiche and the Logic of Late Capitalism

Examples of bricolage are all around us. Hip hop musicians routinely sample from 1970s soul hits and 1950s bop. DJs lay down raga beats over turn of the century gospel. Hollywood directors such as Quentin Tarantino and Robert Rodriguez construct their storylines out of recycled B-movie plots. And tens of thousands of teenagers from around the world piece together YouTube video montages out of television clips and radio hits. This is not just cultural production as usual; it is a particular moment in cultural production, a moment where producers expose, and indeed glory, in their products' assembled quality. Their meaning is derived by their very lack of originality, their deliberate intertextual nature.

Indonesian indie fashion designers, for their part, engage in bricolage through the computer-age methodology of digital "cut and paste." Sometimes cutting and pasting in this context means using the "cut" tool on Corel Draw or Adobe Photoshop to extract an exact copy from a digital image found on a website, then the "paste" tool to apply it to the "canvas" of one of these programs. Sometimes, however, it is done less directly. A designer will scour the Internet for appropriate materials and then attempt to reproduce the images found using the electronic paintbrush and shape tools of Corel Draw.

If, however, the source image is too intricate to recreate on as clumsy a program as Corel Draw, a designer may sketch the image out on paper first and then scan it onto their computer. Or, if he or she is not particularly good at drawing, there are a couple of other possible solutions. Hamid Ariwinata of Triggers Syndicate has his "more-talented" friends sketch out those images he can't quite get right himself. Other designers take digital pictures of the images from which they sample, or print out, images they want and trace them with white paper and a pencil. Some even trace directly off the computer screen.

Like the bricoleurs Lévi-Strauss discusses in *The Savage Mind*, these DIY designers assemble and disassemble, and combine and recombine, instead of creating something wholly from scratch. They tinker with the images they locate through the World Wide Web, put a new spin on them, and remake them for a local audience.

Jameson has attributed the prevalence of such practices of assemblage and recombination in contemporary society to the cultural logic of late capitalism. Aesthetic production, he argues, has become deeply, and irretrievably, integrated into commodity production—that is, "the frantic economic urgency of producing fresh waves of ever more novel-seeming goods [from clothing to airplanes], at ever greater rates of turnover" (Jameson 1992: 4). The result is a cultural tendency toward "pastiche"—Jameson's version of bricolage—an aesthetic with no allegiances, no hidden meanings, and no qualms about borrowing from anything and everything in a continual quest to incite customers to buy. Pastiche, Jameson claims, makes all aesthetics equivalent, mere fodder for capitalist exploitation. It is like parody in that it draws from other peoples' work, but it differs from parody in that is devoid of its "ulterior motives." It is "amputated of satiric impulse" (Jameson 1992: 17), all glossy surface with nothing underneath. It is, he concludes, little more than "a neutral practice of mimicry" (Jameson 1992).

That Indonesian indie fashion design is integrated with commodity production is difficult to deny. Designers sell their work, and they do so in an increasingly competitive environment, in which standing out (*tampil beda*) is of critical importance. The quest for new visual ideas is ongoing, and as Dendy Darman of Unkl347 explains, quite urgent. In Indonesia, he told me, "Ideas only last for about a month." Due to widespread piracy, "Things get staie quickly here." "Outside of the country," he went on, "if you come up with something new, it can last a year or so, but here, after a month, everyone's already wearing it." Bigger companies, he explained, will create a design, and if it does well, sell it continually until it stops selling, but Unkl347 doesn't have that luxury. They only print a design once, with limited editions, before moving on to something else. They have to stay continually fresh or risk becoming irrelevant. Cutting and pasting speeds up the process of design production, makes it quick and easy to crank out new products.

Ahmad Marin of the Bandung label Monik/Celtic tells a similar story to Dendy's. "In design," he tells me "I don't think about how to follow people, but how to innovate, innovate, innovate. That is the key, I think, if you are running [a] design or [other] creative business. You must change change change change. Adapt adapt adapt adapt." And that's exactly what his company does. Every season of Monik/Celtic's products have their own tone, theme, and look. They stray into a number of directions from bright and cheerful to dark and gloomy, but they are always distinctly current. Marin goes to great lengths to keep it that way, taking annual trips to Singapore, Malaysia, and beyond to survey the world of international streetwear and look for new directions for his company to go. He describes his company's design concept (*konsep*) as "simple" or "pop," but for Marin this can mean any number of things, depending on what's happening in streetwear more generally. It can mean disco rabbits, dancing robots, Little Red Riding Hoods making their way through an enchanted forest, owls and unicorns, towering Godzillas, or miniatures poodles.

His work is about as close to Jameson's notion of pastiche as any designer's I encountered in Indonesia. It borrows from anywhere and everywhere, other places and other times, from the disco 1970s of New York to the demure Victorian era of England, without any consistent allegiances or affiliations. It mimics other popular brands, pieces together divergent imagery into a range of designs for sale at distros across the nation. And there is no doubt something "schizophrenic" (Deleuze and Guattari 1996) about this work, the way it seems to flit from one idea to another, as does the postmodern subject of poststructuralist thought.

But Monik/Celtic's work remains immediately recognizable to other Indonesian designers. It has a crisp, clean quality to it, a look that retains its simplicity even as it scavenges from diverse sources. Moreover, despite its schizophrenic content, there is a perspective that emerges from the work. And it's not that of the generic capitalist manufacturer trying to cash in on a trend. Marin, like most designers in the archipelago nation, fervently denies that money has ever been a motivating factor in what he does. His push comes from somewhere else: a desire to set himself and his company apart, a desire to matter in the international arena, to help put Indonesia on the fashion map, not just as a manufacturer of other company's designs, but a design center in its own right. It is, in other words, a perspective on global fashion put forward by someone on its periphery.

Stuck in the Middle

Anthropologist Lila Abu-Lughod has argued that we can "use resistance as a *diagnostic* of power" (Abu-Lughod 1990: 42). Following the lead of Foucault (1978), she suggests that the appearance of resistance itself helps shed light on where power relations lie, gives us a sense of where to look for inequalities and forms of domination. Where there is resistance, there is power, and vice versa. Perhaps the same can be said of cutting and pasting. Where acts of bricolage take on a self-consciously assembled quality, we can be reasonably certain that some sort of power discrepancy is in place. Sometimes, cut and paste serves to reinforce that discrepancy, as is clearly the case with the Indonesian state's appropriation of regional cultural practices. Other times, it challenges it, undermining the authority of the borrowed image or text and re-positioning the appropriator in a new relationship with what is appropriated.

In the case of DIY fashion design, finding the demarcating lines of power is fairly easy. Unkl347, Monik/Celtic—and for that matter, FireFighter Fight!—are tiny companies by world standards, run by a bunch of skaters and surfers from a poverty-stricken industrializing nation, with no real expectations of "making it big." They are small fish in a big sea, even if in Indonesia's fashion scene, they are about as big as brands can get. The source companies from which designers borrow, meanwhile, tend to be major players in the international economy, brands such as Nike, Xerox, and Converse; media companies such as Twentieth Century Fox, Sony, and Viacom. Their products are all over Indonesia, whereas Unkl347 and Monik/Celtic, after ten or so years of relative success at home, have barely managed to begin selling their products in Singapore and Malaysia. The hundreds of other independent clothing companies in the archipelago nation are not doing nearly that well.

This is not a case of literal domination, though. These brands have little direct power over Indonesian designers. Rather, these transnational companies compose a matrix of global brands that assert more and more dominion into the daily lives of Indonesian youth. They dominate the aesthetic landscape of Indonesia, its roadways, its malls, its billboards, its television stations and its Internet content. These brands are all around them, and compose the very fabric of contemporary life. "They are who we are," Dendy told me.

Modern life has become so deeply saturated with international brands that they are integral to the very way contemporary youth conceive of themselves. And not only in the sense that Appadurai delineates, offering glimpses into new "possible lives" (Appaduari 1996: 53), but in the sense of establishing a measure of their own deprivation, a recognition of how little they have in comparison to similarly situated youth in other places. Dendy, Marin, and Ade are comfortably middle class. They are not the poorest of the poor by any means, but they are not the richest of the rich, either. They have a relatively decent economic position by Indonesian standards and are well educated, but by world standards are barely middle class. And these are the most successful among indie designers. The vast majority of them remain well below the poverty line by the reckoning of any industrialized nation. They may be able to afford a cell phone (or two) and a motorbike, but, like Ade, they still tend to live in bleak, student housing units well after graduation, many surviving on less than US$2 a day.

The young Indonesian designers I met while carrying out my fieldwork do their best to live a cosmopolitan lifestyle, of fast food and designer clothes, imported music and fashion, albeit while maintaining something of an ironic, hipster positionality in relation to all these things, but even for Dendy and Marin, their access is still limited. Most young people involved in the Indonesian indie scene can't afford cable television or subscriptions to foreign magazines. Very few have ever left the country. Many don't even own a TV, most don't own a computer, and they still get most of their music through swapping MP3s and burning CDs. Most of them have to rent Internet access by the hour, or share computers with friends and colleagues to keep costs down. This can make cutting and pasting a painfully slow process.

Indonesian indie designers, then, are both empowered and constrained by their middle-class status. They have more money than the average Indonesian, with some degree of access to personal computers, the Internet, foreign media, and the resources of production. But they retain a marginal position in the global economy, particularly the global fashion economy, where Indonesia remains merely an anonymous manufacturing base for outsourced production. They occupy an uncomfortable middle ground between "here" and "elsewhere," the "traditional" and the "modern," the "first" and the "third" world. They can observe global youth cultures from afar, but they are not yet full participants within them. It is a frustrating position, and it speaks volumes about why Indonesian designers do the kind of work they do.

Tributes from Afar

Hamid Ariwinata, like Ade, grew up in Pekanbaru in Sumatra, listening to bands like Motörhead, Metallica, and Slayer. He liked the hard stuff, music with attitude and grit, theatrical atmospherics composed of power chords and screams. It is the kind of music that makes you feel powerful, he told me, like you can do anything. Indonesia, he said, has yet to produce bands like that, and so Hamid has always preferred stuff from the United States and the UK, the old guard of metal, with their loud, abrasive sound and larger-than-life personae. He started growing his hair long in his early teens, joined the headbanger army, those thousands of metal fans scattered throughout Indonesia, and indeed the rest of the world, decked out in a common uniform of black T-shirts and faded jeans. Music was a big part of his self-concept back then. It still is.

For Hamid and his metal-fan friends, though, being a fan just wasn't enough. He wanted to be part of the music in a more direct way, to adopt for himself something of the kind of power such bands emitted. He wanted to be more like his idols, he told me, to "have a strong character and image" that "endures" (*tetap jalan*) and gives other people a frame of reference for understanding who he is and what he's all about. Those of his friends with enough financial resources to do so scraped together whatever instruments they could and began playing in bands. The rest of them just borrowed their instruments from those friends. That's what Hamid had to do. His parents were civil servants, middle-class by local reckoning, but by no means well off. Like most kids in his position, for Hamid sharing resources was just a fact of life (Gerke 2000).

And it worked out okay for him. He played with friends, and practiced when he could. The only trouble was that he was never much of a musician. "I just didn't have any talent," he reported, remorsefully. He took up the guitar briefly, but the strings left his fingers stinging and his ego bruised. He tried singing, but couldn't muster up much of a voice. Eventually, he came to the conclusion that he just wasn't cut out to play music. It was a sad realization, he told me, but it turned out to be a blessing in disguise.

Hamid moved to Yogyakarta in the late 1990s to study economics at UII (the Indonesian Islamic University, and my host institution in Indonesia in 2006–2007). He wasn't all that interested in economics, but his parents—always pragmatic about such things—felt it was an appropriate course of study for someone of his social stature. He wasn't a great student, he admits, but university life provided plenty of opportunities to pursue other passions, most significantly music. He got involved in the local hard rock and metal scene, became friends with bands, went to countless gigs, and spent his evenings lounging around distros such as Reddoor and Slackers.

A number of his friends at the time were beginning to get involved in clothing design, and Hamid would watch them assemble images on Corel Draw. He peered over their shoulders, trying to figure out how to do it himself, and eventually began tinkering with the program. He said to himself, "If other people can [do this] why can't I?" and explained to me that, "everyone is capable [of designing] if they are willing to learn." Over the course of several months of often-frustrating late nights at his friends' boarding houses, he became quite adept at using the Corel Graphics suite, and he experimented with doing posters for his friends' bands. He went on to design album cover art, fliers, and other band merchandise, all in the grand tradition of heavy metal. His work featured lots of skulls and crossbones, decomposing skeletons and coiled snakes. Putting together such pieces took up more and more of his time, until Hamid decided, finally, to drop out of school and make design his full-time occupation.

When one of his friends opened Triggers Syndicate several years back, and he asked Hamid to come on board as the clothing designer, Hamid jumped at the chance. It felt like he finally knew what he wanted to do with his life. His parents weren't too thrilled with this decision, but then, that tends to be the way of things. "At first, my parents questioned it all," he explained, "but now they support me. I was able to show them that I could support myself." In fact, Hamid began to be able to support himself pretty well, bringing in a respectable 3 million rupiah a month (roughly US$312, more than the starting salary of the average civil servant). His parents saw that he was doing well and seemed happy, and eventually they even gave their consent. "They always taught me," Hamid explained, "that you can do whatever you want, so long as you're willing to accept the consequences of it." Hamid was willing, and the consequences didn't turn out to be all that bad. His brother Emil is now the store manager of Triggers Syndicate. The shop is becoming one of Yogya's best-known distros.

The main theme of Hamid's design, as he describes it, is "rock." All of his work "reeks of music" (*berbau musik*). It borrows from the aesthetics of hard rock and heavy metal, occasionally even snippets from his favorite songs. He has channeled his passion for heavy sounds into a visual medium and describes his work as a form of "tribute" to the rock bands and street brands that have had a significant influence over his personal aesthetic.

But more than that, he sees his work as an educational medium, a way of teaching the next generation of music and fashion fans a little something about the inspirations behind what they wear and listen to, the "roots" of the style, as he describes it. "Well, not teach exactly," Hamid corrects himself, characteristically humble in his personal ambitions. "More like just show them."

> I see a lot of kids with a skater or metal image, but if I ask them, "How come you wear that? [Or] what's that a picture of? Do you even have any idea?" They're like, "Oh, it's just that everyone else is wearing it, so I wear it too." I want to create designs that let them know [what it's about].

One of his recent T-shirt designs, for example, features the famous skeleton ripping through a wall motif developed by the legendary Southern California skatewear company Powell Peralta. On the wall itself, he has scrawled the names of bands he likes, groups he considers deeply influential to the Indonesian indie scene, and which he feels the younger generation should be aware of. These include such American punk and hardcore standards as Suicidal Tendencies, Black Flag, and the Misfits. Beneath the image, he has printed "Inspired from Powell 'Ripper.'"

Another line of clothes he has recently completed includes a series of T-shirts and jackets inspired by favorite rock songs. To compose this line, Hamid would first look for inspiration from his substantial CD, cassette, and MP3 collection, then he would select a song he liked, and play it repeatedly until it triggered some sort of visual idea. He then took to the Internet to look for images that could approximately represent his vision. Yahoo proved a reliable place to look, as did Google Image, a whole set of rock T-shirt websites, some graffiti art websites, and the websites of specific companies, such as the California-based skate/punk clothing brand Atticus. When he found what he was looking for—a pointing skeletal hand, perhaps, a scantily clad pin-up, or a cobra ready to strike—he would attempt to recreate the image using Corel Draw.

"Obviously, if you're talking about originality," Hamid told me, as we sat in the black and white-checkerboard backroom of Triggers Syndicate, with Hamid squatting in the floor in his signature knock-off skinny jeans and snugly fitting, black metal band T-shirt, "I can't say I'm original, because I can't even draw … I'm not the one who draws these things. I take pictures [from somewhere else]. But not just randomly, not just any old thing that I have no connection with. And not without changing it." This distinction is critical to Hamid. It is what separates his own appropriative practice from those less-invested, would-be designers who sample haphazardly from the annals of youth culture, and from "pirates" who wholesale copy the designs of major labels. It creates a more substantial link with what he is depicting and who he is. It demonstrates his own engaged awareness of cultural trends. He went on, in a spitfire delivery of slangy Indonesian that took a great deal of concentration to follow. The resulting design, he explained, is more than the image he's "inspired" by. It takes on a new composition. It becomes something else.

For Hamid, then, the practice of cut-and-paste is very much about his own relationship with that which he depicts. For one, his rock-themed design is a way to participate in a musical culture he has long been involved with as a fan and enthusiast but never able to contribute to in a more direct way. It aligns him with a musical lineage beyond the range of the archipelago, and gives him an honorary place within its ranks. For another, it converts him from one of many "mere" consumers of such cultural products into a kind of expert, a connoisseur with knowledge and understanding beyond those other kids whom he seeks to educate about the "roots." Above all, it establishes his place as a creative contributor to this culture, helping determine how it is received, experienced, and understood locally.

As a designer, then, he has been able to assume a more proactive stance toward the cultural products in which he had invested so deeply. He has repositioned himself within the hierarchy of cultural production. Through his "tributes," he leaves his own mark on those images that inspired him. He becomes an active participant in those processes of cultural production on whose sidelines he used to stand.

Designer Vandalism

Hamid's work is a pastiche of heavy metal and rock-themed imagery. It mimics an international repertoire of rock music tropes, assembling them together into new compositions. But it does so without any of the presumed neutrality described by Jameson.

Bricolage like his simply can't help but take a stand. It always positions its practitioner in some sort of new relationship with that which it reproduces. In the most basic sense, bricolage of this sort involves a reconstitution of the consumer as a producer. Ade has placed himself within a pantheon of internationally recognized designers by appropriating their work within his own. Hamid has aligned himself with a global, heavy metal underground by placing its imagery, and lyrics, within his designs.

And sometimes, this re-positioning through cut-and-paste takes on an explicitly oppositional stance, as well. Consider, for example, Unkl347's "Xerox" logo design. It features their "bowl" logo, very familiar to many young Indonesians, disintegrating into pixilated dots. This is a blatant imitation of Xerox's trademark "X," but just in case you missed the reference, the designers at Unkl347 printed the word "Xerox" beneath the image. The effect is jarring. The viewer recognizes the symbol of one brand exhibiting characteristics of another. It creates a momentary visual confusion. Unkl347 appears to have morphed into another brand. They have possessed it, taken it over. And in the process, the world's biggest supplier of copying machines has become little more than a copy itself. They are image fodder for some tiny Indonesian company. They are fair game.

This is distro-label design at its closest to "culture jamming" (Lasn 1999), to anti-commercial agit-prop launching visual tirades against the tyranny of the market. This is designer *détournement* (Debord 1995), "the theft of aesthetic artifacts from their [original] contexts and their diversion into contexts of one's own devise" (Marcus 1989: 168). Like the streetwear designs that inspired it, it turns a corporate logo into a form of personal expression.

This work is irreverent, satirical, even occasionally biting in its commentary. But it is not exactly critique. Its relationship with what it reworks and remixes is much more complex than that. Dendy's work often displays a peculiar reverence for the very thing he appropriates. It pays homage, even as it denies a company's singular right to control its own images. Take another example from Unkl347's collection. In this design, the 347 bowl logo is faded and cracked, some of its resolution lost as in a Xerox transfer. Below the logo is written, this time in past-tense verb form, "XE-ROX**ED**," with the "ED" highlighted. Here, Unkl347 seems to be doing a couple of things: (1) Acknowledging their own debased position in relationship to a global company, their own status as something of a cheap copy; and (2) converting a global brand into a transitive verb, something to be done, carried out, enacted, performed.

XEROXED

Figure 9 One of Unkl347's Xerox designs, featuring their own modified bowl logo.

For Dendy, to Xerox is to take hold of, to make something one's own. It is a tactic of the disenfranchised and left behind. Unkl347 may be a copycat company, they proclaim through this design, but it is a company that turns that status into a term of empowerment.

This is not piracy, Dendy insists. Indonesia has plenty of pirates, a long, and sometimes sordid history of black market entrepreneurs employing the counterfeit as a path out of poverty (see Siegel 1998). Indonesia, after all, has a poor record of copyright enforcement, and taking advantage of the lack of oversight, thousands of Indonesians have gone into business reproducing other peoples' creative labors. The tourist districts of Kuta, Bali, and Yogyakarta, Java, for instance, are chockfull of imitation designer goods and barely redesigned commercial motifs. There are even some knock-off clothing manufacturers operating in similar industrial spaces just down the road from Unkl347. Unkl347, however, doesn't count itself among them. Dendy has nothing personal against pirates. As anthropologist Siegel argues, Indonesians in general have long seen the fake as a "place of possibility" (Siegel 1998: 58), and have accepted piracy as inevitable, even desirable, given the economic circumstances of the island nation. Dendy feels more or less the same way. Pirates are just people who want to support their families, he says. But pirates, Dendy explains, have no real critical intent behind what they do, and no political vision or personal urgency. They imitate, or to use the Indonesian term in vogue for the practice, *nyontek*. It's a term with connotations of both copying and cheating, and it implies a lack of personal investment, a merely pragmatic incentive. Unkl347, however, invests a great deal in what and how they appropriate. "As for us," says Dendy, "we are conscious (*sadar*) of it. And being conscious is good, you know. Now if you're not conscious [like the pirates], that's when it becomes dangerous."

Unkl347 not only choose the designs they appropriate with careful deliberation, they want their customers to know they took their material from somewhere else, and thus, they make their methodology explicit, often visually cite their sources. "We even go so far as to acknowledge it [in our designs] so that people know," says Dendy. One of their designs, for instance, features an almost exact copy of the album cover for "Goo" by the New York art punk band Sonic Youth. A young, modish couple in bowl cuts and sunglasses smoke cigarettes while they lounge in each other's arms. Beside the image, the original handwritten words "I stole my sister's boyfriend" have been replaced with "I stole my Sonic Youth."

Through such work, Dendy and other designers like him engage in what could be called brand vandalism, or "brandalism" (Moore 2007), tagging corporate logos and foreign album covers the way urban gangs mark their territory in the inner city, and declaring in the process the world of international commerce their own home turf. Designers like Dendy contest the very hegemony of transnational corporations over youth trends, taking their designs for their own and manipulating them for their own purposes. They declare the cultural products of transnational capitalism as public domain, rejecting the very idea that such imagery are the exclusive property of their producers at all. Dendy takes recognizable corporate logos and prints his own brand name over them. Ade takes his images from design books, online pamphlets and brochures, and manipulates them for his own use. Hamid borrows from album covers and rock websites, Marin from the trends of Singapore and Malaysia. These designers routinely take other designers' work, chop them up and reassemble them, then put their own stamp on them. And they do so openly, without embarrassment or shame.

One of Ade's creations, for instance, an asphalt-gray hooded sweatshirt he wears all the time, features a series of repeated yellow silhouettes of his favorite mangled, unicorn-deer motif. In the center of the shirt is a bold yellow caption reading "YOU ARE graphic manipulator TARGET." No one, Ade seems to be announcing with his design, is safe from graphic manipulation. If you venture into Indonesian waters, the warning reads, prepare to have your work stolen. But unlike Dendy or Hamid, Ade does not let his viewer know who the target of his attack is. The source material of his work remains anonymous. Authorship is denied.

Back in the late 1970s and early 1980s, it became a common rhetorical move among poststructuralist thinkers to pronounce the "death of the author," the end of that vanity of the Romantic era that an individual can compose a work solely of their own labor (Barthes 1977; Derrida 1988; Foucault 2002; McLeod 2005). Theorists from Barthes to Foucault set about disproving what was no doubt already an antiquated notion, dismissing grandiose claims of autonomous genius in favor of more nuanced theories about the intrinsic sociality of production (Becker 1982), the complex "intertextuality" (Bakhtin 1983) of authorship, and the "structures of feeling" (Williams 1977) in which a work is embedded and out of which it emerges. Cut-and-paste designers such as Ade, Hamid, and Dendy are engaged in a similar project, pronouncing through their work the death of the designer, that vanity of the corporate age that imagery, once created, belongs forever to the holder of its copyright. They see the very concept of originality as problematic, an import from the industrialized world that imposes its obsession with ownership on everyone else. Their cut-and-paste designs restore sociality to the act of production, convert it from a solitary, singular event into an ongoing visual conversation between designers.

We Are the Brands We Consume

Anthropologists have found resistance in nearly every nook and cranny of contemporary lives (Abu-Lughod 1990; Brown 1996). Inspired by such influential thinkers as De Certeau (1984) and Scott (1985), we have had a long, and well-documented, love affair with "the romance of resistance" (Abu-Lughod 1990). But despite a rather large body of critiques against the over-use of the concept, talk of resistance continues to pop up all over the place in ethnographic work. We have yet to come up with an alternative explanation sufficient for making sense of such deconstructive acts of bricolage that are becoming increasingly common in the Information Age (Castells 2000), the remixes of popular songs, the mash-ups and video collages that animate the Internet, and the cut-and-paste designs of Indonesian indie streetwear.

There is, I would argue, an element of resistance to what distro-label designers do, sometimes explicit, sometimes more subtle, but we have to be careful about assigning resistance too liberally to youth aesthetic practice. Indie designer resistance is always an ambivalent resistance, what Kondo, following Hutcheons, has termed "complicitous critique" (Kondo 1997). Indie designers uphold, often even glorify, the source material of their designs. Unkl347's Xerox logo, for instance, both takes over the international brand and declares the brand something worth taking over. Dendy's work, like Hamid's, is often deeply reverential of what he borrows from.

Just as an emphasis on bricolage as an expression of the cultural logic of late capitalism misses a great deal of its subtlety, to call such work "resistant," then, also misses the mark. The principle motivation of designers like Dendy, Hamid, Marin, and Ade is not so much critiquing the source material from which they borrow as with asserting a kind of ownership over it, appropriating commercial imagery in efforts to reproduce themselves as active global citizens. Sometimes, the reconstituted aesthetic objects they produce take on subversive meanings, as in Dendy's Xerox design. Sometimes, they work to reproduce or reinforce an existing meaning, as in Hamid's tributes to the giants of heavy metal. The most compelling feature of indie fashion bricolage, then, is not its utility as a mode of resistance, but the way it re-positions individuals in relationship to those materials from which they sample.

Bricolage is a means of claiming and asserting authority over cultural forms produced by other, generally (though not always) more powerful social actors in other places and other times. It is a technology of cultural production, and what it produces is not only a new set of meanings in association with a borrowed image or idea, but a new relationship between that image and its bricoleur.

Deleuze and Guattari, in their seminal, and notoriously opaque work *Anti-Oedipus*, describe bricolage as "the ability to rearrange fragments continually in new and different patterns or configurations" (1996: 7). It is, for them, a form of production that grafts production onto production that indeed carries out the productive project indefinitely, forever forestalling the possibility of conclusion. In bricolage, there is no end-product to be finally consumed. And there is no clear distinction between production and consumption, either; there is only a continual cycle of production and reproduction. Bricolage, then, thwarts any stabilization of the relations of production into a hierarchy of producer and consumer. It muddies the water, complicates and complexifies, and restores a fluid, frenzied nature to the activity of production. And for this reason, bricolage is the key productive activity of the contemporary "schizophrenic" subject, Deleuze and Guattari's idealized "nomadic" agent, who refuses to be pinned down and resists being fully integrated into any one regime of power.

When we see bricolage in this light, as a productive practice that maintains the activity of production indefinitely, that instills it with a vital sociality, a continual cultural revision, it becomes fairly easy to understand why aesthetic forms that privilege bricolage have become so widespread in our global capitalist era. It is not simply that borrowing from other sources makes capitalism more efficient or provides ready-made models for greedy manufacturers. Rather, bricolage has become so widespread because it empowers consumers—the driving force of late capitalism—to be more than simply consumers. It weaves them into a massive web of dynamic producer/consumers, cultural remixers, and DIYers, and furthers a fundamentally inclusive process of production. Technologies like Corel Draw, or mash-up programs on the Internet give consumers a means of asserting more direct control over what they consume: to affect it, contribute to it, or simply take some sort of direct ownership over it.

Cut-and-paste techniques complicate the very notion of innovation itself, the conceit of originality, independence, and creative autonomy. They may not threaten the smooth functioning of the capitalist economy, or even the continuation of global corporate domination of apparel design and manufacture, but they do challenge the power relationships operating within it. They destabilize the distinctions between producer and consumer, designer and knock-off artist, creator and remixer, and ultimately, as the next chapter will argue, global and local.

–6–

On Site and Sound: Music and Borders in a DIY World

Kita tak kenal Pancasila. Kita hanya kenal Punkasila.

We don't know the five principles of the Indonesian state ideology. We only know the principles of punk.

—Armada Racun, "Drakula," from the album *La Peste* (2010)

Here's Three Chords and a Nirvana CD. Now Go and Form a Band!

For rock critic and indie music historian Michael Azerrad, the American "indie movement was changed forever when [Nirvana's] *Nevermind* hit number one on the *Billboard* charts" (Azerrad 2001: 8). The "sprawling cooperative" (Azerrad 2001: 3) of zines, bands, labels, radio stations, and alternative venues that made up the American indie music scene was thrust into the spotlight, capturing, for the first time, and with all its scruffy, self-consciously unkempt splendor still intact, the attention of mainstream America. There was no turning back. Suddenly, major labels were scouring the seediest Seattle nightclubs for new talent, and when those were exhausted, sending A&R emissaries to every conceivable indie enclave for fresh blood. Small indie outfits from Athens, Georgia; Olympia, Washington; Omaha, Nebraska; and other, once exceedingly unlikely sources of new Top-40 acts were appearing on the covers of major magazines, shooting videos for MTV, trading in their beat-up vans for luxury tour buses, and searching painstakingly for some loophole in their indie ideology that would allow them to reconcile their newfound success with their anti-commercial rhetoric. In this narrative, the once carefully policed boundary between indie "authenticity" and pop culture vacuousness had been irreparably breeched, and indie culture, for better or for worse, would never be the same.

I have my doubts about this story. It is simply too clean and neat, and it is so commonly told in indie circles as to have become something of a cliché. In truth, the line between indie and mainstream has always been much blurrier than this story would allow. There were dozens of border crossings in both directions for decades before Nirvana, often in much subtler forms, and there were numerous "break-through" bands before Nirvana, as well, from The Sex Pistols to Suede, crystallizing momentarily in public consciousness before fading back into semi-obscurity. Nonetheless, the scale of Nirvana's success was unprecedented for an indie band. They brought a great deal of attention to "alternative" music and fashion, and gave a face and voice to the Generation X so many journalists and pop psychologists had been theorizing about for months beforehand.

And there's no question that *Nevermind* had an enormous impact on Indonesia, as well. Where it allegedly brought a thriving American underground to its symbolic end—and subsequent resurrection in even more "alternative" form—in Indonesia, it seems to have supplied a template for a whole new underground. David Tarigan, founder of the Jakarta indie label Aksara Records, claims that when he and his friends first saw Nirvana perform on Indonesian state television (TVRI) in 1991, it felt like something of a revelation. "Just imagine," he told me, as we chatted in his recording studio in South Jakarta in 2007. "What happened in '91 in Indonesia was probably a lot like what happened in the Western world in '77, you know, the punk explosion."

> It was like the kids suddenly realized, "Oh, actually, you don't have to be [professional musicians] to be in a band." You don't have to be that great at playing guitar. You don't have to be this or that. Before '91 the whole idea of being in a band seemed really remote . . . but when we saw Nirvana on TVRI [playing] "Smells Like Teen Spirit" . . . [We thought] wow this is crazy, a band with only four chords and these nihilistic lyrics! . . . It taught us a whole new attitude. [We said to each other], "Hey tomorrow, let's form a band, huh!"

There were a lot of cover bands at first, David recalls. Bands developed their chops replicating the sounds of prominent grunge, punk, and metal groups they heard on the newly christened MTV Indonesia or discovered through cassettes passed hand-to-hand among friends. Then, as their skill and their confidence improved, these bands began playing their own songs, mostly fast, aggressive, and simple. Acts like Puppen, Full of Hate, and Koil assaulted their Bandung audiences with dense blasts of noise. They stuck to those heavy, abrasive genres that felt the most appropriate for the times, the most equipped to sound the alarms of revolt and rebellion. And the lyrics only contributed to the mood, calling for an end to tyranny and critiquing the New Order regime for its corruption, nepotism, and enthusiastic selling out of the Indonesian people to the aims of global corporations (see Wallach 2003). The end of the Suharto era was coming fast, and these bands wanted to be part of its demise. They furiously recorded their albums in the lo-fi, truly DIY fashion of old-school anarcho-punk (see O'Connor 2008), using whatever media were available to them, often four-tracks rented by the hour at low-brow local studios, or even just home cassette recorders. What they lacked in subtlety, the early Indonesian underground more than made up for in enthusiasm and volume.

This was not, however, always the most cutting edge of music. Many underground bands quite un-self-consciously promoted themselves as the local version of an international act. The hugely popular pop-punk group Superman Is Dead, for instance, launched themselves into the musical ether back in the late 1990s as the Balinese version of Green Day, then reinvented themselves several years later as the Balinese Social Distortion. Cherry Bombshell was something like Bandung's The Cranberries. Koil was its Nine Inch Nails. Bands tended to wear their influences on their sleeves, to dress in imitation of their idols, and to carefully study and mimic their antics on stage as accurately as they could. They were punk rock neophytes. They wanted to get it right. On occasion, they even seemed to enter into the domain of accidental parody. Balinese bands like The Hydrant and Suicidal Sinatra enacted a Stray Cats–filtered rendition of 1950s rockabilly that bordered on cabaret, complete with stand-up basses, greased-back pompadours, and between-song hair-combing sessions. Bandung's Gabba Gabba were one step away from being a fairground tribute band version of The Ramones.

But this, too, began to change, as Indonesian young people gained greater and greater access to informational resources about new sounds and styles. Like the American indie scene in whose footsteps it followed, Indonesia's indie underground started out blunt, simple, and alienating, and gradually diversified into a far more inclusive, and difficult to characterize, set of genres. David Tarigan, once again, attributes this initial push toward diversification to the opening of mass media, and, in particular, to local radio programs showcasing alternative bands (see also Barendregt and Zanten 2002), and newly imported shows such as *Alternative Nation* on MTV.

"It's like Blur [the melodic Britpop group popular in the 1990s] opened up our eyes," he said. "Our [musical] attitudes became way more eclectic. Music doesn't have to be just one thing [we realized]. It can be hard; it can also be soft . . . And so a lot of bands like that started popping up." Britpop-influenced indie bands like Pure Saturday, The Milo, and Sajama Cut began playing alongside punk, metal, and hardcore acts on crowded, rent-by-hour stages. Other bands dug up used analog synthesizers and added new wave elements to their sound. Even others began incorporating elements of jazz, folk, reggae, and bossa nova into theirs.

Then, when the Internet became readily available in Bandung back in around 1996, the musical floodgates were thrown wide open. "With insane ease," recalls David, "we were able to get information that we didn't even ask for." The Internet supplied a ready means for thousands of young people, at least those middle-class college and high school kids with enough time and money to regularly access it, to become hip to international aesthetics in real time. Plus, the increased availability of computer hardware, combined with open-source and pirated recording software, enabled a larger and larger number of bands to begin recording their own music on their own terms, either at home, or at one of a number of newly established independent recording studios popping up toward the end of the millennium (Barengregt and Zanten 2002). A wider variety of bands, occupying a growing number of musical niches, were able to have their music heard by a significant population, no matter how bizarre or novel their sound may have been.

The marked tendency of indie bands became musical pastiche, idiosyncratic assemblages of international sounds. Cranial Incisored hit the Yogyakarta scene in the early 2000s as a brash hybrid of death metal and bebop; Airport Radio as a fusion of down-tempo, ambient, and pop. The Jakarta band The Brandals describe themselves as "rockabilly mixed with 12 bar blues, punk rock and attitude" (from the liner notes of their eponymous first album), Bandung's Hollywood Nobody as "bossa nova, jazz, and indie." "Bands actually sound too eclectic now," claims Iyo of Pure Saturday and *Ripple* magazine. Gone were the days of blatant imitation, the efforts to precisely reproduce foreign styles on local shores. Indonesian indie musicians began to draw from all sorts of sources, to combine styles and sounds into new, often-unexpected configurations.

Gone, too, was the explicit political content of earlier underground music (see also Barendregt and Zanten 2002). This was music about music, music engaged in a continual game of references with other music. It seemed to revel in its diversity as if it were an end in itself.

This does not, however, mean that indie music stopped being political. Its political orientation simply changed with the times. When the New Order government fell from power at the end of the 1990s, the politics of indie music began to shift from a politics of regime change to a politics of access and mobility. What mattered to indie scenesters was being part of something larger than Indonesia, not simply attacking the Indonesian state. The indie music emerging from the early 2000s on was above all about autonomy (Baredreft and Zanten 2002; Wallach 2003)—from governmental meddling, from corporate control, and from the borders and boundaries that prevent easy movement across places and times. Indie musicians began to assert their eclecticism as evidence of their very independence.

Popular and academic discussions of DIY and independent music have tended to focus on the threat it poses (or fails to pose) to the existing business model of the international music industry (Shank 1994; McLeod 2005; Fonarow 2006; Mason 2008; Lessig 2009). Authors express anxiety over the use of indie music in television commercials for Subarus, question the ability of bands to define the terms of their exploitation, and ponder just how independent indie labels that feed their most successful bands to the majors can really claim to be. This work makes some important points. To some extent, however, it misses a larger one. The music industry was always as much a symbol as an explicit target of indie practice. To indie bands it represented power—over cultural production, over creative practice, and over the very constitution of personal taste. As Azerrad puts it, "Rebelling against the major labels was a metaphor for rebelling against the system in general" (Azerrad 2001: 9). Being independent of the majors, thus, was as much an existential as a practical claim. It was never really about the music industry. It was about seizing control over creative expression, and by extension, forging one's own, autonomous way of being and living in the world.

This chapter takes DIY musical practice beyond the rather tired, and stubbornly complicated question of its independence from major labels, exploring the way musical aesthetics become implicated in the reproduction and refutation of power relations more generally. It demonstrates the contributions of indie musicians to the very re-making of identity and place. Indie music, the chapter concludes, has become an important medium for the deterritorialization of the self from colony and nation-state, a means of forging new alliances, networks, and commercial flows that challenge the governing bodies of global politics as much as the inflexible structure of an old-fashioned music industry. DIY, in music as in fashion, is about establishing self-sovereignty and claiming one's rightful place on the world stage, as a producer of culture, not just another marginalized recipient biding time in the global peripheries.

I'll begin my discussion with one of indie Indonesia's biggest success stories to date, a band that has become something of the poster child for a new wave of Indonesian independent music: the Bandung-based "indie pop" group Mocca.[1]

This Is Not World Music!

Mocca has accomplished something few other Indonesian recording artists have managed to do. They have reached an international audience, selling more than 150,000 copies of their first album alone, and touring through Singapore, Malaysia, Thailand, Korea, and Japan, without either signing onto a major label or marketing themselves as an "ethnic," "traditional," or "world music" act. In fact, listening to their sugary, English-language songs, which combine elements of crooner jazz, swing, and folk with lo-fi indie rock, there is little to identify them as Indonesian at all. Songs like "Dear Diary" or "Once Upon a Time," which propelled them to fame in their home country and beyond, could have been written nearly anywhere by nearly anyone. That, of course, is the point. "I want people to respond to the music first," guitarist and song-writer for the group Riko Prayitno told me, "then later think to themselves, 'Oh wow! This is from Indonesia?'"

Like a number of contemporary pop and rock bands to emerge out of the Indonesian indie scene in recent years, Mocca has stripped their sound and their image of overt ethnic signifiers. They experiment with a wide range of musical sources, but never those associated with their own backgrounds. They sing in English. Their lyrics stick principally to broad human themes unspecific to time and place. And in so doing, they defy easy categorization for consumption by a niche audience of "world music" fans. They not only don't play up their ethnicity, they drop it altogether like a bad habit or an outdated trend. And why not? these young musicians assert. It's not like kids in Bandung grow up listening to *degung* anymore.[2] These are children of a globalized world, raised on MTV and the Internet, and they insist on being taken seriously on the same terms as other international pop artists. If Swedish indie pop bands like Club 8 and Radio Dept. are not expected to sing in Swedish and play the *nyckelharpa*, then why should Mocca don sarongs and play kettle gongs?

It's not as if Mocca is ashamed of who they are or where they come from, though. Over the last decade, they have stepped forward as one of the most prominent public faces of the Indonesian indie scene, doing more than just about any other band to instill local pride in its music. They have, in fact, like a number of other bands from the scene, become something of informal ambassadors for an Indonesian "buy local" movement, participating in events, expositions, and workshops that incite youth from all over the archipelago to "support the local brand revolution!"[3]

But let's not confuse our terms. The "local" Mocca advocates is not the "local" they grew up with, the cut-and-paste construction of region and ethnicity taught in schools, paraded in public festivals, or broadcast on government television channels. And their "local" is not the "local" of a continuous indigenous tradition, either, a conception of space and place passed down from one generation to the next. Instead, theirs is a "local" reinvented and re-imagined by contemporary Indonesian youth, a "local" dissociated from the classificatory schema of nation-state and colony, and built instead from the tropes and typologies of transnational popular culture.

There has been a marked tendency in anthropology, ethnomusicology, and related disciplines to read the "local" as if it were a kind of default mode of resistance against the hegemonic forces of global capitalism. By sticking with tradition despite pressures to "modernize" (Kingston 1991; Adams 1998; Tsing 1993), or hybridizing imported cultural forms with indigenous genres (Miller 1992; Appadurai 1996; Condry 2001; Diehl 2002; Kulick and Willson 2002), marginalized ethnic groups and citizens of developing countries maintain regional distinctiveness in the face of an emergent transnational order. In many anthropological texts, "localization" appears as a sort of "weapon of the weak" (Scott 1985), a form of insulation against an encroaching neoliberal regime. Although most anthropologists long ago discarded a theoretical framework of cultural imperialism (Schiller 1976; Hamelink 1983; Mattelart 1983) as simply "too blunt an instrument" (Timothy D. Taylor, personal communication, 2008) to describe the complexity, ambiguity, and ambivalence (Bhabha 1994) of the postcolonial encounter, it lives on in many ethnographic accounts as the implied threat of integration. Localization is read as a nearly heroic act of refusal.

This, however, is not always how localization is experienced on the ground. Appadurai reminds us that there is "a moment of colonization" in locality building (1996: 183), particularly in a case such as Indonesia's, where the territory of the modern nation-state was superimposed onto a Dutch colony and trade network. As I argued in chapter 1, convincing the incredibly diverse, 300-plus ethnic groups of the archipelago that they are all part of the same community is a massive task that remains decidedly unfinished. There is a violence embedded within this process, an imposition. And for hip, educated, middle-class youth in relatively cosmopolitan cities like Bandung, West Java, the kind of people who form indie bands, the "local" of the nation-state often feels like a trap, a barrier between Indonesia and the rest of the world. Bands like Mocca find ethnic, regional, and national traditions untenable as resources for creative expression, as such traditions serve to further isolate them from global youth culture and bring them into line instead with nationalist projects toward which they often feel distrust and disconnection. Such bands, then, tend not so much to "localize" transnational aesthetics, as previous anthropologists might have suggested, mixing them with indigenous cultural forms in order to instill them with local meaning and significance; rather, they use transnational aesthetics to challenge existing constructions of locality, supplanting the "local" of the national and colonial past with a chosen, empowering positionality grounded in a dialectical relationship with the global.

Nostalgia for Other Peoples' Memories

I first met Mocca's manager, Buddy, one day in July 2007 when I was hanging out at Setiabudi, Ahmad Marin's family home, which he had converted into a production, warehouse, and distribution site for both FFWD Records and his clothing label Monik/Celtic. Setiabudi is the Bandung indie scene's unofficial capitol. Spend enough time there, I had discovered, and I would eventually meet almost everyone who had anything to do with indie music or fashion in the city.

I was watching a couple of the employees iron shrinkwrap around a stack of merchandise piled up on the patio (The S.I.G.I.T.'s new album, *Visible Idea of Perfection*) when Buddy came over to chat. He was a laidback kind of guy, with a shaved head, dirty jeans, and a casual, plain white T-shirt, and we talked about Mocca's touring schedule, the recent use of one of their songs in a Korean television commercial,

Figure 10 The Bandung indie pop band Mocca, one of the Indonesian indie scene's biggest success stories to date. Photo by Firman N.I.

and their hopes of breaking into an international market beyond East and Southeast Asia. He invited me and my partner Jessica to come watch Mocca rehearse the following day, and we gladly took him up on his offer.

Mocca's studio was modest, to be sure, tucked away behind a fading turquoise-blue house that had been converted into a *warung*. The carpet was peeling. The walls had been covered over in egg cartons to keep the sound in. Buddy offered us some bottles of iced tea, and we sat in folding chairs facing the instruments, and greeted the members of Mocca as they slowly filtered in.

Mocca performed their set as consummate professionals, playing with both precision and passion, and they were friendly, too, with a humility and down-to-earth quality I have seldom encountered in rock bands back home, even in those substantially less-well known than Mocca. Arina Ephipania Simangunsong, the vocalist and principle lyricist for the band, had just picked up a couple of DVDs of *The Muppet Show* that she had ordered off of Amazon.com, and she told us about how some of the inspiration for the band's sound had come from these Jim Henson productions for children. Their latest album, for instance, included a cover of the song "Sing" by The Carpenters, which Arina first encountered on the soundtrack of the children's show *Sesame Street*. She dedicated the last song in their set, "Tomorrow," from the musical *Annie,* to us.

The theme of childhood nostalgia runs deep through Mocca's music and projected image. Their latest album's CD case was shaped like a colored pencil box. Their first album's was decorated like a hardcover children's book, complete with illustrations of a little (white) girl dancing with a man in a sheep suit. Made by hand by FFWD employees, the album art evokes Lewis Carroll or Maurice Sendak, authors thoroughly outside the Indonesian literary canon. Their songs, too, written primarily by Riko with lyrics by Arina, are structured with simple melodies that echo the style of European and American kid songs. It is a decidedly soft sound, utilizing instrumentation of a guitar, an upright bass, a trumpet, drums, and a keyboard, and drawing influence from a variety of light genres from a variety of places. This is a far cry from what most people think of as DIY music, and it has little in common with the earlier sounds of the Bandung underground. It's listenable, it's likeable, and it's recorded with high-fidelity precision.

Arina grew up with this some of this stuff, watching *Sesame Street* and listening to Broadway tunes and "old standards," and to some extent Mocca's music simply reflects her own relatively privileged background, the access to Western pop culture she had from an early age, her education (in interior design from the National Institute of Technology, Bandung), and her high-level of facility with English. But the rest of it she and the other members of the band learned about from friends and through actively searching the Internet and used record bins for novel sounds. This is not the music she heard on the streets of Bandung, the sounds rising organically from the participatory culture of urban life, but a carefully selected assemblage of musical attributes that "gesture elsewhere" (Baulch 2003: 586).

Consider their song "Secret Admirer" off their first album. "Oh . . . secret admirer," Arina sings liltingly to a jazz flute and acoustic bass, "when you're around the autumn feels like summer. How come you're always messing up the weather? Just like you do to me." Putting aside for the moment that Arina is singing cute, possibly ironic lyrics in well-studied English to musical styles originating far away, the song describes seasons Indonesia does not even have. With the year divided into two moderately different tropical seasons—hot and dry and hot and wet—Indonesians like Arina can only experience autumn in other countries, or, more likely, in the fertile grounds of their book and movie-fueled imaginations. This is light, summery music, with the sweetness of a childhood ditty, the sass of a *Seventeen* magazine cover, and the postmodern tendency to "flatten" musical history into a single sonic moment (Jameson 1992). It displays many of the preoccupations with cuteness Allison and others have noted in Japanese popular culture, a fetishization of girlhood and innocence lost (McVeigh 2000; Allison 2002) that probably accounts for some of their success in East Asia. And it also displays American and English indie's pronounced nostalgia for childhood (Fonarow 2006). But one thing this music is *not* is reminiscent of life in Bandung, with its stable tropical weather system, its crowded, tree-lined streets, its vendors selling spicy rice dishes out of tents of plastic tarp. This is music nostalgic for other people's memories.

Mocca is not at all unique in the Indonesian indie scene for promoting this kind of placeless longing, though. Such *dislocated nostalgia* is common in Indonesian indie music. The Jakarta band The Adams, dressed in oppressively thick argyle sweaters with disheveled, untucked dress shirts sticking out, earth-toned pleated slacks, and black-framed glasses, recall the 1950s American dream of the good life, the early rock 'n' roll of Buddy Holly, and the British Invasion sounds of The Animals and The Yardbirds. Bali's The Hydrant, with their combed-back pompadours and cigarette packs rolled up into white T-shirt sleeves, mines American rockabilly for theirs. Yogyakarta's Southern Beach Terror, in their plain white Ts and khaki chinos, market themselves as an homage to 1960s surf guitar acts such as The Ventures and Dick Dale.

I was particularly struck by this phenomenon when I visited the office of *Rolling Stone Indonesia* magazine in Jakarta to talk about the rising indie pop stars The Upstairs with their manager Wendi Putranto, also a writer and editor for the magazine, and once the zine writer behind *Brainwashed*, an influential underground metal publication. The Upstairs, Wendi told me, burst onto the scene with their self-produced debut album in 2002. Their singer and songwriter, Jimi Multazham, had just dropped out of Jakarta's art institute (IKJ) to pursue his own, idiosyncratic tribute to the new wave sounds of 1980s pop bands such as Flock of Seagulls and Depeche Mode. With an art school sensibility, Jimi envisioned the band as a grand, vibrantly colored performance art experiment. Their live shows combine ironic rock star bravado with mindless dumb fun.

The retro theme became the principle musical and performance *konsep* of the band. They all dress in pastels, wear moptop haircuts, thick white belts, and psychedelic shirts, and era-blend mod scooter-driving aesthetics with the large, white sunglasses and furry legwarmers of 1980s MTV. The mix has worked well for them. Over the early part of the new millennium, The Upstairs rose up to become one of the biggest bands in Indonesia, with their second, full-length album released on Warner Music.

The Upstairs' wild "retro" look and fun nostalgic sound is continually cited as their appeal in popular magazines and television shows. Everyone is crazy for their throw-back fashion. But the thing is, this is not a nostalgic look or sound for many Indonesians. During its heyday in the 1980s, new wave got close to no airtime on Indonesia's government-monitored radio stations and was difficult to find in cassette shops. To the fans that made The Upstairs big, this music was fresh and new, not old and reminiscent.

And it wasn't reminiscent for Jimi, either. Born in the 1970s, Jimi was raised on a musical diet of rock and metal. He didn't discover new wave until art school in his 20s, where so many of his friends from IKJ were digging into retro sounds and forming bands of their own—White Shoes and the Couples Company, Naif, and The Adams, among them (Putranto 2006). He got into punk, then post-punk, then indie rock, and began to trace the musical lineages of contemporary bands he was into. So many of the bands he liked cited groups like Devo, Joy Division, and New Order as influences in magazine interviews or on their MySpace profiles, that Jimi decided to check out their music for himself. He liked what he found, and so now The Upstairs are bringing their brand of other peoples' nostalgia to the rest of Indonesia.

As if reversing the terms of the "imperialist nostalgia" anthropologist Renato Rosaldo has famously discussed (Rosaldo 1989), The Upstairs, as with Mocca before them, seems to long for the childhood musical experiences that form the backdrop of other peoples' bands, for access to those varieties of cultural and symbolic capital (Bourdieu 1977; 1984) that afford a dominant position in the pop culture hierarchy to groups from America, Europe, and (occasionally) Japan. These bands exhibit a kind of fascination with Western pop culture, both past and present, which belies their own position as relatively well-off kids in a country still on the margins of the world economy, a lifestyle that, as Liechty has put it, "is simultaneously the object of intense local desire and always [just] out of reach" (Liechty 2003: xi).

Indie musicians, then, in aligning themselves with an internationalist aesthetic, adopting other people's musical nostalgia as their own, work to carry out a distinctly "middle-class project" (Liechty 2003) of hipster retro-historicizing. They actively position themselves within a shifting hierarchy and an evolving lineage, and, in doing so, carve out a tentative place for themselves on what remains unsteady social terrain. They work to demonstrate their own hard-earned cosmopolitanism as testimony to their own global relevance, their taste and style as markedly different from some colossal, but perpetually vague, Indonesian Other. Whereas "most Indonesians," particularly those from lower-class backgrounds, listen to *dangdut* and *pop Indonesia* (Fredrick 1982; Lockard 1998), indie kids prefer the relatively obscure styles popping up in the global underground. Whereas the imagined "mainstream" (Thornton 1996) of Indonesian youth adopt as their personal aesthetic whatever is currently popular, indie hipsters actively construct their personal tastes by exhaustively searching the Internet, combing through the dust bins of musical history for a style that sets them apart from the hordes, makes them *tampil beda* (stand out) and appear *unik* (unique).

The nostalgia of indie bands, then, is a strategic nostalgia, a nostalgia of those denizens of the industrializing world seeking to take their place on the global stage, while simultaneously positioning themselves locally as sophisticated in their tastes and middle-class in their sensibilities. It is as much a spatial as a temporal nostalgia, a longing for what lies just beyond easy reach.

Beyond Nation and Colony

Of course, this longing for a life beyond the boundaries of the archipelago is nothing new for Indonesians. Mrázek (2002), as mentioned in chapter 4, describes the "Indonesian dandy" as a character type that appeared in the Netherlands Indies as early as 1915. In contrast to the peasant majority of the archipelago, the dandy donned the garb of Western European fashions and adopted a "new theatricality" (141) in his movements, speech, and style. He dove "into things modern" (143), developed an obsession with neatness (144), and constructed a persona of "somebody in between, an enigma" (149), neither of the archipelago nor the Western world toward which he so ardently strived.

It can also be argued that Indonesian nationalism itself has always been part of a similar project. Just as communism sought to free the masses from the opiate of religion, nationalism sought to free Indonesians from the shackles of regional traditions. For its early subscribers, Indonesian nationalism implied a transcendence of the bounded space, a promise of newfound mobility based on a faith in modernity and progress. It sought to construct an "imagined community" (Anderson 1983) out of the hodgepodge ethnicities that peopled the more than 13,000 islands of the Netherland Indies, to unify the archipelago behind a utopian fantasy.

Locality, expressed in Indonesia through the concept of *daerah* (region), first emerged as a classificatory scheme of Dutch colonialism, a way of dividing up the archipelago into different, but manageably different, regions. It was a useful way of conceptualizing the colony, enabling Dutch authorities to modify their patterns of government according to local social and cultural demands. It also helped keep the people of the archipelago from conceiving of themselves as a single social unit, and hence rising up united against the Dutch.

Early Indonesian nationalists, however, sought to overthrow this "divide and conquer" version of regional diversity by forging the idea that the incredibly diverse residents of the archipelago could be conceived of as a single people (Anderson 1972; Siegel 1997). *Daerah*, the region, was made subservient to *negara*, the nation. Under such conditions, outlined in detail in chapter 1, the individual ethnic group became little more than an expression of national identity.

In the process, ethnic traditions often became stale, hollow version of themselves, museumified, standardized, and frozen in time (Kuipers 1998)—hardly the kind of dynamic, living force that makes alternative definitions of self possible. In the case of ethnic identities outside the canon of official representation, locality became a force of marginalization and exclusion, which, as Tsing points out, may serve as a rallying cry for resistance (Tsing 1993), but more often perpetuates the feeling of isolation and powerlessness. And the nation has hardly fared better as a unit of identification for contemporary youth. Nations have a way of creating their own cages. The promise of mobility found its limits in the *fiskal* tax (of around US$100) imposed on anyone hoping to leave the country. It found its limits in the longtime domination of national airwaves by a government monopoly, by an ingrained regime of self-monitoring and censorship. And it found its limits in an unstable local economy unable to fulfill its promise of progress and development.

It is no wonder, then, that young people in the urban centers of Indonesia find few resources for creative expression in such local identification. The "local" they have known has become almost irredeemably tainted, first by colonial authority, and later by the nationalist project. For Indonesia's new middle-class, it is simply too easy to see beyond the confines of the nation-state, and yet it remains difficult to move beyond them. The middle class remains, in the words of Iyo from Pure Saturday, *di tengah-tengah* (in the middle), no longer content with what Indonesia can provide, but unable to become full citizens of the "world community."

It should be no surprise, then, that Indonesian DIYers often feel disconnected from the identity resources of nation, region, and ethnicity, find them ill-equipped to the task of self-making and scene-making, and prefer instead to enact through their music and fashion what Lipsitz has referred to as "strategic anti-essentialism" (Baulch 2007; Lipsitz 1994), that is, of intentionally complicating, ignoring, or avoiding inherited identity types.

The Local in "Localization"

A good deal of scholarship in cultural anthropology, ethnomusicology, and related disciplines has been devoted to disproving the alarmist notion, popular among critics of capitalism and anti-globalization activists, that globalization is homogenizing the world's population, replacing dynamic cultural and ethnic diversity with an undifferentiated Americanized blandness (Miller 1992; Appadurai 1996; Hefner 1997).

Anthropologists such as Condry (2001) and Diehl (2002) remind us that Western musical forms do not simply assert themselves over existing musical traditions; they are incorporated into local life in complex ways, "localized" to make sense in new social and cultural contexts. When music is separated from its source of origin, the messages encoded in the music itself are destabilized, and thus, decoded in often-unpredictable ways in their specific sites of reception (Hall 1980; Feld 1994).

Under the anthropological gaze, with its focus on specific localities rather than sweeping global processes, the fear that that world's population is homogenizing has begun to disintegrate, and locally specific practices of contestation and hybrid-ization have become more and more evident (Dickey 1998; Ginsburg et al. 2002; Hahn 2002; Larkin 2002). Anthropologists working in Indonesia in particular have stressed that the island nation, as a centuries-old trading center and diverse collec-tion of ethnic groups, is particularly given to syncretic cultural forms. The tradition of *wayang kulit* (shadow puppetry) attests to the influence of Hindu elements (Keeler 1987) on the largely Muslim Javanese, and the diverse practices of Islam through-out the archipelago, even the most fundamentalist, remain infused with mysticism and local animism (Geertz 1960; Bowen 1993; Beatty 1999). In Indonesian popular music like *kroncong* (Becker 1975), *jaipongan* (Manuel and Baier 1986), and *dang-dut* (Fredrick 1982), hybridized aesthetics are the norm, combining imported musical styles with indigenous sensibilities and languages.

This anthropological emphasis on localization has served as an important the-oretical counterweight to popular theories of cultural imperialism, attesting to the creativity and ingenuity of situated social actors operating within myriad regional contexts. But it too often ignores the historical specificity of the "local," seeming to take for granted a pre-existing indigenous conception of self and Other, here and elsewhere that somehow imposes itself onto imported cultural forms or fuses with them to produce syncretism and hybridity. Much of the literature fails to elucidate the fluid and often-contradictory processes that constitute place-making in the first place. The "local," after all, is a highly unstable construct, produced in dialogue with larger abstract spatial units—the nation, the colony, the global economy—and it is continually being remade, reinforced, and challenged by those situated social actors who live with it everyday.

As such, it is unclear in much of the contemporary anthropological literature ex-actly what is meant by the "local" in "localization." Who's local are we talking about here? The "local" of the nation-state? The former colony? The local as it is imagined by an outside observer or as it is understood by the people occupying a particular location?

It should be mentioned that the term "local," borrowed directly from English or sometimes Indonesianized as *lokal*, actually appears quite frequently in indie scene discourse. It routinely popped up in conversation, was peppered throughout nearly all of my interviews, and was pasted onto T-shirts, printed onto posters and fliers. It has become something of a power word in the scene, an incitement to action.

"SUPPORT UR LOCAL MOVEMENT," commands a flier for the Yogyakarta distro expo. "SUPPORT TO OUR LOCAL PRODUCT," exclaims a sticker for Eighty-Three Clothing Company. But the term, as they use it, is not a neutral description of place. It has nothing to do with tradition or nation, with any kind of "essence" that could sum up a people and present them in a tidy little package to the rest of the world. This not the local of the colonial or nationalist past, nor is it the "local" discussed in so many anthropological accounts, the local that rises up in imagined opposition to a hostile cultural takeover.

The "local" circulating through indie scene discourse describes a relationship with the global, rather than a region, nation, colonial state, or even indigenous cultural tradition. It is a term of participation over isolation, autonomy over autocracy, and as such, it seeks to replace the earlier terms of *daerah* (region) and *negara* (nation) still imposed from on high. This "local" describes a position on the global map, rather than a distinct, regional body. It is a "local" about place, but not bounded by place, a term of participation in global culture, supplanting older models of distinction and isolation.

It simply does not make sense, then, to describe the indie scene appropriation of global aesthetics as "localization." Indie scenesters use the global to construct a new model of the local, rather than fit transnational forms into pre-existing "local" configurations. They are actively internationalizing their music, not localizing international music.

The indie pop emerging from the Indonesian indie scene is hybrid to be sure. It is a mixture of diverse musical elements. It's got jazz in it, vocal styles borrowed from the "old standards" of the American song book, some new wave, some post-punk, some samba, some British and Swedish pop—but it is a *deterritorialized hybrid*, a hybrid devoid of any intentional contribution from the cultural aesthetic of its producers. This is music intentionally indiscernible from music happening elsewhere.

When I asked Indonesian indie musicians about what distinguished their music from similar music being produced in other countries, the answer I almost uniformly got was "nothing" (*tidak ada*). Members of Sleepless Angel told me that since the music (in this case, thrash and metal) comes from "over there" (the United States and Europe), there isn't really anything locally distinctive about it. Alfonso, the Reddoor regular and vocalist for the Yogyakarta indie rock band Nervous, answered the question of whether there was anything locally distinctive about his music with a brief "no" and added "it's all from the West" (*semua dari Barat*). The foreign origin of his music is, in fact, a point of pride. Nervous trace their musical lineage directly through the New York indie rock band Interpol back to British post-punk legends Joy Division, even going so far as to don the NYC band's signature suits and ties on stage to make the connection explicit.

In this, the Indonesian indie sound has a good deal in common with sounds emerging from elsewhere in the DIY diaspora. Early British indie bands often emulated the accent and swagger of American rock 'n' roll. American indie bands, in contrast, have occasionally copped a fake British accent to maximize their twee credibility. Ditto with Swedish indie bands. The Swedish indie crooner Jens Lekman told *The Jakarta Post* that back in the 1990s Swedish indie bands were far too interested in sounding English. "People were [even] sending their vocalists to London so they could pick-up the accent right" (Haswidi 2010). In all these cases, there seems to be an embedded insecurity in indie about place and authenticity, a preferencing of the international as somehow more genuine and real than its local variants. Indie has yet to escape its entrenched Americo-centrism and Anglophilia.

Nowhere, however, is the importance of internationalism to the indie construction of locality as apparent as in the use of English in indie songs, both in Indonesia and nearly everywhere else with a large indie music scene. Wallach (2003) has pointed out that "underground" bands in Indonesia have historically used English for a variety of reasons, including bypassing government censors and reaching out to an international audience. In today's indie scene, no longer faced with the strict censorship of the past, the latter goal has decidedly eclipsed the former. English, it was often explained to me by Indonesian indie bands, is the language of indie music, whether in Spain, Sweden, Brazil, or wherever. The bands that influenced Indonesian bands sing in English, so they do, too.

To sing in a regional language, on the other hand, would classify a band instantly as *musik daerah* (regional music), of interest only to a small, regional audience, and by extension as *kampungan*, or provincial. To sing in the national language of Bahasa Indonesia, similarly, is to sing in the language of *pop Indonesia* and *dangdut*, the most popular musical styles in the country. It runs the risk of making a band sound pedestrian and commonplace, no different than all the other musical acts broadcast in heavy rotation over the mainstream radio. It aligns a band with the commercial interests of the national recording industry, promotes an aesthetic too easily palatable and comprehensible to "most Indonesians." In many bands' minds, to do so is to "sell out" one's indie integrity. To sing in Bahasa Indonesia is to attempt to attract as large audience an audience as possible. It is a cynical act.

To sing in English, then, is to thumb one's nose at commercial interests. It cements a band's goal of remaining on the margins of the Indonesian recording industry, positions them as middle-class and cosmopolitan, and aligns them with other bands in the larger indie diaspora. But it also has the added, and seemingly contradictory benefit of making it at least theoretically possible for a band to extend their audience base beyond the boundaries of the archipelago. "The fantasy of global success" (Silvio 2007) is a significant motivating factor for most indie bands. It is always on bands' minds, no matter how unrealistic the goal may be. Bands, after all, are not against *sukses*, as such. No one wants to have to keep their day job. But they are against *sukses* that compromises their self-concept, success that exposes them as provincial and out of touch.

There is little doubt, then, that Indonesian indie music, like indie music in Scandinavia or Latin America, has occidentalist (Carrier 1992; Coronil 1996) and "xenocentric" (Wallach 2002) tendencies. This is music whose musicians see the symbolic indicators of place as tainting their authenticity, ethnic, regional, and national markers as unnecessary cultural baggage. Consequently, Indonesian indie bands play an active role in promoting the cultural ascendancy of international cultural forms. They become de facto advocates for the innumerable aesthetic streams that accompany the spread of free market capitalism worldwide, and they help secure the status of ethnic and regional traditions as irrelevant at best, déclassé and complicit with the state agenda at worst. Like the "local" in national, colonial, and scene discourse, the "global" has become something of an "ideal type" (Weber 1978) for Indonesian youth, an imagined, unified field (Weiss 2002) of deterritorialized culture, a borderless utopia composed of an infinite number of elsewheres.

Constructing New Localities

Indonesian indie bands have become active agents in the construction of a new formulation of Indonesian locality, a locality depleted of "local" aesthetics, devoid of references to ethnicity, region, and nation, which revels in its diversity and flaunts its liberation from place as its defining features.

But if the global has become the basis for this reconstituted local, then what does this say about the fate of older aesthetics or cultural forms, those markers of ethnic, regional, and national placehood that used to be so intrinsic to local identity? Do they have any place in contemporary youth culture at all? And if not, isn't this evidence of widespread cultural imperialism, the domination of regional cultural forms by an encroaching global capitalist regime?

The short answer, I would concede, is "yes." The recurrent devaluation of indigenous aesthetic forms evident in indie music combined with a marked preoccupation with individuated expression reminiscent of "the culture of neoliberalism" described by Comaroff and Comaroff (2001) and Harvey (2005) strongly point to the scene's incorporation into an emergent, global economic order. The cultural logic (see Jameson 1992) of indie practice is not only compatible with the aims of global capitalist expansion, it seems to actively buttress and support it.

The problem, however, with applying a cultural imperialist argument to Indonesian indie music is that it ignores the role youth themselves have played in establishing and maintaining the ascendant status of international musical styles. It presents youth as victims, rather than active agents of social change, and ignores the ways Indonesian youth actually encounter and make use of global aesthetics in daily life.

This is, after all, hardly the New Order Indonesia of the early 1990s, where young Indonesians had only one government television station and a single private channel to choose from. This is an Indonesia faced with the politics of "plenitude" (Mc-Cracken 1997), where the potential resources for the formation of personal taste are nearly infinite. The deregulation of media and the expansion of Internet resources have substantially weakened any single would-be media hegemony.

These days, young, relatively well-off Indonesians, like millions of youth from similar backgrounds nearly everywhere, can readily access media products from all over the world. They don't have to wait until they are available on national stations or in corporate-owned record stores, and they don't have to settle for overblown Hollywood productions either. They can, and do, draw from a truly international selection, that includes media products from the United States, the UK, Sweden, Japan, Korea, Jamaica, and Brazil, among other places, and from all scales of production, from the truly DIY to the undeniably corporate. Moreover, they have more power than ever before to manipulate the texts and products that come their way. They can post their own media productions online, network with other amateur producers, and use readily-available open-source or pirated software to remix and rework any number of existing media texts, all with relative autonomy from corporate or state control. Transnational media conglomerates still produce and disseminate a disproportionate percentage of media texts, but more than ever their hegemony is being contested by competing independent producers.

Today most urban middle-class Indonesians discover new music groups and genres through scouring online databases, downloading and trading MP3s, or picking their friends' brains for their own recent musical acquisitions, not simply by tuning into MTV or taking *Rolling Stone*'s word as gospel. Adorno and Horkheimer's conception of a culture industry that manufactures the tastes of its audiences (Horkheimer and Adorno 1944) is hardly an apt description in this case. Establishing one's own taste, rather, is done both consciously and reflexively, and is practically a part-time job in the indie scene. It requires hours a week devoted to finding and assessing foreign music, alongside new local indie bands, and hours more debating its merits with friends.

I would suggest, then, an alternative reading to those models of globalization that continue to understand the forces of global capital as a monolithic power to be resisted at all costs through myriad forms of localization. Indonesian indie pop groups are not the victims of globalization; they are its accomplices, its co-conspirators. Their preference for international musical elements over local musical forms probably does reveal an internalization of inequality, the subjugation of Indonesian youth to new, diffuse forms of transnational power (Yang 2002), but it is not a passive subjugation. Instead, middle-class Indonesian youth are active agents in both establishing the ascendant position of transnational cultural forms in local life and devaluing local aesthetic and cultural forms as unusable and déclassé. They are consciously working to build a transnational soundscape of deterritorialized aesthetics, a domain of personal expression and experimentation that is detached from the imposition of "the local."

Indonesian indie musicians, like DIY fashion designers, forge a collective definition, not through the resources of ethnicity, region, or nation, not from the distinctive experiences of their own upbringing, but from the international pop culture discourses that define contemporary experience for youth nearly everywhere. They assert citizenship in a flexible world economy, de-marginalizing and de-isolating in a transnational context in which being bounded by place has become "a sign of deprivation and degradation" (Bauman 1998: 2).

No doubt, then, the social ramifications of indie production are a mixed bag. On the one hand, the young people involved in the indie scene, whether in Indonesia or elsewhere, are helping break down the hegemony of international corporations over youth trends. They have provided a viable alternative to both the major label music industry and state-run media, producing a much greater variety of sounds and enabling a much broader range of youth to participate directly in the industry. Moreover, they have promoted a range of identities for youth to occupy outside the scope of official representation, undermining in the process those imposed national and colonial versions of ethnic authenticity that young people have come to find oppressive and limiting.

On the other hand, indie scenesters have themselves constrained the scope of permissible subject positions to occupy and live through, rendering irrelevant any form of expression associated with the regional, the rural, or the poor. And in doing so, they are actively upholding the hegemony of transnational aesthetics over indigenously produced ones. The middle-class Indonesian youth behind the Indonesian indie scene are actively engaged in the construction of a "territory" beyond the boundaries of region and nation, a global field of power relations that perpetuates and reinforces social differences on the ground-level based on one's ability to participate in transnational culture. In the long run, such a regime may prove to be equally oppressive, even for the middle-class youth who have the upper hand in this game of aesthetics and style. But for now, for the Indonesian indie scenesters taking part in it, this act of shedding the baggage of colonialism and nation-state, of deterritorializing the self through dislocated sounds, is at least experienced as an act of liberation.

Conclusion: The Indie Mainstream

Support Your Local Brand Revolution!

—A flier for KICKfest 2008

Fashion's Peripheries

The Modex Independent Clothing Expo was held at a stuffy exhibition hall with badly functioning air-conditioning near downtown Makassar, South Sulawesi, in early May 2007. In hindsight, it seems an unlikely spot for an event like this to take place: a rundown, dusty warehouse on the outskirts of town in a city some thousand miles from Bandung or Jakarta. Makassar is pretty far off the radar of Indonesian fashion, let alone international fashion, a port city better known for its sea cucumber industry than its contribution to youth trends. But the event was evidence of just how and far and wide the scene has spread in recent years and how deeply the DIY ethos has taken root in the archipelago. As Ardi, founder of Chambers, one of the main distros affiliated with the event, explained, Makassar is just beginning to see the potential in DIY production. It only has a few indie clothing labels, a few prominent bands, but a great deal of interested youth. It is a scene still very much in formation.

Indie brands from all the major design centers in Indonesia showed up at Modex, showing off their designs and hawking their wares, doing their best to *tampil beda*, or stand out, from the hordes of competing clothing labels. Everyone had their own modestly unique take on international commercial culture, their own plot staked out for harvesting global trends. Nearly every semi-obscure subcultural aesthetic from Europe, Japan, Jamaica, and the United States from the last fifty years had taken on a second life at Modex, and was present somewhere, in some incarnation or other, among the vinyl-draped stalls and bins of discounted clothes. Punk, funk, and hip hop were referenced in loud, clashing color combinations, as were death metal, black metal, and grindcore through hundreds of menacing flames and decomposing skulls. New wave, indie, and mod lent their catchy pop look to target signs, robots, and disco rabbits. There was even a sizable collection of rasta-inspired boxer shorts, decked out in African colors and silhouetted Bob Marleys. Global youth culture at Modex had been converted into material form, cut up, and reassembled in thousands of different garments. This was bricolage as merchant fair, cut-and-paste meets warehouse sale.

Modex sent out a hundred billowing smoke signals to a hundred different, but interconnected, scenes. The fashion was diverse, eclectic, moderately experimental, even occasionally visually arresting, and yet, the effect of all of it together was somehow vague and incoherent. Walking through the rows of stalls, my senses were overwhelmed, and individual flavors began to merge into one indistinct mass, one mammoth processed cheese blend of global pop. All that standing out had somehow managed to make everything look the same, all dissociated bright colors and garish imagery. Maybe that's just how it is with DIY. Cultural democratization equals lots more of the same old crap. Certainly that is critic Andrew Keen's position (2008). Only so many new voices can enter the conversation before it turns into a cacophonous, collective drone.

Or perhaps that's simply how culture works: individual practices become patterned and predictable. Innovations become *habitus* (Bourdieu 1977; 1980) and the "serious games" (Ortner 1996) of indie fashion cohere into stale conventions and trends. It's also possible that youth subcultural fashions were never really that different from each other to begin with, sharing a deeper underlying sensibility expressed through subtle variations in aesthetic form.

Or maybe I was just in a bad mood. I had arrived in Makassar several hours before the launch party for Modex in pretty bad shape. A few recent bouts of food poisoning had left me weak and emaciated. Some skin infection had set in on the left side of my face—an occupational hazard of anthropology in the tropics—leaving long maroon scabs that made it look like I had been clawed by a tiger. I had to change planes in Surabaya on the way there, and I had not eaten anything in hours, for fear of getting sick at an inopportune time.

When the plane finally landed, I had more or less no idea where I was going to stay, or what I was going to do. Luckily, I had the cell phone number of a friend of mine who was also attending the event, Diana of Slackers Distro in Yogyakarta, and I gave her a ring when I got off the plane. Some other designers from Yogya she knew had just arrived as well and were about to be picked up by a shuttle sent by the *panitia* (organizing committee) of the expo. I tagged along. We introduced ourselves and conducted small talk, and I tried to hide my sorry state behind a pulled-down trucker cap and a pair of aviator sunglasses.

When we got to the lodgings the *panitia* had organized, my mood shifted from tired to despondent. It was the grim dormitory of an Islamic high school, dirty, loud, and crowded with bunk beds full of unhappy young designers. The widespread sentiment was that the *panitia* clearly could have used the 1 million rupiah (roughly US$105) they had paid as registration fees to better effect. But these were mostly people in their late teens to early 30s, current university students and recent graduates, urban bohemians living in self-imposed poverty, and they were used to similarly unglamorous living.

This was not New York Fashion Week. There were no celebrities in attendance, no limousines, no football-field-size catwalks. It was a modest get-together of DIY designers, a collection of like-minded, middle-class Indonesian youth, without much financial backing behind them, and without any (or at least many) giant egos to get in the way. People complained about the meager conditions, but didn't do much to remedy the situation. "*Gimana lagi*?" I heard someone say, "What can be done about it?"

I, however, in my weakened state, was not feeling quite as tolerant of grime and noise. I was eager to get out of there. I found Diana Slackers and took refuge for a while in the musty green room she, her husband, and several of her employees' were staying in. We all watched TV and plotted our escape. But none of us knew the town, and we seemed to be somewhere on the outskirts of it anyway, far from passing taxicabs and alternative lodging options. Eventually, standing outside their doorway and watching the rush of designers arrive by *panitia* van, I ran into Uchok, the head honcho over at *Suave Street Brand Catalogue* (now *Suave Magazine*), whom I had interviewed a month or two before. He invited me to come stay at the rented house he and his friends from the Bandung clothing label Invictus had managed to secure for free from a local entrepreneurial couple in the real estate business. The couple, hoping to capitalize on the indie movement while it was still hot, were about to open up their own distro—much to the not-so-disguised disdain of the *Suave* and Invictus crowd. *Suave*, the free catalog that features ads for most major (and many minor) distro brands, is one of the surest promotional ventures for launching a clothing label. The couple wanted to get in good with them, and as I did not have any better plans, I went along.

It turned out to be both a blessing and a curse. I had a nice room in a very modern, comfortable house (with only the slightly annoying drawback of losing power several times a night), and got to have great conversations with people right at the center of the indie fashion universe, but I had also incurred significant social debt through the arrangement and an even heavier social schedule that kept me from getting the rest I undoubtedly needed. The entrepreneurial couple were eager to drag us around to the coolest nightclubs, the most popular neighborhood cafes for *sop daging* (meat soup) and *coto makassar* (buffalo intestine stew), and since they were paying for everything, we had very little say in the matter. Maybe this is what Bourdieu (1980) means by "soft domination." But who was dominating whom in this arrangement? Who was more effectively manipulating the uncomfortable relationship between indie idealism and venture finance? I still don't know the answer to these questions.

Conspicuous Creative Production

Needless to say, when the kids from *Suave* and Invictus and I all arrived at the launching party at Chambers Distro, sponsored, incidentally, by Unkl347 in honor of their recent incursion into the South Sulawesi market—a homecoming of sorts for Dendy—I was a pretty sad sight to behold, worn-out and beat up, like a feather-weight boxer on a losing streak.

If there was anything I had learned from hanging out with Indonesian indie kids over the previous eight months, though, it is to flaunt what you've got, even if what you've got isn't much to look at. The DIY ethos is all about making do, tinkering with available materials, making the best of a difficult situation. It is about turning disadvantage into advantage, the unintentional into the intentional. My scabs and almost scary skinniness were by no means glamorous, but looked at in the right light, I decided, they lent me a kind of bar-brawl authenticity. All I needed was attitude to back it up. So after an iced café mocha from a coffeeshop next door, a couple of beers handed to me by the staff of Unkl347, and some puff pastries from the buffet table, I worked the room as best I could, scanning the crowd for people I knew and people I felt I should.

This was, after all, what everyone was doing. Everyone knew there were important connections to be made, alliances to be forged, and they put on their tightest T-shirts, their skinniest jeans, teased their hair, and underwent all the various arcane rites that comprise the ritual of *berdandan* (getting made up). I settled on the movie star hiding from the paparazzi look: sunglasses and trucker cap in full effect. Clothes were not the only thing on display at Modex; we all were.

It didn't take me long to realize, dodging the inquiring eyes of dozens of young designers, that Modex was not just an advertising venue for promoting activities that happened elsewhere; *it* was the main event. People don't just go to Modex to make connections or market their designs; they also design so they can go to events like Modex, which, every year that passes by, become bigger, more boisterous spectacles, what Indonesians approvingly call *rame*. The goal of being there was to be on display, to be seen as part of the scene. Young designers come together at events like Modex, of course, to network, forge alliances, and solidify social ties, but they also come there for the purpose of simple recognition. They want to be seen as designers. They want others to recognize them as kin. And they walk away from these events feeling like designers, like they were finally on the right path toward creative self-actualization, the end game of DIY. Tbonk Weimpy, designer and owner of Starcross distro in Yogyakarta, told me years later that it was Modex that convinced him to finally stop pursuing a career in industrial engineering and make fashion his full-time gig. Showing alongside Unkl347, Ouval, and the like, and getting compliments from other designers, he says, gave him the drive and the spirit (*semangat*) he needed to re-fashion himself into a designer. By 2010, he had three distros, one in Yogya, another in Bandung, and one in the north coast Javanese city of Semarang. He was widely recognized as one of the strongest emergent voices in the scene.

The nineteenth-century cultural critic Thorstein Veblen (1994) coined the term "conspicuous consumption" to describe the wasteful spending habits of the idle elite, those socially conscious aristocrats concerned with distinguishing themselves from the less financially endowed masses. Indonesianist scholars have bandied about the term for years now to describe the materialism of Indonesia's growing middle classes, their penchant for BMWs and name-brand fashion. But in the Indonesian indie scene today, and among the larger middle-class crowd of which they form a significant part, conspicuous consumption increasingly takes a back seat to displays of *conspicuous creative production*. In the urban hubs of Indonesia, it seems like everyone's got their own clothing label these days. Everyone wants to be a designer, musician, writer, or some kind of artist or other, and they want everyone else to know that is what they are. They want to see themselves reflected back in other peoples' eyes as a creative contributor, an active producer, someone who matters because they are a part of something larger, not simply because they stand on a higher rung of the class ladder. As Indonesia develops its own "creative economy," and shifts from industrial manufacture to postindustrial and more immaterial forms of labor, being cool is no longer as easy as buying the latest fashions, hanging out at the hottest nightclubs, or staying hip to the latest trends. These days, it is way cooler to be seen as an active cultural producer in one's own right.

The Cultural Influence of the Indonesian Indie Scene

No one is more keenly aware of the cultural ascendancy of collaborative, creative production in Indonesia than is Dendy Darman, the owner and cofounder of Unkl347. He played a significant role in making it that way, inciting youth through workshops, concerts, and unsubtle messages in his clothing designs to take up the banner of DIY production. "I, Xerox, Go" read a projection over the door of Dendy's Bandung store at a party in 2007, and that about sums up his philosophy for me. Dendy is all about doing, no matter how primitive the technology, no matter how simple the product.

That night, before the opening of the Modex Expo, beat-up, sick, and running on almost no sleep, was the first time I met Dendy, one of many subsequent meetings in Bandung. Although I had never so much as seen a picture of him, I recognized the influential DIY designer and entrepreneur almost immediately. He is just not the kind of guy you miss, heavyset in a country of skinny people, outgoing in a society that values discreteness, a man who truly stands out in a crowd. As it turned out, Dendy seemed to have some idea of who I was, too. Gossip about this American anthropologist doing research on the scene had circulated well beyond my control, so when I introduced myself to him, it wasn't all that awkward. He even pretended not to notice the tiger marks on my face, looking me directly in the eye so that his gaze didn't wander too far toward the more pathetic portions of my countenance.

Several years have gone by since then. I finished my PhD, started a position at Drexel University, and published articles on the scene, all the while maintaining e-mail and IM (instant message) contact with my friends and informants back in Indonesia. The last time I saw Dendy was in the summer of 2010 as I was putting the finishing touches on this book. I met up with him again at Unkl347's flagship store on Jalan Trunojoyo in Bandung, and I was around ten minutes late to our appointment, not because I was caught up or running behind, but because I had been practicing at being late. It's not something that comes naturally to me. This is usually not a problem in the life of an American academic, but in Indonesia, I had learned, being too punctual can be impolite, or if not impolite, then at least inconvenient. Things have a tendency to linger there, to dwell indefinitely. Time stretches itself back like a slingshot. *Jam karet*, the locals call it, "rubber time."

Indonesia's indie scene, however, had done anything but linger since I had concluded my fieldwork. Indie brands had risen to become some of the most recognizable names in a budding national fashion scene, even participating in Jakarta Fashion Week, Indonesia's premier industry event. Malls in Bandung now frequently have an upstairs section devoted to local independent brands, and throughout the archipelago, mass-produced imitations of distro-style apparel show up in chain stores like Unite Shop, Counter Culture, and BlackID. Jakarta's newest, arguably most exclusive mall, Grand Indonesia Shopping Town, has a whole section devoted to local indie brands, simply and pragmatically labeled "Level One." "Premium" indie retailers like SatCash (the upscale division of longtime distro brand Satellite Castle), Hunting Fields, Monday to Sunday, and Magic Happens line a long, polished corridor with gleaming marble floors. Other premium labels show their work at Brightspot Market, a curated independent fashion and craft exhibition put on several times a year in prominent retail establishments. Brightspot now has a permanent venue, as well, the Goods Dept, at the older more established, and even more upscale Plaza Indonesia next door to Grand Indonesia. Many of the labels that show at Brightspot and the Goods Dept. have no other physical retail venue. They maintain only an online presence, to keep overhead down. Brightspot and the Goods Dept. have become the go-to resource for those in the know seeking up-market Indonesian brands, "the place," according to the Goods Dept.'s website, "to find all things cool under one roof." Elang Eby sells his Easton and Cool Caps lines there. The artsy and currently trendy Monstore label sells their hand-drawn T-shirts there. Designers have described it to me as a place where people who truly *apresiasi* (appreciate) quality products shop. In contemporary indie scene lingo, "appreciate" seems to mean willing to spend extra money.

As for indie music, most national cassette outlets now sell albums by FFWD, and occasionally a few other, newer indie labels such as De Majors and Lil' Fish Records. Indie bands such as Efek Rumah Kaca and The Trees and the Wild have produced some of the most critically acclaimed albums of the last couple of years, earning continual write-ups in national newspapers such as *The Jakarta Post*, *The Jakarta Globe*, and *Kompas*, along with music and lifestyle magazines such as *Trax*, *Rolling Stone Indonesia*, and *Hai*. Aksara Records in Jakarta, however, is no more. They went defunct in 2009 after disappointing sales. This doesn't mean there's no market for indie music anymore, simply that indie bands are disbursed among so many labels now that no one label can hold any kind of claim to market domination.

Plus, there is a significant movement in the indie scene away from older models of distribution. Indie record labels now face competition from online labels, or "netlabels," some of which, such as Yes No Wave out of Yogyakarta, have opted not to sell their music at all. Their eclectic range of bands, including the pyschobilly punk group Coffin Cadillac, the fuzz-laden shoe-gazers Shorthand Phonetics, and the tongue-in-cheek "old school death metal" act Bvrtan, post their albums for free download on their website. For Yes No Wave and its bands, the profit incentive has simply been removed from the equation. "This is an action of the 'gift economy,'" claims Wok the Rock, founder of Yes No Wave on the "About" section of their website, "an experiment in applying a free music model for music lovers in a capitalistic world."

But removing the profit equation from musical distribution has not meant a reduction in cultural influence. One band that has achieved a good deal of success without either selling albums or signing onto a label, indie or otherwise, is bottlesmoker, a Bandung-based two-piece that specializes in layered instrumental electronica composed out of toy keyboards and old thrift store synthesizers. Bottlesmoker is as DIY as they come, a no-budget "bedroom music" duo with little interest in being the next Justin Bieber Internet sensation. They are not fishing for a record deal. There is, they claim, "no recording company that suits with their music concept" (from the band's tumblr page, bottlesmoke.tumblr.com). They are, instead, attempting to build their own audience in a grassroots fashion, without intermediaries and without compromise. They use the social networking website MySpace as their distribution hub, where they encourage potential fans to write to them asking for a virtual copy of their album in wav or MP3 format. They happily oblige all requests.

As Marcel Thee, himself a longtime vocalist for the indie pop outfit Sajama Cut, reported in the *Jakarta Globe*, bottlesmoker has followed in Mocca's footsteps to become one of the most successful Indonesian bands ever at touring internationally (Thee 2011). They have been invited to do performances (all expenses paid) in the Philippines, Kuala Lumpur, Beijing, Shanghai, Hong Kong, and Brunei, and not just in embassies and consulates, as has been the fate of most touring pop acts in the past, but at electronica and indie festivals, a range of events driven by groundswells of fans. Bottlesmoker has demonstrated that commerce simply does not have to be a part of music production, and music need not be subject to the constraints and expectations of capital. They are working to carve out perhaps the most truly autonomous path Indonesian DIY music has experienced so far.

For me, however, perhaps the most obvious sign that the DIY movement had reached a new height of power and influence in Indonesia lay with its many regional clothing and music festivals. Modex was my first, but it was already considered small potatoes by the time I left Indonesia in September 2007. By 2006, the era of the indie mega-festival had already dawned on Indonesia. I attended my first about a month before the end of my fieldwork, KICKfest 2007, an event sponsored by the Kreative Independent Clothing Kommunity and the largest of its kind up to that point. Around

150 clothing labels participated in the event. Tens of thousands of people were in attendance over the course of three days, and more than 3 billion rupiah (around US$325,000) in clothing was sold. Many of Indonesia's top indie bands, including Pure Saturday, The S.I.G.I.T., and Vincent Vega, turned out to play the festival, a variety of prominent filmmakers, artists, and skateboarders showed off their stuff; and a steady stream of visitors crowded the street behind Gedung Sate, the Bandung governor's office, to shop, loiter, or simply observe the spectacle firsthand. There are now several regional KICKfests, the largest of which is held in Yogyakarta, in addition to a variety of other mega-festivals, including, most notably, those put on by the Indonesian Independent Clothing Association (IICA) in Jakarta. These are the distro red tag sales, the biggest opportunities to shop and save. Teenagers, I'm told, save up for months beforehand. Billboards advertise the events for weeks in advance. And these festivals secure big corporate sponsorships, mainly from cigarette companies like LA Lights and X Mild, further complicating the proclaimed "independent" status of the scene.

I went to my most recent KICKfest in the summer of 2010 a few days before I last saw Dendy, and it had only expanded in the meantime. According to KICK spokespeople, it had somewhere around 56,000 visitors over the course of a weekend with about 170 distinct brands represented, all monitored for "quality" control by the KICKfest steering committee. They had to turn dozens of applicants away. That year it was held in the large field behind Stadion Siliwangi, a sparse space in Northern Bandung crowded with stalls, hardly any grass covering the ground. When the rains started, it quickly turned into a swamp. Denim-clad hipsters tromped through mud, seeking the best deals they could find on T-shirts and hoodies. Local indie superstars like Mocca, Shaggy Dog, and Koil took the stage, while crowds took cover beneath plastic white tents. I ran into lots of old friends, designers from Bandung and Yogya, zinesters and scenesters. "This is like our Woodstock," one of them commented to me, "only everyone's wearing clothes!"

Jalan Trunojoyo, where Unkl347's store is located, had changed, as well, more densely packed than before, with flashier signs, and more upscale interiors. Real estate prices had gone up substantially. But in Bandung by 2010, if you didn't have a shop on Jalan Trunojoyo, you simply didn't matter. The local scene had consolidated itself there. Anonim was now located there, as were up-and-coming brands such as Starcross and Tosavica.

The façade of Unkl347's store had also been remodeled since I had last seen it. This was not a big surprise. It had been remodeled several times during the year of my initial research, updated to reflect whatever campaign the brand was currently conducting. This remodel was a bit more substantial, though. In addition to repainting the sign above the shop into a simple, bold set of thick lines, Unkl347 had taken over the space next door. The shop Eat, once owned by Ade, Dendy's former partner when the label was called Eat347, was no more. In its place was a new store, stretching over the space of two or three older shops, called Family Affair, Dendy's new effort to promote some of the best work by friends and colleagues in the larger indie fashion network. The name was meant to reflect the continuing family atmosphere of the scene, despite its conspicuous change in fortune.

The More Things Change . . .

When I arrived at Unkl347, I found a film crew sitting on the concrete steps in front of the store. A guy wearing a baseball cap and holding a tripod-mounted digital video camera was seated, bored and waiting, next to a clipboard-carrying youngish woman in a Muslim headscarf, while another woman in her late 20s, clad in a professional black suit, was having her make-up done. A news anchor, I figured. I passed by them into the shop, inquired at the counter as to whether Dendy had already arrived, and was directed into the room next door, now devoted to Unkl347's shoe line, Indicator. There was Dendy, standing before a large, wall-size map of Indonesia in a basic brown, rather formless T-shirt; matching, loose-fitting trousers; and a pair of green suede shoes. It was almost the exact same outfit he had been wearing the first time I met him at Modex three years earlier. His hair was cut in the same scruffy, over-his-ears look, and his goatee was as scraggly as ever. He waved at me and smiled, while he held up in front of his chest a gray Unkl347 T-shirt. Across the room was another mounted video camera, behind which was another cameraman in a baseball cap.

As it turned out, the film crew was recording a twenty-minute episode on Dendy and Unkl347 for a documentary television series called *Kenali Anak Negri* (Meet the Youth of the Nation). It is a program on Trans TV, one of five privately owned national television stations in Indonesia, that does video profiles on "inspiring young people [under age 35], who are successful or of a high status within their field" (Transtv.com). Dendy had been selected as an influential young entrepreneur, an example for other young Indonesians to look up to and emulate. One of several prominent indie scene members to be profiled on the national television series in its still short run, Dendy, it seems, has become more than just an icon of the indie scene; he has taken on the status of a model figure of Indonesian modernity, a new social and cultural "type" (see Siegel 1997; Barker et al. 2009) for Post-Reformasi Indonesia.

I spent the rest of the day following Dendy and the film crew from the store to lunch to Unkl347's warehouse office and, finally, to Dendy's suburban home, where they added his wife and two kids to the mix. As we traveled from place to place, Dendy filled me in on some of the changes his company, and the scene itself, had undergone since I had last been there.

Unkl347, Dendy explained to me, is no longer in the business of selling clothes. Everyone sells clothes these days. There is nothing all that interesting in that anymore. Instead, he said, Unkl347 sells concepts (*konsep*), visual prototypes that can be printed onto any variety of clothing, bags, or everyday items. They are in the process of re-branding Unkl347 as a design, rather than a clothing company, taking to an extreme the already graphic orientation of Indonesian streetwear. They will keep doing clothing, he told me, since that's where the money is and it supports their other, more personally fulfilling projects, but what he is really passionate about these days is architecture and interior space. He, along with his Singaporian architect friend Zaki, who rode along in Dendy's Toyota SUV with us, has been envisioning a kind of domestic aesthetic overhaul for Indonesia, a new vision of the bourgeois lifestyle that, frankly, looked to me a lot like the "Apartment" home goods collection of the Philadelphian "alternative" retail giant Urban Outfitters. Dendy knew this would mean catering to a much more up-market crowd than they had in the past, and he was okay with that, so long as he didn't have to compromise his vision or his way of doing business. That's the way the indie scene in general seems to be going. In truth, the bourgeoisie and the bohemians are increasingly difficult to tell apart in urban Indonesia, just as they are in New York or London (see Brooks 2000).

The single biggest thing that has changed in the scene recently, Dendy told me, is the set of resources at their disposal. When Dendy and crew were starting out, all they had were what they could muster up for themselves, mainly their personal ingenuity, their creativity, and their still-limited access to technology. Today, there are a variety of government and corporate resources to turn to. The Ministries of Tourism, Development, and Industry hold lots of forums and events, many of which specifically cater to indie production. Occasionally, they even provide grants. Local governments are much more willing to issue permits for events, as well, which had been a major barrier in the past. No more over-crowded, rent-by-hour stages for indie shows. Indie fits more comfortably into upscale urban nightclubs these days.

For Unkl347, specifically, Dendy said, the biggest change is that now they have the money to actually do what they have wanted to do all along: have an interior design division, a shoe line, and be involved in a wide variety of external collaborations, such as recent book and music ventures with indie musicians Vincent Vega, White Shoes & the Couples, Rock N Roll Mafia, and Efek Rumah Kaca. They've even developed their own publishing division, S.C.A.N.D.A.L, which puts out the semi-regular glossy magazine *Still Loving Youth*, and has now become its own, autonomous company, specializing in design publications. "We used to dream of doing this stuff," Dendy told me, and "now the dream has been realized." "The mainstream," Dendy offered, "is already fully aware of what we used to call the subculture," and in practical terms, this means they can produce much higher-quality products than before. "We can be idealistic, while getting money at the same time" (*Kita bisa idealis sama dapat duit*). They now use organic cotton, have experimented with soy-based inks, and have, he admits, dropped the old standard of printing no more than seventy or so editions of a single line. It took them years to get to this point, he told me, but they are enjoying being there.

The new crop of clothing labels popping up, on the other hand, are able to do from the outset what it took Dendy and his friends years to accomplish. They come up with an idea, get financing—either from parents, outside investors, or banks—and immediately make high-quality products. Indie production, it seems, is already considered a safe investment in Indonesia. Plenty of financial institutions are willing to support creative ventures that would have once seemed like colossal risks. This doesn't mean that the DIY spirit is dead, however. The new crop of indie labels maintains the DIY ethos, Dendy insists, and are still part of the indie community. They have, he told me, "the idealism of before with the [means of] execution of now" (*idealis yang dulu dengan eksekusi sekarang*); "the substance is the same but the quality's better" (*Intinya sama tapi quality lebih bagus*). "It's like a new era," he said. The new labels, like Sixteen D-Scale in Bandung and Pot Meets Pop in Jakarta, go "straight to premium," producing high-quality clothing that more closely resembles lowbrow couture than indie streetwear. "This is a new generation," one that takes DIY for granted as the single most obvious way to produce their wares and do their business. Self-marketing is now second nature.

I asked Dendy if, despite their mainstream success, Unkl347 is still cut-and-paste. He smiles and leans back on the couch. "We have to keep being cut-and-paste" (*harus cut-and-paste terus*), he answered, "because inspiration is always changing. You have to take from what you're into at the moment. The spirit stays the same, even as our taste changes" (*spiritnya sama tapi taste bisa berubah*). "Unkl has gone major" (*Unkl jadi major*), he adds, "but we are still Unkl."

Becoming the Media

Indie is underground no more, in Indonesia, or for that matter, in Europe, Asia, or the United States. Just ask Wendy Fonarow, the American anthropologist who studies British indie rock. When she first started asking her classes at the University of California, Los Angeles (my alma mater) back in the mid-1990s if they had heard of indie, she would get one or two raised hands at best. As of the early 2000s, she says, almost everyone raised their hands (Wendy Fonarow, personal communication, 2011). Or ask Kaya Oakes's UC Berkeley freshmen composition class, the ones who insisted that indie is "just a bunch of hipsters in skinny jeans" (Oakes 2009: 194). The indie ideal, so important to Oakes, reads as just another mundane style possibility to them. It is an image promulgated by a broad swath of companies from American Apparel to Converse and Levis, cheapened by overuse, hackneyed by buzz. Bedroom recorded singer/songwriters now get nominated for Grammys. Once-underground publications such as *Giant Robot* and *Dazed and Confused* have tens of thousands of readers worldwide. And major fashion publications routinely feature the dirty hair, undersize T-shirts, and oversize glasses once held close by indie scenesters as their own signature brand of ironic detachment. Not only have indie bands and brands achieved a new level of prominence, but also the conceptual divide between "independent" and "mainstream" has been hopelessly corroded. The idea of independence is now vague, at best. With respected indie bands from The Black Keys to Edward

Sharpe and The Magnetic Zeroes using their sound to hawk Ford Fiestas on network TV, the difference between indie rock bands and regular rock bands remains largely aesthetic. The charge of "selling out," in this context, just doesn't pack the same punch it once did. Autonomy may still be the ideal of DIYers everywhere, and yet it is not always clear what autonomy means when the very websites used to promote one's product "on one's own terms" are owned by Fox NewsCorp and funded by Goldman Sachs.

The conceptual unity of indie and mainstream became especially clear to me when I visited Wendi Putranto, the manager of Indonesian new wave pop darlings, The Upstairs, at his office at *Rolling Stone Indonesia*, the local licensee of the international music magazine in Jakarta. The two-story building, with its iconic sign dominating the visual landscape of the small, southern Jakartan road, is occupied by a staff of kids from the Bandung underground, punk and metal musicians, writers for zines, even former designers for local clothing labels.

Wendi disputes the idea that indie has sold out or been co-opted by the mainstream. He gave me an alternative explanation to this popular indie scene lament, as we chatted at the elongated oval table in the *Rolling Stone* conference room, giant digital prints of John Lennon and Mick Jagger dominating the walls. It is simply that the war between indie and the mainstream is over, and it is the indie scene that has come out victorious. They have infiltrated the halls of media corporations, snuck in through the back door, and taken over. Wendi himself has been working as an editor and writer for the transplanted American publication since its inception a few years back. He is now Executive Editor, and he is happy to use the position to promote local bands that he believes in. A large percentage of the bands *Rolling Stone* features are from the indie scene. That, Wendi says, is simply where the talent is these days, and so that's where magazines like his look for source material. *Rolling Stone* has little interest in the prefabricated pop of the Jakarta recording industry. And plus, the editors and writers for *Rolling Stone*, with their DIY pedigrees, tend to prefer stuff that is a little rougher around the edges. These formerly self-conscious outsiders to the mainstream have become some of its highest profile gatekeepers.

Wendi spent years fighting the good fight on behalf of the indie cause. He managed the Jakarta hardcore outfit Step Forward, the first such local band with a female lead singer, before going on to manage The Upstairs, and he still considers himself a staunch opponent of the commercial media, with its money-driven, soul-sucking agenda. Ultimately, however, Wendi decided that the best way to change the media was to join it. He no longer sees a contradiction between anti-commercial sentiments and conspicuously commercial enterprises. Instead, he sees the latter as a potential means of disseminating the former. As I shook his hand and stepped into my taxi after our interview was over, Wendi switched from Indonesian to English and said to me, conspiratorially, quoting San Francisco punk icon Jello Biafra: "Don't hate the media; become the media." And this seems to have become a mantra for today's Indonesian youth, as it has perhaps for youth throughout the industrial and industrializing world.

The point, these days, is not to resist the media. Resistance is futile. It is to make the media work for you. Make your own stuff, today's DIYers insist. Get it out there. Get it noticed. Become the voice of your generation. Let other people worry about whether you've sold out or not.

From the Fringes to Front and Center

DIY, after all, has long since crossed over from a fringe cultural practice to a mainstream moral ideal. Having one's own video blog seems as natural to today's youth as writing in a diary. It has become normalized, status quo even, at least among the world's middle-class urban population with easy access to the Internet.

It is impossible to say just how many DIYers there are out there, because there are no longer any clear lines of demarcation between DIY and everything else. We would, of course, have to count YouTube amateur video makers as DIY, along with bloggers, craftivists, hardware hackers, guerilla gardeners, and basement scientists. And we would have to make room in our definition for the homeschoolers, the urban farmers, graffiti bombers, and billboard-altering culture jammers. And what about the pirates, the knock-off artists, and the Internet scammers? Aren't they doing it themselves, too? Aren't they seizing the means of production for their own ends?

Sometimes, the difference between DIYer and public menace is murkier than we might like to admit (see Wohlsen 2011), as is the line between ordinary "prosumer" and "authentic" DIYer. Inveterate quilters and knitters are a relatively easy case, but what about gamers who customize their characters in virtual worlds (see Boellstorff 2008)? What about Home Depot shoppers building their own shelves or repairing their own roofs? What about amateur photographers posting their family pictures on Flickr? Or microbloggers thinking out loud on Twitter? When we expand the definition of DIY to include any kind of voluntary, unpaid, non-professional production, suddenly we are all DIYers. Just try ordering a piece of patio furniture online without having to assemble it yourself.

There remains, nonetheless, a stubborn conceptual division between the self-professed DIYer and the occasional handyman, the idealistic indie instigator and the casual craft-maker, but it is a harder and harder distinction to maintain. And why would we want to maintain it, anyway? If DIY is to be a truly egalitarian enterprise, a fully democratic mode of cultural participation, what right have any of us to deny someone else's DIY's credentials? Better to grant them the benefit of the doubt. We are all DIYers, at least sometimes, and those sometimes either get more and more frequent, or weigh more and more heavily upon us.

The DIY ethos insists that we all get up off the couch and go do something. It nags. It pleads. It berates. It promises self-contentment and a sense of personal fulfillment, like a carrot on a shoestring always just three paces ahead. This isn't some schizophrenic fantasy, some repressed paranoid delusion whispering from the inner recesses of the mind; it is the emergent voice of moral authority, perhaps even the newly dominant mode of thinking, a superego for the age of immaterial production. If we aren't contributing something creative to the community at large, this new voice of reason suggests, we aren't worth much of anything to anyone.

Not everyone, of course, is a DIYer in any earth-shaking, world-altering sort of way. Most of us are casual DIYers, at best. Some of us, perhaps, not even that. Even the Internet—the cheapest, fastest route to incurring DIY street cred—is far from ubiquitous. Internet use may be up to some seventy-eight percent of the American population and sixty-five percent of the European Union's, but it still hovers around thirteen percent of the Indonesian population, even less for countries in sub-Saharan Africa, and of regular internet users, less than a quarter have their own blog, let alone their own channel on YouTube. Few people ever start their own record labels, their own clothing lines, or film production studios. Most of us don't have the time, the energy, or even the inclination. We may dream of writing and self-publishing our first novel or putting together an album of our greatest Karaoke hits available through our MySpace page, or even just crafting our own dining room table or sewing our own drapes, but for the vast majority of us, these dreams are never realized. They are stocked away on the dusty shelves of projects yet to be completed. In Indonesia alone, there may be three thousand independent clothing lines, dozens of indie record labels, and perhaps millions of engaged youth pushing in some way against the terms and limits of participation in popular culture, but that leaves some 230 million people apparently content to watch and consume. This assumes, of course, that they even have access to a television or radio, not by any means a given. Die-hard DIYers are hardly the majority—in Indonesia, the United States, or anywhere else.

Nonetheless, we have ample reason to believe their numbers are increasing at an impressive, if not unprecedented, rate. Internet users have grown exponentially over the last decade, and as they have, new netlabels and indie clothing lines pop up everyday, advertising their goods on Facebook, selling their wares on Etsy. Sites devoted to assisting with DIY projects or providing forums for discussion on such projects are now so numerous, it is anybody's guess as to how many there are. The Maker Faire, the United States' largest exposition for DIYers, has more than tripled in attendance since its launch in 2005, drawing in 75,000 visitors to its 2009 San Mateo, California event (Frauenfelder 2010: 222). It now has several other regional fairs bringing in similar numbers. The displays exhibited range from sculpted objects to Petri dish experiments and homemade robots, but even in more traditional crafts like knitting, the trend is toward substantial growth. The Craft Yarn Council of America documented a thirteen percent increase in knitting among people aged 25–34 in 2004 (Turney 2009: 1). Quilting, too, is experiencing a dramatic upswing (Stalp 2008). And one can only venture a guess about the number of bands there are out there, plotting their global takeover from the auspices of their parents' garage.

Devoted DIYers may not yet be the mainstream, but their ideology appears to be, an international ethic supporting creative practice and collaborative production.

"Woven from threads of anarchism, libertarianism, and Thoreau-style radical self-reliance" (Wohlsen 2011: 120), the DIY ethos, once installed, is not easily removed, demanding that we all should be contributing more actively to the production of the culture around us. We all already, to greater and lesser degrees, feel the pull of DIY. It challenges our complacency, tugs at our idle hands, and reminds us that if we want to stand up and be counted, we better have something to show.

Even Hipper Capitalism

Popular historian Thomas Frank rather presciently argues in *The Conquest of Cool* that in the United States back in the 1960s, "hip became central to the way American capitalism understood itself and explained itself to the public" (Frank 1997: 26). Brands like Volkswagen and 7-Up recognized the potential of the counterculture's critique of the mainstream to sell their products. They took on its romantic obsession with personal passions as their own, its language of self-expression and "living in the moment." The counterculture, with its disdain for all that is conventional, enduring, or overtly moralistic, became the perfect ideological justification for the pursuit of endless novelty. It "served corporate revolutionaries as a projection of the new ideology of business, a living embodiment of the attitudes that reflected their own" (Frank 1997: 27).

Frank argues, then, that the counterculture should probably be understood not as a movement running counter to the currents of the bloated bourgeoisie, but as a "stage in the development of the values of the American middle class, a colorful installment in the twentieth century drama of consumer subjectivity" (Frank 1997: 29). Not only did the 1960s counterculture fail to overturn the culture of late capitalism, it became its dominant logic, "a symbolic and musical language for the endless cycles of rebellion and transgression that make up so much of our mass culture" (Frank 1997: 31).

In this book, I have made a similar case for indie culture and DIY practice. DIY, I have argued, is the emergent ethos of the global middle-class at a moment when production is increasingly decentralized, deregulated, and immaterial, and when the tools and technologies of active participation are evermore widely distributed. If the counterculture was a phase in the American middle-class, DIY may very well be a phase in the production of a new global elite, an elite residing over a historical moment of unsurpassed connection across borders, of flexible accumulation and expansive creative participation, an elite, in fact, whose very DIY sensibility undermines the notion of being elite in the first place.

On the one hand, this is a welcome development, an expansion of the terms of participation, a democratization of popular culture. On the other hand, it is hard to argue that it poses a genuine threat to the existing configurations of power in a global neoliberal economy. It may weaken the hold of the nation-state, but it only expands the reach and influence of consumer capitalism. It is even a fair question to ask whether the Indonesian indie scene described in this book directly serves the interests of capital, as something such as Indonesia's "creative class," the innovative backbone, as it were, of an Indonesia moving beyond outsourced manufacture and large-scale agriculture as its primary modes of production. In such a reading, DIYers, despite an entrenched anti-corporate rhetoric, support the very economic system they ostensibly reject. DIYers solidify and expand its domain. As far as capitalism is concerned, they are with the tide, not against it.

It is also possible to see the emerging international indie scene as something of a training ground for the next generation of young capitalists. Most participants, of course, move on after a few years, get jobs in the corporate world, or move up into the commercial media. Their work in the scene teaches them a skill-set that will be fundamentally useful in their future careers, and it inculcates in them a *habitus* of flexibility and risk, quirkiness and creativity, critical to achieving success in a late capitalist workplace (Martin 1994; Ong 1999; Lloyd 2006). Hence, all my indie rock friends from back in Santa Cruz in the 1990s who now work as designers of some sort or other in the Silicon Valley, and all the Indonesian scenesters I know who have gone on to more financially lucrative endeavors. Among my informants from Reddoor Distro, for instance, one is now the store manager of another prominent Yogyakarta Distro, another works for a commercial design firm in Kalimantan, another as a promotional materials designer for a cigarette company in Pekanbaru, another for an independent record label in Jakarta, and several others now run their own premium distro and clothing label on Yogyakarta's Ring Road.

Nonetheless, I am wary of the enthusiasm with which writers such as Frank, or his over-eager disciples Heath and Potter (2005), dismiss the subversive potential of such purportedly countercultural movements as punk and indie rock. While it is true that the Indonesian indie scene never steers too far from the ethic that drives contemporary capitalist practice or the neoliberal ideals reforming the marketplace, its participants demonstrate far more self-awareness than these authors would give them credit for. They know they are capitalists. They know, in the final analysis, that what they do is sell music, magazines, and clothes. They know that they probably won't change the world in any profound way.

They are also, however, smart enough to know that capitalism is not a fixed system. It undergoes changes. It develops. It evolves. Neoliberalism is not the endgame of capitalism. In the wake of the current foreclosure crisis, international recession, and anti-Wall Street protests now 900 cities strong as this book goes to press, it is beginning to look more like a botched social experiment than an inevitable outcome of our economic course. There will be history beyond neoliberalism, just as there was history before it. And the youth involved in DIY culture want to be part of determining the course that history takes. They hope to push capitalism in a new direction, away from the atomistic pull of an alienated, competitive individualism, away from the materialist temptations of unrestrained greed, and toward something else, something more cooperative, expressive, and uplifting, which values creativity and community as their own rewards.

In classic Marxist thought, the seeds of capitalism's undoing are already planted within it. Its own internal contradictions, its cleavage of society into two great oppositional social classes, and its ceaseless production of unfulfillable desires, will eventually coalesce into proletariat uprising. The have-nots will overtake the haves, seize the means of production, eliminate private property, and establish, by force if necessary, a truly egalitarian state. Today's generation of DIY youth have, in fact, already seized the means of production. They have taken advantage of modern technologies and made themselves into cultural producers in their own right, found forms of non-alienated labor, and forged an alternative capitalism right under the nose of its bigger, corporate brother.

But this is not the proletariat revolution Marx and his followers were waiting for. Kids these days just don't believe in anything so grandiose. For most of them, there is no after or beyond capitalism. There is no Utopia waiting on the other side of revolt. There is just more of the same. The very tools with which we imagine Utopia, this generation of youth seems to acknowledge, were supplied for us by corporate media anyway, by clever ad campaigns and Hollywood fantasies. And even if there were something better and brighter on the other side of ownership, would we really want it? Are we really ready or willing to get rid of all our cool stuff, or to stop having access to boundless media, entertainment, and information? How good could Utopia really be if it has no video game consuls or satellite dishes? And if said Utopia were ever constructed, won't someone figure out how to capitalize on it?

The question for today's DIY movement, then, is not "how do we move beyond capitalism?" Such a quandary has already been rendered irrelevant. It sounds preposterous to this generation's ears. In the hearts and minds of youth in nearly every nation, capitalism has already won. It may leave us cold, alienated, and aching for something more meaningful and fulfilling, but it is the system we have to work within. The question for them, then, perhaps for all of us, is: "Since capitalism has already won, what do we do now?" How do we make it something we can live with? How do we make it our own?

Notes

Preface

1. Although the network of young DIYers that I refer to as the "indie scene" goes
   by a number of different names in Indonesia, from "the underground" to "the
   subculture" (*subkulturnya*) to "the community" (*komunitasnya*), I have chosen
   to call it a "scene" in this book, following the example of Mahon (2004), Shank
   (1994), Straw (1997), and others; as for me, the term captures something of its
   flexibility and impermanence. A "scene" describes a social "field" (Bourdieu
   1977, 1980, 1993) characterized by interconnections between multiple, differently situated social actors, with varying degrees and types of participation. It
   can be local or trans-local, national or international. It has no clear boundaries
   or borders, no obvious points of rupture. It describes, in other words, an unstable configuration, rather than a tightly knit social unit. The term "scene," borrowed from English and sometimes Indonesianized as *skena,* is in widespread
   circulation in Indonesia, as well.

Introduction

1. Lou Pearlman was the music impresario most famous for putting together the
   chart-topping boy bands NSYNC and the Backstreet Boys in the early 1990s.
2. In 1992 Virgin was purchased by EMI. As of 2007, EMI/Virgin merged with
   Capitol Records to become the Capitol Music Group.

Chapter 2— DIY Capitalism: Class, Crisis, and the Rise of Indie Indonesia

1. I use the term "kids" to describe participants in the Indonesian indie scene,
   because it most closely corresponds in meaning to the term participants use
   to describe themselves, *anak.* It is not meant to be demeaning or imply that
   participants have not yet reached adult status. Incidentally, "kids" is a term
   participants in indie scenes in Europe and the United States also commonly use
   to describe themselves.

2. All quotations by indie scene members, unless otherwise noted, were stated originally in Indonesian and translated into English by the author. In the case of idiosyncratic, ambiguous, or difficult to translate passages, I have also included the original Indonesian statement in parentheses.
3. The name Anonim Wardrobe means "Anonymous Wardrobe," a play, like No Label Stuff's name, on the fact that Anonim doesn't consider itself a conventional clothing shop, with the conventional emphasis on brand name fashion. Dede has taken on the name of her shop as her last name.
4. These T-shirts were also clearly a reference to one of Dendy's favorite bands, Joy Division, a British post-punk band from the late 1970s, whose cult hit "Love Will Tear Us Apart" continues to play in distros throughout urban Indonesia.
5. By way of comparison, *Maximumrocknroll*, the Berkeley-based publication, widely regarded as the most influential punk zine worldwide, had a readership of around 15,000 at its mid-1990s peak (O'Connor 2008: 7).

Chapter 6—On Site and Sound: Music and Borders in a DIY World

1. The term "indie pop," most closely associated with bands like The Smiths and Primal Scream, was originally used to describe a style of popular music emerging out of the UK in the mid-1980s. It was a genre deeply influenced by 1960s rock, folk, and psychedelia, and tended to use quirky and often-ironic lyrics. The term is used in Indonesia today, however, to describe a broader variety of melodic and accessible genres produced on independent record labels. It describes less a style of music than a style of production.
2. A gamelan musical ensemble from Sunda, the western region of Java, that utilizes a pelog musical scale, a variety of kettle gongs, hanging gongs, a bamboo flute, and a stringed rebab, among other instruments. Degung is one of the most melodic and recognizable of Indonesian gamelan styles.
3. From a poster for KICKfest, an annual independent fashion event put on by the Kreative Independent Clothing Kommunity (KICK).

References

Abu-Lughod, Lila. 1990. The Romance of Resistance: Tracing Transformations of Power Through Bedouin Women. *American Ethnologist* 17(1): 41–55.

Adams, Kathleen M. 1998. More Than an Ethnic Marker: Toraja Art as Identity Negotiator. *American Ethnologist* 25(3): 327–51.

Ahmad, Sara. 2006. *Queer Phenomenology: Orientations, Objects, Others*. Durham, NC: Duke University Press.

Allison, Anne. 2002. The Cultural Politics of Pokemon Capitalism. In *Media in Transition 2: Globalization and Convergence*. Massachusetts Institute of Technology.

Anderson, Benedict R. O. 1972. *Java in a Time of Revolution: Occupation and Resistance 1944–1946*. Ithaca, NY: Cornell University Press.

Anderson, Benedict R. O. 1983. *Imagined Communities: Reflections on the Origin and Spread of Nationalism*. London: Verso.

Anderson, Benedict R. O. 1990. *Language and Power: Exploring Political Cultures in Indonesia*. Ithaca, NY: Cornell University Press.

Ang, Ien. 1996. *Living Room Wars: Rethinking Media Audiences for a Postmodern World*. London: Routledge.

Appadurai, Arjun. 1996. *Modernity at Large: Cultural Dimensions of Globalization*. Minneapolis: University of Minnesota Press.

Aronowitz, Stanley. 2003. *How Class Works: Power and Social Movement*. New Haven, CT: Yale University Press.

Aspelund, Karl. 2009. *Fashioning Society: A Hundred Years of Haute Couture by Six Designers*. New York: Fairchild Publications.

Atkinson, Jane Monnig. 1996. Quizzing the Sphinx: Reflections on Morality in Central Sulawesi. In *Fantasizing the Feminine in Indonesia,* ed. L. J. Sears, 163–90. Durham, NC: Duke University Press.

Atkinson, Jane Monnig. 2003. Who Appears in the Family Album? Writing the History of Indonesia's Revolutionary Struggle. In *Cultural Citizenship in Island Southeast Asia: Nation and Belonging in the Hinterlands*, ed. R. Rosaldo, 134–61. Berkeley: The University of California Press.

Azerrad, Michael. 2001. *Our Band Could Be Your Life: Scenes from the American Indie Underground 1981–1991*. New York: Back Bay Books.

Bakhtin, Mikhail. 1983. *The Dialogic Imagination: Four Essays*. Austin: The University of Texas Press.

Banet-Weiser, Sarah, and Marita Sturken. 2010. The Politics of Commerce: Shepard Fairey and the New Cultural Entrepreneurship. In *Blowing Up the Brand: Critical Perspectives on Promotional Culture*, eds M. Aronczyk and D. Powers. Vol. 263–284. New York: Peter Lang.

Bannister, Mathew. 2006. 'Loaded': Indie Guitar Rock, Canonism, White Masculinities. *Popular Music* 25(1): 77–95.

Barendregt, Bart, and Wim van Zanten. 2002. Popular Music in Indonesia since 1998, in Particular Fusion, Indie, and Islamic Music on Video Compact Discs and the Internet. *Yearbook for Traditional Music* 34: 67–113.

Barker, Joshua, Johan Lindquist, et al. 2009. Figures of Indonesian Modernity. *Indonesia* 87(April): 1–38.

Barthes, Roland. 1977. *Roland Barthes by Roland Barthes*. Berkeley: University of California Press.

Baulch, Emma. 2003. Gesturing Elsewhere: The Identity Politics of the Balinese Death/Thrash Metal Scene. *Popular Music* 22: 195–215.

Baulch, Emma. 2007. *Making Scenes: Reggae, Punk, and Death Metal in 1990s Bali*. Durham, NC: Duke University Press.

Bauman, Zygmunt. 1998. *Globalization: The Human Consequences*. Cambridge: Polity.

Bauman, Zygmunt. 2003. *Liquid Love*. Cambridge: Polity.

Beatty, Andrew. 1999. *Varieties of Javanese Religion: An Anthropological Account*. Cambridge: Cambridge University Press.

Beck, Ulrich. 1992. *Risk Society: Towards a New Modernity*. London: Sage.

Becker, Howard. 1982. *Art Worlds*. Berkeley: University of California Press.

Becker, Judith. 1975. *Kroncong*, Indonesian Popular Music. *Asian Music* 7(1): 14–19.

Benjamin, Walter. 1955. The Work of Art in the Age of Mechanical Reproduction. In *Illuminations*, ed. H. Arendt, 219–53. New York: Harcourt, Brace & World.

Benjamin, Walter. 2002. *The Arcades Project*. New York: Belknap Press.

Bhabha, Homi K. 1994. Of Mimicry and Man: The Ambivalence of Colonial Discourse. In *The Location of Culture*, 121–31. London: Routledge.

Bhabha, Homi K. 2005. Looking Back, Moving Forward: Notes on Vernacular Cosmopolitanism. In *The Location of Culture*, ix–xxxi. London: Routledge.

Boellstorff, Tom. 2005. *The Gay Archipelago: Sexuality and Nation in Indonesia*. Princeton, NJ: Princeton University Press.

Boellstorff, Tom. 2008. *Coming of Age in Second Life: An Anthropologist Explores the Virtually Human*. Princeton, NJ: Princeton University Press.

Borland, John. 2010. Transcending the Human, DIY Style. In *Wired*. Vol. Blog— www.wired.com/threatlevel/2010/12/transcending-the-human-diy-style/.

Bourdieu, Pierre. 1977. *Outline of a Theory of Practice*. Cambridge: Cambridge University Press.

Bourdieu, Pierre. 1980. *The Logic of Practice*. Stanford, CA: Stanford University Press.

Bourdieu, Pierre. 1984. *Distinction: A Social Critique of the Judgment of Taste*. Cambridge, MA: Harvard University Press.

Bourdieu, Pierre. 1993. The Field of Cultural Production, or: The Economic World Reversed. In *The Field of Cultural Production: Essays on Art and Literature*, ed. R. Johnson, 29–73. New York: Columbia University Press.

Bourdieu, Pierre. 1997. *Pascalian Meditations*. R. Nice, transl. Stanford, CA: Stanford University Press.

Bourdieu, Pierre. 1998. *The Essence of Neoliberalism*. Vol. 2008. Le Monde Diplomatique: http://mondediplo.com/1998/12/08bourdieu.

Bowen, John R. 1993. *Muslims Through Discourse: Religion and Ritual in Gayo Society*. Princeton, NJ: Princeton University Press.

Brenner, Suzanne. 1999. On the Public Intimacy of the New Order: Images of Women in the Popular Print Media. *Indonesia* 67: 13–38.

Brooks, David. 2000. *Bobos in Paradise: The New Upper Class and How They Got There*. New York: Simon & Schuster.

Brown, Michael F. 1996. On Resisting Resistance. *American Anthropologist* 98(4): 729–35.

Burke, Meredith Melling. 2010. Logged On. *Vogue* (March): 514–23.

Caldwell, John Thornton. 2008. *Production Culture: Industrial Reflexivity and Critical Practice in Film and Television*. Durham, NC: Duke University Press.

Campbell, Colin. 1987. *The Romantic Ethic and the Spirit of Modern Consumerism*. Oxford: Blackwell.

Carbone, Bradley, and Noah Johnson. 2011. An Oral History of the Graphic T-shirt. In *Complex*. Vol. 2011: www.complex.com.

Carrier, James G. 1992. Occidentalism: The World Turned Upside-down. *American Ethnologist* 19(2): 195–212.

Castells, Manuel. 2000. *The Information Age: Economy, Society and Culture*. Malden, MA: Blackwell Publishers.

Chandler, David P., William R. Roff, John R. W. Smail, David Joel Steinberrg, Robert H. Taylor, Alexander Woodside, and David K. Wyatt. 1987. *In Search of Southeast Asia: A Modern History*. Honolulu: University of Hawaii Press.

Chao, Emily. 1999. The Maoist Shaman and the Madman: Ritual Bricolage, Failed Ritual, and Failed Ritual Theory. *Cultural Anthropology* 14(4): 505–34.

Clarke, John. 1976. The Skinheads and the Magical Recovery of Community. In *Resistance through Ritual: Youth Subcultures in Postwar Britain*, eds S. Hall and T. Jefferson, 99–102. Birmingham: University of Birmingham.

Clarke, John, Stuart Hall, Tony Jefferson, and Brian Roberts. 1976. Subcultures, Cultures, and Class: A Theoretical Overview. In *Resistance Through Rituals*, eds S. Hall and T. Jefferson, 9–74. London: Routledge.

Clayton, Jace. 2010. Vampires of Lima. In *What Was the Hipster? A Sociological Investigation*, eds M. Greif, K. Ross, and D. Tortorici, 24–30. New York: n+1 Foundation.

Clifford, James, and George E. Marcus. 1986. Introduction: Partial Truths. In *Writing Culture: The Poetics and Politics of Ethnography*, eds J. Clifford and G.E. Marcus, 1–26. Berkeley: University of California Press.

Comaroff, Jean, and John L. Comaroff. 2001. Millennial Capitalism: First Thoughts on a Second Coming. In *Millennial Capitalism and the Culture of Neoliberalism*, eds J. Comaroff and J. L. Comaroff, 1–56. Durham, NC: Duke University Press.

Condry, Ian. 2001. Japanese Hip-Hop and the Globalization of Popular Culture. In *Urban Life: Readings in the Anthropology of the City*, eds G. Gmelch and W. Zenner, 357–87. Prospect Heights, IL: Waveland Press.

Coronil, Fernando. 1996. Beyond Occidentalism: Towards Nonimperial Geohistorical Categories. *Cultural Anthropology* 11(1): 51–87.

Debord, Guy. 1995. The *Society of the Spectacle*. D. Nicholson-Smith, transl. New York: Zone Books.

De Certeau, Michel. 1984. *The Practice of Everyday Life*. Cambridge: Cambridge University Press.

Deleuze, Gilles, and Félix Guattari. 1987. *A Thousand Plateaus: Capitalism and Schizophrenia*. B. Massumi, transl. Minneapolis: University of Minnesota Press.

Deleuze, Gilles, and Félix Guattari. 1996. *Anti-Oedipus: Capitalism and Schizophrenia*. Minneapolis: University of Minnesota Press.

Derrida, Jacques. 1980. Structure, Sign, and Play in the Discourse of the Human Sciences. In *Writing and Difference*, 278–94. London: Routledge.

Derrida, Jacques. 1986. *Memoirs for Paul Demain*. New York: Columbia University Press.

Derrida, Jacques. 1988. *Limited, Inc*. Evanston, IL: Northwestern University Press.

Dick, H. W. 1985. The Rise of a Middle Class and the Changing Concept of Equity in Indonesia: An Interpretation. *Indonesia* 39: 71–92.

Dick, H. W. 1990. Further Reflections on the Middle-Class. In *The Politics of Middle-Class Indonesia*, eds R. Tanter and K. Young, 63–70. Glen Waverly, Australia: Aristoc Press.

Dickey, Sara. 1998. Anthropology and Its Contributions to Studies of Mass Media. *International Social Science Journal* (153): 413–27.

Diehl, Keila. 2002. *Echoes from Dharamsala: Music in the Life of a Tibetan Refugee Community*. Berkeley: University of California Press.

Duncombe, Stephen. 1997. *Notes from Underground: Zines and the Politics of Alternative Culture*. London: Verso.

Durkheim, Emile. 1984. *The Division of Labor in Society*. W. D. Halls, transl. New York: The Free Press.

Eco, Umberto. 1972. *Towards a Semiotic Inquiry into the Television Message*. W.P.C.S.3. Birmingham, UK: University of Birmingham.

Elliot, Anthony, and Charles Lemert. 2006. *The New Individualism: The Emotional Costs of Globalization*. London: Routledge.

Errington, Shelly. 1990. Recasting Sex, Gender, and Power: A Theoretical and Regional Overview. In *Power and Difference: Gender in Island Southeast Asia*, eds J. M. Atkinson and S. Errington, 1–58. Stanford, CA: Stanford University Press.

Evans, Caroline. 2007. *Fashion at the Edge: Spectacle, Modernity, and Deathliness*. New Haven, CT: Yale University Press.

Feld, Steven. 1994. From Schizophonia to Schismogenesis: On the Discourses and Commodification Practices of "World Music" and "World Beat". In *Music Grooves*, eds S. Feld and C. Keil, 257–89. Chicago: University of Chicago Press.

Fiske, John. 1987. *Television Culture*. London: Routledge.

Florida, Richard. 2002. *The Rise of the Creative Class*. New York: Basic Books.

Fonarow, Wendy. 2006. *Empire of Dirt: The Aesthetics and Rituals of British Indie Music*. Middletown: Wesleyan University Press.

Foucault, Michel. 1978. *The History of Sexuality: An Introduction*. New York: Random House.

Foucault, Michel. 1986. *The History of Sexuality: The Care of the Self*. New York: Random House.

Foucault, Michel. 1994. What Is Enlightenment? In *Ethics: Subjectivity and Truth*, ed. P. Rabinow, 303–19. New York: The New Press.

Foucault, Michel. 2002. What Is an Author? In *Reading Architectural History*, ed. D. Arnold, 71–82. New York: Routledge.

Foulcher, Keith. 1990. The Construction of an Indonesian National Culture: Patterns of Hegemony and Resistance. In *State and Civil Society in Indonesia*, ed. A. Budiman, 301–320. Glen Waverly, Australia: Aristoc Press.

Frank, Thomas. 1997. *The Conquest of Cool: Business Culture, Counterculture, and the Rise of Hip Consumerism*. Chicago: University of Chicago Press.

Frank, Thomas. 2000. *One Market Under God: Extreme Capitalism, Market Populism, and the End of Economic Democracy*. New York: Anchor Books.

Frauenfelder, Mark. 2010. *Made by Hand: Searching for Meaning in a Throwaway World*. New York: Portfolio.

Frederick, William H. 1982. Rhoma Irama and the Dangdut Style: Aspects of Contemporary Indonesian Popular Culture. *Indonesia* 34: 103–30.

Freeman, Carla. 2007. The "Reputation" of Neoliberalism. *American Ethnologist* 34(2): 252–67.

Gates, Henry Louis Jr. 1988. *The Signifying Monkey: Towards a Theory of African-American Literary Criticism*. Oxford: Oxford University Press.

Gauntlett, David. 2011. *Making Is Connecting: The Social Meaning of Creativity, from DIY and Knitting to YouTube and Web 2.0*. Cambridge: Polity.

Geertz, Clifford. 1960. *The Religion of Java*. Chicago: The University of Chicago Press.

Geertz, Clifford. 1973. Deep Play: Notes on the Balinese Cockfight. In *The Interpretation of Cultures*, 412–53. New York: Basic Books.

Geertz, Clifford. 1981. *Negara: The Theatre State in Nineteenth-Century Bali*. Princeton, NJ: Princeton University Press.

Geertz, Clifford. 2000. *Available Light: Anthropological Reflections on Philosophical Topics*. Princeton, NJ: Princeton University Press.

Gelber, Steven M. 1997. Do-It-Yourself: Constructing, Repairing and Maintaining Domestic Masculinity. *American Quarterly* 49(March): 66–112.

Gellert, Paul K. 2008. What's New with the Old? Scalar Dialectics and The Reorganization of Indonesia's Timber Industry. In *Taking Southeast Asia to Market: Commodities, Nature, and People in the Neoliberal Age,* eds J. Nevins and N. L. Peluso, 43–55. Ithaca, NY: Cornell University Press.

Gerke, Solvay. 2000. Global Lifestyles under Local Conditions: The New Indonesian Middle-Class. In *Consumption in Asia: Lifestyles and Identities*, ed. B.-H. Chua, 135–58. London: Routledge.

Giddens, Anthony. 1979. *Central Problems in Social Theory: Action, Structure and Contradiction in Social Analysis*. Berkeley: University of California Press.

Giddens, Anthony. 1991. *Modernity and Self-Identity: Self and Society in the Late Modern Age*. Stanford, CA: Stanford University Press.

Ginsburg, Faye D., Lila Abu-Lughod, and Brian Larkin. 2002. Introduction. In *Media Worlds: Anthropology on New Terrain*, eds F. D. Ginsburg, L. Abu-Lughod, and B. Larkin, 1–38. Berkeley: University of California Press.

Gladwell, Malcolm. 2000. *The Tipping Point: How Little Things Can Make a Big Difference*. New York: Back Bay Books/Little Brown and Company.

Goldstein, Carolyn. 1998. *Do It Yourself: Home Improvement in 20th Century America*. Princeton, NJ: Princeton Architectural Press.

Gramsci, Antonio. 1971. *Selections from the Prison Notebooks*. New York: Lawrence and Wishart.

Greif, Mark. 2010. Positions. In *What Was the Hipster? A Sociological Investigation*, eds M. Greif, K. Ross, and D. Tortorici, 4–13. New York: n+1 Foundation.

Hahn, Elizabeth. 2002. The Tongan Tradition Goes to the Movies. In *The Anthropology of Media: A Reader*, eds K. Askew and R. R. Wilk, 258–69. Malden: Blackwell Publishers.

Hall, Stuart. 1977. Culture, the Media, and the "Ideological Effect." In *Mass Communication and Society*, eds C.J.M. Gurevitch and J. Woollacott, 315–48. London: Edward Arnold.

Hall, Stuart. 1980. Encoding/Decoding. In *Culture, Media, Language: Working Papers in Cultural Studies: 1972–79*. University of Birmingham, The Centre for Contemporary Cultural Studies, 128–38. London: Hutchinson.

Hamelink, C. 1983. *Cultural Autonomy in Global Communications*. New York: Longman.

Hardt, Michael, and Antonio Negri. 2001. *Empire.* Cambridge, MA: Harvard University Press.

Harvey, David. 2005. *A Brief History of Neoliberalism.* Oxford: Oxford University Press.

Haswidi, Andi. 2010. In the 1990s, the Swedish Indie Scene Had a Low Self-Esteem. *The Jakarta Post Online,* Sunday, April 11.

Hatton, Elizabeth. 1989. Lévi-Strauss's "Bricolage" and Theorizing Teacher's Work. *Anthropology & Education Quarterly* 20(2): 74–96.

Hatley, Barbara. 1990. Theatre as Cultural Resistance in Contemporary Indonesia. In *State and Civil Society in Indonesia,* ed. A. Budiman, 321–48. Glen Waverly, Australia: Aristoc. Press.

Heath, Joseph, and Andrew Potter. 2005. *The Rebel Sell: How the Counterculture Became Consumer Culture.* Sussex, England: Capstone.

Hebdige, Dick. 1979. *Subculture: The Meaning of Style.* London: Routledge Press.

Hefner, Robert W. 1997. Print Islam: Mass Media and Ideological Rivalries among Indonesian Muslims. *Indonesia* 64: 77–104.

Heider, Karl G. 1991. *Indonesian Cinema: National Culture on Screen.* Honolulu: University of Hawai'i Press.

Henley, David. 1993. Nationalism and Regionalism in Colonial Indonsia: The Case of Minahasa. *Indonesia* 55: 91–112.

Heryanto, Ariel. 1990. State Ideology and Civil Discourse. In *State and Civil Society in Indonesia,* ed. A. Budiman, 289–300. Glen Waverly, Australia: Aristoc Press.

Heryanto, Ariel. 1999. Kelas Menegah yang Majemuk. In *Kelas Menengah Bukan Ratu Adil,* ed. Hadijaya, 3–16. Yogyakarta, Indonesia: Pt. Tiara Wacana Yogya.

Heryanto, Ariel. 2008. *State Terrorism and Political Identity: Fatally Belonging.* London: Routledge.

Hesmondhalgh, David. 1999. Indie: The Institutional Politics and Aesthetics of a Popular Music Genre. *Cultural Studies* 13(1): 34–61.

Hesmondhalgh, David. 2007. *The Cultural Industries.* London: Sage.

Hill, David T., and Krishna Sen. 2005. *The Internet in Indonesia's New Democracy.* London: Routledge.

Hills, Matt. 2002. *Fan Cultures.* New York: Routledge.

Horkheimer, Max, and Theodor W. Adorno. 1944. *Dialectic of Enlightenment.* J. Cumming, transl. New York: The Seabury Press.

Hoskins, Janet. 1987. The Headhunter as Hero: Local Traditions and Their Reinterpretation in National History. *American Ethnologist* 14(4): 605–22.

The Jakarta Post. 1999. Kaum Yuppie Menuai Buah Boom Ekonomi. In *Kelas Menengah Bukan Ratu Adil,* ed. Hadijaya, 63–66. Yogyakarta, Indonesia: Pt. Tiara Wacana Yogya.

Jameson, Fredric. 1992. *Postmodernism, Or, the Cultural Logic of Late Capitalism.* Durham, NC: Duke University Press.

Jenkins, Henry. 1997. Television Fans, Poachers, Nomads. In *The Subcultures Reader*, eds K. Gelder and S. Thornton, 506–22. London: Routledge.

Jenkins, Henry. 2006. *Convergence Culture: Where Old and New Media Collide.* New York: New York University Press.

Joyce, Patrick. 1995. Introduction. In *Class*m, ed. P. Joyce, 3–16. Oxford: Oxford University Press.

Keane, Webb. 1997. Knowing One's Place: National Language and the Idea of the Local in Eastern Indonesia. *Cultural Anthropology* 12(1): 37–63.

Keeler, Ward. 1987. *Javanese Shadow Plays, Javanese Selves*. Princeton, NJ: Princeton University Press.

Keeler, Ward. 1990. Speaking of Gender in Java. In *Power & Difference: Gender in Island Southeast Asia*, eds J. Monig Atkinson and S. Errington, 127–52. Stanford, CA: Stanford University Press.

Keen, Andrew. 2008. *The Cult of the Amateur: How Blogs, MySpace, YouTube, and the Rest of Today's User-Generated Media Are Destroying Our Economy, Our Culture, and Our Values*. New York: DoubleDay.

Kingston, Jeffrey. 1991. Manipulating Tradition: The State, Adat, Popular Protest, and Class Conflict in Colonial Lampung. *Indonesia* 51: 21–46.

Kitley, Philip. 2000. *Television, Nation, and Culture in Indonesia*. Athens: Ohio University Center for International Studies.

Klein, Naomi. 2007. *The Shock Doctrine: The Rise of Disaster Capitalism*. New York: Picador.

Kompas. 1990. Young Professionals of Jakarta: Millions in Salary Lack of Hard Work. In *The Politics of Middle-Class Indonesia*, eds R. Tanter and K. Young, 167–74. Glen Waverly, Australia: Aristoc Press.

Kompas. 1999 Survei Kompas tentang Kelas Menengah Jakarta. In *Kelas Menengah Bukan Ratu Adil*, ed. Hadijaya, 271–88. Yogakarta, Indonesia: Pt. Tiara Wacana Yogya.

Kondo, Dorrine. 1997. *About Face: Performing Race in Fashion and Theater*. New York: Routledge.

Kuipers, Joel C. 1998. *Language, Identity, and Marginality in Indonesia: The Changing Nature of Ritual Speech on the Island of Sumba*. Cambridge: Cambridge University Press.

Kuipers, Joel C. 2003. Citizens as Spectators: Citizenship as a Communicative Practice on the Eastern Indonesian Island of Sumba. In *Cultural Citizenship in Island Southeast Asia: Nation and Belonging in the Hinterlands*, ed. R. Rosaldo, 162–91. Berkeley: The University of California Press.

Kulick, Don, and Margaret Willson. 2002. Rambo's Wife Saves the Day: Subjugating the Gaze and Subverting Narrative in a Papua New Guinea Swamp. In *The Anthropology of Media: A Reader*, eds K. Askew and R. R. Wilk, 270–85. Malden: Blackwell Publishers Ltd.

Laing, Dave. 1985. *One-Chord Wonders: Power and Meaning in Punk Rock.* London: Open University Press.

Lamont, Michéle, and Marcel Fournier. 1992. Introduction. In *Cultivating Differences: Symbolic Boundaries and the Making of Inequality,* eds M. Lamont and M. Fournier, 1–17. Chicago: University of Chicago Press.

Lanham, Robert. 2003. *The Hipster Handbook.* New York: Anchor Books.

Larkin, Brian. 2002. The Materiality of Cinema Theaters in Northern Nigeria. In *Media Worlds: Anthropology on New Terrain,* eds F. D. Ginsburg, L. Abu-Lughod, and B. Larkin, 319–36. Berkeley: University of California Press.

Lasch, Christopher. 1979. *The Culture of Narcissism: American Life in An Age of Diminishing Expectations.* New York: W.W. Norton & Company.

Lash, Scott. 1994. Reflexivity and Its Doubles: Structure, Aesthetics, Community. In *Reflexive Modernization: Politics, Tradition, and Aesthetics in the Modern Social Order,* eds U. Beck, A. Giddens, and S. Lash, 110–69. Cambridge: Polity Press.

Lash, Scott, and John Urry. 1994. *Economies of Signs and Space.* London: Sage.

Lasn, Kalle. 1999. *Culture Jam: How to Reverse America's Suicidal Consumer Binge—And Why We Must.* New York: Harper Collins.

Latour, Bruno. 2005. *Reassembling the Social: An Introduction to Actor-Network Theory.* Oxford: Oxford University Press.

Lazzarato, Maurizio. 1996. Immaterial Labor. In *Radical Thought in Italy: A Potential Politics,* eds P. Virno and M. Hardt, 133–50. Minneapolis: University of Minnesota Press.

Leland, John. 2004. *Hip: The History.* New York: Harper Perennial.

Lessig, Lawrence. 2004. *Free Culture: The Nature and Future of Creativity.* New York: Penguin Books.

Lessig, Lawrence. 2009. *Remix: Making Art and Commerce Thrive in the Hybrid Economy.* New York: Penguin.

Lev, Daniel S. 1990. Intermediate Classes and Change in Indonesia: Some Initial Reflections. In *The Politics of Middle-Class Indonesia,* eds R. Tanter and K. Young, 25–43. Glen Waverly, Australia: Aristoc Press.

Lévi-Strauss, Claude. 1966. *The Savage Mind.* Chicago: University of Chicago Press.

Levine, Faythe, and Cortney Heimerl. 2008. *Handmade Nation: The Rise of DIY Art, Craft, and Design.* Princeton, NJ: Princeton Architectural Press.

Levy, Pierre. 1997. *Collective Intelligence: Mankind's Emerging World in Cyberspace.* Cambridge, MA: Perseus Books.

Li, Tania Murray. 1999. Compromising Power: Development, Culture, and Rule in Indonesia. *Cultural Anthropology* 14(3): 295–322.

Li, Tania Murray. 2007. *The Will to Improve: Governmentality, Development, and the Practice of Politics.* Durham, NC: Duke University Press.

Liechty, Mark. 2003. *Suitably Modern: Making Middle-Class Culture in a New Consumer Society.* Princeton, NJ: Princeton University Press.

Lipovetsky, Gilles. 2002. *The Empire of Fashion: Dressing Modern Democracy*. Princeton, NJ: Princeton University Press.

Lipsitz, George. 1994. *Dangerous Crossroads: Popular Music, Postmodernism and the Poetics of Place*. London: Verso.

Lloyd, Richard. 2006. *Neo-Bohemia: Art and Commerce in the PostIndustrial City*. New York: Routledge.

Lockard, Craig. 1998. *Dance of Life: Popular Music and Politics in Southeast Asia*. Honolulu: University of Hawai'i Press.

Lustig, R. Jeffrey. 2004. The Tangled Knot of Race and Class in the United States. In *What's Class Got to Do with It? American Society in the Twenty-First Century*, ed. M. Zweig, 45–60. Ithaca, NY: ILR Press.

Luvaas, Brent. 2006. Re-Producing Pop: The Aesthetics of Ambivalence in Contemporary Dance Music. *International Journal of Cultural Studies* 9(2): 167–87.

Luvaas, Brent. 2010. Designer Vandalism: Indonesian Indie Fashion and the Cultural Practice of Cut 'n' Paste. *Visual Anthropology Review* 26(1): 1–16.

Maffesoli, Michel. 1996. *The Time of the Tribes: The Decline of Individualism in Mass Society*. London: Sage.

Mahon, Maureen. 2004. *Right to Rock: The Black Rock Coalition and the Cultural Politics of Race*. Durham, NC: Duke University Press.

Mankekar, Purnima. 2008. Unsettling India: Media, Mobility, and Impersonation. In *Culture, Power, and Social Change*. Los Angeles: University of California, Los Angeles.

Manovich, Lev. 2001. *The Language of New Media*. Cambridge, MA: The MIT Press.

Manuel, Peter, and Randall Baier. 1986. Jaipongan: Indigenous Popular Music of West Java. *Asian Music* 18(1): 91–110.

Marcus, Greil. 1989. *Lipstick Traces: A Secret History of the Twentieth Century*. Cambridge, MA: Harvard University Press.

Marcuse, Herbert. 1991. *One-Dimensional Man: Studies in the Ideology of Advanced Industrial Society*. Boston: Beacon Press.

Martin, Emily. 1994. *Flexible Bodies*. Boston: Beacon Press.

Martin-Iverson, Sean. 2008. "C'mon Commodify Us!": Commodity Fetishism and Resistant Practice in the Bandung DIY Hardcore Scene. In *Youth, Media, and Culture in the Asia Pacific Region*, eds U. M. Rodrigues and B. Smaill, 177–94. Newcastle, UK: Cambridge Scholars Publishing.

Marx, Karl. (1867) 2009. Capital. In *The Craft Reader*, ed. G. Adamson, 69–77. Oxford: Berg.

Marx, Karl, and Friedrich Engels. (1849) 1998. *The Communist Manifesto*. New York: Signet Classic.

Mason, Matt. 2008. *The Pirate's Dilemma: How Youth Culture Is Reinventing Capitalism*. New York: Free Press.

Massumi, Brian. 2002. *Parables for the Virtual: Movement, Affect, Sensation*. Durham, NC: Duke University Press.

Mattelart, A. 1983. *Transnationals and the Third World: The Struggle for Culture*. South Hadley, MA: Bergin and Garvey.

Mbembe, Achille. 2001. *On the Postcolony*. Berkeley: University of California Press.

McCracken, Grant. 1997. *Plenitude*. Toronto: Fluide.

McLeod, Kembrew. 2005. *Freedom of Expression: Resistance and Repression in the Age of Intellectual Property*. Minneapolis: University of Minnesota Press.

McKay, George. 1996. *Senseless Acts of Beauty: Cultures of Resistance Since the Sixties*. London: Verso.

McRobbie, Angela. 1998. *British Fashion Design: Rag Trade or Image Industry?* London: Routledge.

McRobbie, Angela. 2004. 'Everyone Is Creative': Artists as Pioneers of the New Economy. In *Contemporary Culture and Everyday Life*, eds E. Silva and T. Bennett, 186–99. New York: Routledge.

McVeigh, Brian. 2000. How Hello Kitty Commodifies the Cute, Cool, and Camp: 'Consumutopia' Versus 'Control' in Japan. *Journal of Material Culture* 5(2): 225–45.

Miller, Daniel. 1992. The Young and the Restless in Trinidad: A Case of the Local and the Global in Mass Consumption. In *Consuming Technologies: Media and Information in Domestic Spaces*, eds R. Silverston and E. Hirsch, 163–82. London: Routledge.

Milner, Murray, Jr. 2004. *Freaks, Geeks, and Cool Kids: American Teenagers, Schools, and the Culture of Consumption*. New York: Routledge.

Moore, Elizabeth Anne. 2007. *Unmarketable: Brandalism, Copyfighting, Mocketing, and the Erosion of Integrity*. New York: The New Press.

Moore, Ryan. 2010. *Sells Like Teen Spirit: Music, Youth Culture, and Social Crisis*. New York: New York University Press.

Morris, William. 2009. The Revival of Handicraft. In *The Craft Reader*, ed. G. Adamson, 148–55. Oxford: Berg.

Mrázek, Rudolf. 2002. *Engineers of Happy Land: Technology and Nationalism in a Colony*. Princeton, NJ: Princeton University Press.

Muggleton, David. 2000. *Inside Subculture: The Postmodern Meaning of Style*. Oxford: Berg.

Mulder, Niels. 1996. *Inside Indonesian Society: Cultural Change in Java*. Amsterdam: The Pepin Press.

Muther, Christopher. 2009. Hipster Fatigue. *Boston Globe* (online edition). http://www.boston.com/lifestyle/fashion/articles/2009/07/16/putting_the_hate_on_hipsters/.

Neilson, William A. W. 1999. The Rush to Law: The IMF Legal Conditionalities Meet Indonesia's Culture Realities. In *Indonesia After Soeharto: Reformasi and*

Reaction, eds D. Duncan and T. Lindsey, 4–15. Victoria, BC: Centre for Asia-Pacific Initiatives, University of Victoria.

Nevins, Joseph, and Nancy Lee Peluso. 2008. Introduction. In *Taking Southeast Asia to Market: Commodities, Nature, and People in the Neoliberal Age*, eds J. Nevins and N. L. Peluso, 1–24. Ithaca, NY: Cornell University Press.

Newman, Michael Z. 2009. Indie Culture: In Pursuit of the Authentic Autonomous Alternative. *Cinema Journal* 48(3): 16–43.

Oakes, Kaya. 2009. *Slanted and Enchanted: The Evolution of Indie Culture*. New York: Henry Holt and Company.

O'Connor, Alan. 2008. *Punk Record Labels and the Struggle for Autonomy: The Emergence of DIY*. Lanham, MD: Lexington Books.

Ong, Aihwa. 1999. *Flexible Citizenship: The Cultural Logics of Transnationality*. Durham, NC: Duke University Press.

Ong, Aihwa. 2006. *Neoliberalism as Exception: Mutations in Citizenship and Sovereignty*. Durham, NC: Duke University Press.

Ortner, Sherry B. 1996. Making Gender: Toward a Feminist, Minority, Postcolonial, Subaltern, etc., Theory of Practice. In *Making Gender: The Politics and Erotics of Culture*, 1–20. Boston: Beacon Press.

Ortner, Sherry B. 1998. Generation X: Anthropology in a Media-Saturated World. *Cultural Anthropology* 13(3): 414–40.

Ortner, Sherry B. 2006. *Anthropology and Social Theory: Culture, Power, and the Acting Subject*. Durham, NC: Duke University Press.

Pemberton, John. 1994. *On the Subject of Java*. Ithaca, NY: Cornell University Press.

Pink, Sarah. 2007. *Doing Visual Ethnography: Images, Media, and Representations in Research*. 2nd ed. London: Sage.

Polhemus, Ted. 1994. *Streetstyle: From Catwalk to Sidewalk*. London: Thames and Hudson.

Polhemus, Ted. 1996. *Style Surfing: What to Wear in the 3rd Millennium*. London: Thames and Hudson.

Priyono, A. E. 1999. Konsumtivisme Kelas Menengah Perkotaan. In *Kelas Menengah Bukan Ratu Adil*, ed. Hadijaya, 223–28. Yogyakarta, Indonesia: P.T. Tiara Wacana Yogya.

Putranto, Wendi. 2006. School of Rock. In *Rolling Stone*. Vol. August, 57–61. Indonesia.

Ray, Paul H., and Sherry Ruth Anderson. 2000. The *Cultural Creatives: How 50 Million People Are Changing the World*. New York: Three Rivers Press.

Reynolds, Simon. 2004. *Rip It Up and Start Again: Postpunk 1978–1984*. New York: Penguin.

Robinson, Geoffrey. 1995. *The Dark Side of Paradise: Political Violence in Bali*. Ithaca, NY: Cornell University Press.

Robison, Richard. 1996. The Middle Class and the Bourgeoisie in Indonesia. In *The New Rich in Asia: Mobile Phones, McDonalds, and the Middle-Class Revolution*, eds R. Robison and D. S. G. Goodman, 79–101. London: Routledge.

Robison, Richard, and David S. G. Goodman. 1996. The New Rich in Asia: Economic Development, Social Status, and Political Consciousness. In *The New Rich in Asia: Mobile Phones, McDonalds, and Middle-Class Revolution.* eds R. Robison and D. S. G. Goodman, 1–18. London: Routledge.

Rosaldo, Renato. 1989. *Culture and Truth: The Remaking of Social Analysis.* Boston: Beacon Press.

Rudnyckyj, Daromir. 2009. Spiritual Economies: Islam and Neoliberalism in Contemporary Indonesia. *Cultural Anthropology* 24(1): 104–41.

Rudnyckyj, Daromir. 2010. *Spiritual Economies: Islam, Globalization, and the Afterlife of Development.* Ithaca, NY: Cornell University Press.

Ruskin, John. 2009. The Nature of Gothic. In *The Craft Reader*, ed. G. Adamson, 139–45. Oxford: Berg.

Rutherford, Danilyn. 1996. Of Birds and Gifts: Reviving Tradition on an Indonesian Frontier. *Cultural Anthropology* 11(4, Resisting Identities): 577–616.

Sale, Kirkpatrick. 1995. *Rebels Against the Future: The Luddites and Their War on the Industrial Revolution. Lessons for the Computer Age.* New York: Perseus Books.

Sartre, Jean-Paul. 1963. *Search for a Method.* H. E. Barnes, transl. New York: Vintage Books.

Schactman, Noah. 2009. Combatting Satellite Terrorism, DIY Style. *Popular Mechanics* (online edition). http://www.popularmechanics.com/technology/military/4205155.

Schiller, H. 1976. *Communication and Cultural Domination.* White Plains, NY: International Arts and Sciences.

Scott, James C. 1985. *Weapons of the Weak: Everyday Forms of Peasant Resistance.* New Haven, CT: Yale University Press.

Sen, Krishna, and David T. Hill. 2000. *Media, Culture and Politics in Indonesia.* Oxford: Oxford University Press.

Shank, Barry. 1994. *Dissonant Identities: The Rock'n'Roll Scene in Austin, Texas.* Middleton: Wesleyan University Press.

Siegel, James T. 1986. *Solo in the New Order: Language and Hierarchy in an Indonesian City.* Princeton, NJ: Princeton University Press.

Siegel, James T. 1997. *Fetish, Recognition, Revolution.* Princeton, NJ: Princeton University Press.

Siegel, James T. 1998. *A New Criminal Type in Jakarta: Counter-Revolution Today.* Durham, NC: Duke University Press.

Silvio, Teri. 2007. Remediation and Local Globalizations: How Taiwan's "Digital Video Knights-Errant Puppetry" Writes the History of the New Media in Chinese. *Cultural Anthropology* 22(2): 285–313.

Sims, Josh. 2010. *Cult Streetwear.* London: Laurence King.

Spencer, Amy. 2005. *DIY: The Rise of Lo-Fi Culture.* London: Marion Boyars.

Stalp, Marybeth C. 2008. *Quilting: The Fabric of Everyday Life.* Oxford: Berg.

Stevens, Dennis. 2009. DIY Revolution 3.0-Beta. *American Craft* (Oct/Nov).

Stewart, Kathleen. 2007. *Ordinary Affects*. Durham, NC: Duke University Press.

Straw, Will. 1997. Communities and Scenes in Popular Music. In *The Subcultures Reader*, eds K. Gelder and S. Thornton, 494–505. London: Routledge.

Sutton, R. Anderson. 1999. *Local, Global, or National?: Popular Music on Indonesian Television. Media, Performance, and Identity in World Perspective*. Madison: University of Wisconsin Press.

Sutton, R. Anderson. 2002. *Calling Back the Spirit: Music, Dance, and Cultural Politics in Lowland South Sulawesi*. Oxford: Oxford University Press.

Tanter, Richard, and Kenneth Young. 1990. Editor's Introduction. In *The Politics of Middle-Class Indonesia*, eds R. Tanter and K. Young, 7–21. Glen Waverly, Australia: Aristoc Press.

Taylor, Chris, Peter Turner, Joe Cummings, Brendan Delahunty, Paul Greenway, James Lyon, Jens Peters, Robert Storey, David Willett, and Tony Wheeler. 1997. *South-East Asia on a Shoestring*. Melbourne: Lonely Planet.

Thompson, E. P. 1963. *The Making of the English Working Class*. New York: Vintage.

Thompson, Stacy. 2004. *Punk Productions: Unfinished Business*. Albany: State University of New York Press.

Thee, Marcel. 2011. "Look Out World, Here Comes Bottlesmoker." *The Jakarta Globe*, February 09, 2011. Available at www.thejakartaglobe.com.

Thornton, Sarah. 1996. *Club Cultures: Music, Media, and Subcultural Capital*. Hanover: Wesleyan University Press.

Toffler, Alvin. 1980. *The Third Wave*. New York: Bantam Books.

Tsing, Anna Lowenhaupt. 1993. *In the Realm of the Diamond Queen: Marginality in an Out-of-the-Way Place*. Princeton, NJ: Princeton University Press.

Tsing, Anna Lowenhaupt. 2003. The News in the Provinces. In *Cultural Citizenship in Island Southeast Asia*, ed. R. Rosaldo, 192–222. Berkeley: The University of California Press.

Tsing, Anna Lowenhaupt. 2005. *Friction: An Ethnography of Global Connection*. Princeton, NJ: Princeton University Press.

Turkle, Sherry. 1995 *Life on the Screen: Identity in the Age of the Internet*. New York: Simon & Schuster.

Turkle, Sherry. 2011. *Alone Together: Why We Expect More from Technology and Less from Each Other*. New York: Basic Books.

Turney, Joanne. 2009. *The Culture of Knitting*. Oxford: Berg.

Tyler, Steven A. 1986. Post-Modern Ethnography: From Document of the Occult to Occult Document. In *Writing Culture: The Poetics and Politics of Ethnography*, eds J. Clifford and G.E. Marcus, 122–40. Berkeley: University of California Press.

Uttu. 2006. Distro: Independent Fashion Moves From Margins to Mainstream. *Inside Indonesia* 85 (Jan–Mar). http://www.insideindonesia.org/edition-85-jan-mar-2005/distro-1507105.

Veblen, Thorstein. 1994. *The Theory of the Leisure Class*. London: Dover Publications.

Vickers, Adrian. 1989. *Bali: A Paradise Created*. Singapore: Penguin Books Australia.

Vickers, Adrian. 2005. *A History of Modern Indonesia*. Cambridge: Cambridge University Press.

Vogel, Steven. 2007. *Streetwear: The Insider's Guide*. San Francisco: Chronicle Books.

Volkman, Toby Alice. 1990. Visions and Revisions: Toraja Culture and the Tourist Gaze. *American Ethnologist* 17(1): 91–110.

Wagner, Jon. 1990. "Bricolage" and Teachers' Theorizing. *Anthropology & Education Quarterly* 21(1): 78–81.

Wallach, Jeremy. 2002. Exploring Class, Nation, and Xenocentrism in Indonesian Cassette Retail Outlets. *Indonesia* 74(October): 79–102.

Wallach, Jeremy. 2003. 'Goodbye My Blind Majesty': Music, Language, and Politics in the Indonesian Underground. In *Global Pop, Local Languages*, eds H. M. Berger and M. T. Carrol, 53–86. Jackson: University of Mississippi Press.

Wallach, Jeremy. 2008a. Living the Punk Lifestyle in Jakarta. *Ethnomusicology* 52(1): 98–116.

Wallach, Jeremy. 2008b. *Modern Noise, Fluid Genres: Popular Music in Indonesia, 1997–2001*. Madison: University of Wisconsin Press.

Wayne, Teddy. 2010. Drilling Down: Age Gap Narrows on Social Networks. *New York Times* (online edition). http://www.nytimes.com/2010/12/27/business/media/27drill.html.

Weber, Max. 1930. *The Protestant Ethic and the Spirit of Capitalism*. T. Parsons, transl. London: Routledge.

Weber, Max. 1978. *Economy and Society*. G. Roth and C. Wittich, transl. Berkeley: University of California Press.

Weinzierl, Rupert, and David Muggleton. 2004. What Is 'Post-subcultural Studies' Anyway? In *The Post-Subcultures Reader*, eds D. Muggleton and R. Weinzierl, 3–23. Oxford: Berg.

Weiss, Brad. 2002. Thug Realism: Inhabiting Fantasy in Urban Tanzania. *Cultural Anthropology* 17(1): 93–124.

Werner, Silvia. 1999. Mendefinisikan Kelas Menengah Baru. In *Kelas Menengah Bukan Ratu Adil*, ed. Hadijaya, 59–62. Yogyakarta, Indonesia: Pt. Tiara Wacana Yogya.

Wibowo, S. Kunto Adi. 2006. Metroseksual: Sebuah Situs Resistensi. In *Resistensi Gaya Hidup: Teori dan Realitas*, ed. A. Adlin, ed185–215. Bandung: Forum Studi Kebudayan ITB.

Williams, Raymond. 1977. *Marxism and Literature*. Oxford: Oxford University Press.

Wohlsen, Marcus. 2011. *Biopunk: DIY Scientists Hack the Software of Life*. New York: Current.

Wrekk, Alex. 2005. *Stolen Sharpie Revolution: A DIY Zine Resource.* Portland, OR: Microcosm Publishing.

Yampolsky, Philip. 1989. 'Hati Yang Luka,' An Indonesian Hit. *Indonesia* 47: 1–17.

Yang, Mayfair Mei-hui. 2002. Mass Media and Transnational Subjectivity in Shanghai: Notes on (Re) Cosmopolitanism in a Chinese Metropolis. In *Media Worlds: Anthropology on New Terrain*, eds F. D. Ginsburg, L. Abu-Lughod, and B. Larkin, 189–210. Berkeley: University of California Press.

Index

Italicized page numbers indicate reference to a photograph of or relating to the subject of the entry.